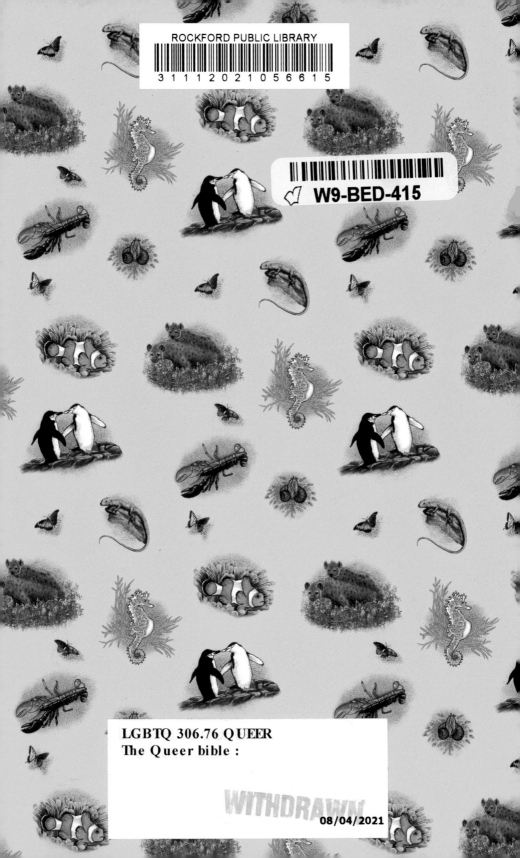

The Queer Bible

The Queer Bible

ESSAYS

EDITED BY JACK GUINNESS

DEY ST.

An Imprint of WILLIAM MORROW

This book is dedicated to my
queer ancestors who went before me,
that I never knew existed,
whose stories we'll never know.
I hope that I'm making you proud.

Contents

Foreword **8**

One

WORDS TO DANCE TO

Paul Flynn—Choose Life: George Michael **13**

Freddy McConnell—David Bowie **33**

Mykki Blanco—Radical Genius: Vaginal Davis **43**

Mark Moore—Quentin Crisp **57**

David Furnish—Sylvester **67**

Elton John—Divine **81**

Two

WORDS OF JOY

Jack Guinness—RuPaul **95**

Courtney Act—*Priscilla, Queen of the Desert* **107**

Graham Norton—Armistead Maupin **119**

Gus Kenworthy—Adam Rippon **129**

Lady Phyll—Moud Goba: My Sister's Keeper **139**

Matthew Todd—Harvey Fierstein **147**

Three

WORDS TO INSPIRE CHANGE

165 Munroe Bergdorf—*Paris Is Burning*

177 Mae Martin—Tim Curry

187 Hanne Gaby Odiele—Pidgeon Pagonis

195 Paris Lees—Edward Enninful

207 Tan France—*Queer Eye*

225 Paula Akpan—Black British Lesbians

Four

WORDS OF WISDOM

241 Amelia Abraham—Susan Sontag

257 Hans Ulrich Obrist—Ever Félix González-Torres!

267 Juliet Jacques—Pier Paolo Pasolini

279 Joseph Cassara—Pedro Almodóvar

293 Russell Tovey—David Robilliard

303 Paul Mendez—A Love Letter to James Baldwin

312 Artists

318 A Note on the Endpapers and Maps

Foreword

by Jack Guinness

The book you hold in your hands is a love letter to the queer community. Each essay is by a personal hero of mine, in which they write about a queer figure who has inspired them, illustrated by a queer or ally artist. All our lives are richer because of the works of queer people: everyone is indebted to LGBTQIA people, whether they know it or not, and reading this book will shine a light on the impact of these queer figures on shaping the world around us.

I can't quite believe we've got all these amazing people in one book. Our contributors are activists, artists, sports people, models, musicians, hosts, comedians, writers, and curators. They've made me laugh my arse off, educated me about gender and sexuality, comforted me during breakups, made music I've cried and danced to, expanded my mind, and, hopefully, won me a gold medal at the Olympics (I'm looking at you, Gus Kenworthy!). Our subjects were chosen by our contributors because they made a deeply personal impact on their lives; their enthusiasm and insights will hopefully inspire you to go off and do your own research and learn about each of their lives and works.

The moment young people realize that they're LGBTQIA they can instantly feel cut off from those around them. They feel separated from the very people they should feel closest to—their friends and families. Isolation and rejection led me down a path of self-destruction. This is the book I wish I'd read when I was growing up. To know where you're going, you need to know where you've come from. So often LGBTQIA histories have been hidden, in order to protect people's safety, or forcibly erased in acts of cultural vandalism and oppression. Let's bring those stories into the light. Let's connect with our past and be filled with the power of those who went before us. I am handing you your sacred history. A physical holy text that shows you not only are you seen and loved and are enough, but that anything is possible, not in spite of who you are, but because of it. Your wonderful uniqueness is beautiful. I want queer people to not just survive, but to thrive, knowing that they walk in the footsteps of the bravest, fiercest, most inspiring people to walk the face of the planet. We stand on the shoulders of giants. It's time to learn their names.

The person I am today has been shaped and influenced by so many queer heroes. The soundtrack to my life has been queer culture: laughter with my first gay best friend, Kele; solace in the writings of James Baldwin; Walt Whitman's magic words made me fly; Bronski Beat released my tears; Audre Lorde gave me strength; I sang karaoke to George Michael's "Freedom," I worshipped the stars of *Paris Is Burning*, I drank with drag queens till sunlight when I ran off to New York aged 18. You have been my family, my inspiration, and my joy. This book is for all of you. Thank you.

In these politically unstable times, with LGBTQIA rights under threat the world over, this book couldn't be more necessary—connecting us through our shared history and allowing people to tell their own stories, in their own voices. From the outset, I saw *The Queer Bible* as a platform to elevate, celebrate, and amplify the voices of our community. As a white cis man I benefit from so much unearned privilege. I'm very happy that this collection shines a light on members of our community who so often aren't given the attention or accolades they deserve. I hope that the range of voices, the varied stories, and the memories shared speak to the richness and diversity of our global queer community. Putting this book together was harder than it needed to be. The importance of this work was never plainer to me than when one of our contributors was violently assaulted in a homophobic hate crime. Our Trans contributors had to deal with horrific daily attacks online and in the press. Homophobic and transphobic people want to silence us. They want to question our very existence, fill our heads with their negativity, and to stop us from being who we are. So our greatest victory, in the face of hatred and intolerance, is to live our best lives. Don't let them stop you doing the work.

Be completely you. Be happy. Be fabulous.

Words to Dance to

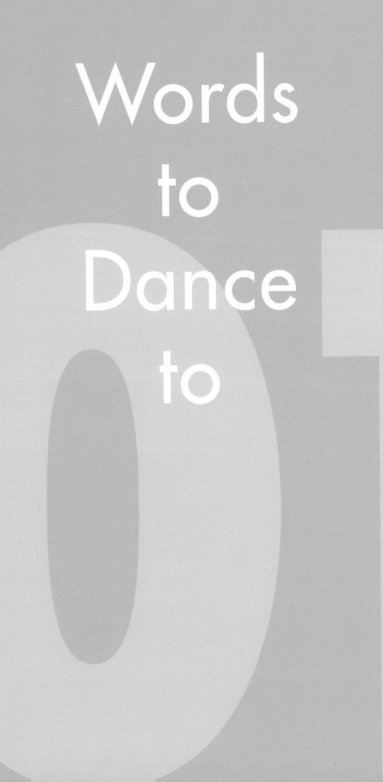

When I was a teenager, I went traveling. My sister made me a series of cassettes (I'm showing my age here). Each one had an abstract title scrawled onto that little label carefully placed along the center of the cassette—names like "Music to Fly Kites To" and "Music to Mend a Broken Heart." I didn't realize their significance until months later, when I found myself sitting at the summit of a mountain in Vietnam, exhausted, lonely, and exhilarated. I pushed the Walkman's "play" button, and after a whirl, my sister's cassette played. I immediately understood that she had curated a soundtrack for every possible one of my moods. I'm not as amazing as my beautiful, kind sister, but I've tried to collect these essays into sections that will make your soul dance, lift your spirits, spur action, and raise you up when you're feeling down.

"Words to Dance To" isn't only about performers. These essays are about the originators, the innovative rebels who challenged the status quo, moved culture forward, and got us on our feet! They'll position people you thought you knew in a fresh light and introduce you to changemakers you'll fall in love with. I hope these words connect you with the joyous rhythm of life and inspire you to create yourself.

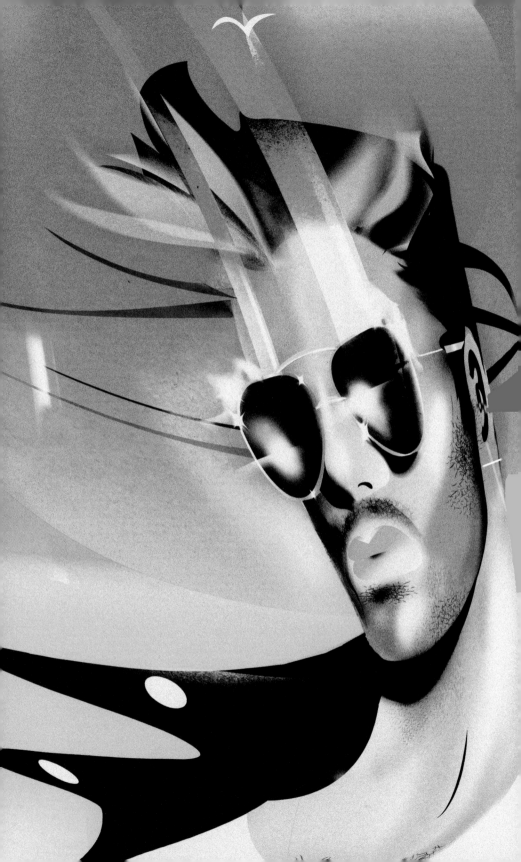

CHOOSE LIFE: GEORGE MICHAEL

by Paul Flynn

It is early 1985 and I am sat, bored, at the back of a South Manchester classroom. I'm guessing it's raining outside. When I think of that school now—its grubby windowpanes, misfiring adventures in teenage deodorant, and hours of detention—I see mostly the teachers, staring out at a gray sea of hopelessness, trying their hardest to encourage some method of escape for us all. Everybody needs good teachers.

We were taught by a cascading rota of staff during English lessons. For a spell, there was a witty young Black woman called Miss Black, a literalism no fiction would dare invent for the depressed northern comprehensives of the time. And someone with thinning hair whose name I've long forgotten was soon shipped in from a stint teaching adult literacy classes at Strangeways prison. She told us during her first lesson that we were considerably more charmless than her inmates. Then there was my favorite: a

---

Illustration by James Davison

ruddy-faced, thickset Scotsman with a moustache who would get misty-eyed when reading aloud, especially sensitive stanzas of wartime poetry.

I cannot begin to tell you how much I loved their company. They opened up other worlds beyond the drizzle of our immediate sightline on the simple act of turning a page. I am 13. Today's lesson is for 30 schoolboys to rein in our collective ADD and sit in the humming, itchy quiet of bored pubescence, reading the opening passages from Franz Kafka's *Metamorphosis*. For homework, the Scotsman wants to encourage our writing valves, our imaginative capacity. We are instructed to go home and write our own metamorphosis, a transcendental change in which we are no longer who we are, transposing our lives into those of others. Nothing appeals more.

(Do I know I'm gay by this point? Certainly, the initial inklings are present enough to get a brief, spinal twitch at this early intimation of complete personal reinvention, which may or may not be connected to the new urges I've developed concerning Lewis Collins every time a repeat of *The Professionals* appears on TV.)

A week hence and a pile of schoolbooks sits on the teacher's desk, annotated with wobbly handwritten care and attention. All but one follows the same predictable sequence of events, in which our little protagonist turns from scruffy oik into star striker at Manchester's United or City football clubs. If a collective dream can be located among our class, this is it. Local heroism located below the ankles.

My work that day broke the mold. From a head buried mostly in the pages of *Smash Hits* magazine and schooled in the extra-curricular music TV shows *Top of the Pops* and *The Tube*, I conjured "The Day I Turned into George Michael." That was my idea of the most fantastical metamorphosis a grown man could experience, at the furthest removes of glamour and excess from my first teenage year. George was my favorite pop star. He was still in the last of his brief Wham! years, a joyous, youthful place of suntans, Speedos, and Fila tracksuit tops, arced by blue-sky melody and killer couplets.

George Michael was the first everyman pop star to pierce me deeply, at an age when I could not fully control the depth of the incision. His story was shaped out of complete suburban escape, close enough to touch yet still miles beyond my ken. With his best friend, Andrew Ridgeley, he fashioned a run of effortless white-bread pop classics that owed everything to the Black music of his instruction. He sang like an angel and danced like a lunatic with a hairbrush in the bedroom mirror. His gift for song and poetry cut swiftly through to the premium mass market, a place he never left until his dying day. He was still only just out of his teens and had turned his ludicrously prolific talent for the connectivity of music into something luxurious, soulful, aspirational, immediate, and loved.

> My work that day broke the mold. From a head buried mostly in the pages of *Smash Hits* magazine and schooled in the extra-curricular music TV shows *Top of the Pops* and *The Tube,* I conjured "The Day I Turned into George Michael."

George was always with his best friend, everywhere he went. That was Wham! Two boys together. There was something soft, gorgeous, and open-armed about the duo, framed by the three-minute pulse of hit noise. They contained every gay man's camaraderie with the best friend he loves, sometimes wordlessly; the one who is so near but so far. Platonic, yes, but more so. They were Bushey's Bodie and Doyle, ramped up on naïve Home Counties' ambition. Their buoyant *cri de coeur* spoke of soul on the dole, the Bee Gees, cigarettes and love bites, death by matrimony, guilty feet, and rays of sunshine.

There are lines George Michael wrote back then, at the start of his incredible pop life, that still make me shiver—silver-lined and gilt-edged with instructive possibilities. For a long time after his death, these were the songs that cut the deepest, not his later, more mature work. Because they spoke of a blind faith in his own transformation, an osmosis which turned out to be so much trickier than he'd imagined. As he grew later as a lyricist, he became a poet. There were early hints. I loved the way he sang "wise guys realize there's danger in emotional ties," long before I had any idea what it implied.

When we think of Wham! now, we think of a proto-boyband, a confection, something lightweight and innocuous. But a handsome duo opening their hit deck with an anti-Thatcherite rap about rejecting the system that middle England carved for them in favor of a life on the DHSS had more in common with the later work of another gay man and his best friend, Sleaford Mods, than it did One Direction.

George Michael had fired himself an atypical starting gun on the pop blocks. He wasn't the man who was lost in the hunt and heartache of love. That was to come. He was the assiduous best friend warning his buddy about girls who'd trap them into the boredom of domesticity, robbing them of spark and fire, a curious vantage point to first position his pop life. Sometimes it was as if his tenacity alone turbocharged him along. In "Everything She Wants" ("And now you're telling me that you're having my baby/I'll tell you that I'm happy if you want me to") he had sculpted a work of indisputable, hard-bitten, blue-eyed soul genius. This idiosyncratic kitchen-sink drama played out in pop couldn't—and didn't—last long. At the time I turned into George Michael on the lined pages of a homework essay, they were well into their final furlong, four years after their keen sprint began. By 1985, Wham! was comfortably the biggest band in the world, the first to gleefully leapfrog the iron curtain and play in China.

> **They contained every gay man's camaraderie with the best friend he loves, sometimes wordlessly; the one who is so near but so far. Platonic, yes, but more so. They were Bushey's Bodie and Doyle, ramped up on naïve Home Counties' ambition.**

Teen pop could not have been any more tribal back then. This was not about preferences for me. I wanted to swallow the whole giddy, gay canvas of British pop oddities, fashioned to alert each one of my newly developing adolescent senses in one gulp. Wham! pricked something so specific in me, a sensation I could taste before I could get close to articulating. They had just released their second album, *Make It Big*, a droll bit of wordplay on their tumescence. They were cocksure from the groin out, electrified by a sexuality percolating just below boiling point.

Wham! was supposed to be hetero-sexy but it looked like something more complex. George had hair like Princess Di and was always dressed in white. He wore a crucifix earring, appealing to the rejecting Catholic in me. His chest was emblazoned with the positivity slogan, *Choose Life!*, an edict the designer Katharine Hamnett stole from some Buddhist tract or another, a slogan which cut at right angles against the messaging of the government AIDS leaflets ("Silence=Death") posted through every British letterbox at the start of the pandemic. Amid the hits George wrote for that record was a cover of the Isley Brothers' "If You Were There," a song I loved from the opening bars. It found in me a new flavor of personal ache and hope that is almost certainly realer and harder in the imagining than it is played out in your twenties, when the adrenalized drama of life itself takes the place of tough, formless projection. The inescapable ballad "Careless Whisper" hinted at some of his commercial plaudits to come as a solo star; the sad, lonely lament "A Different Corner" at his incumbent artistic greatness. The sun shone in summer, the snow fell at Christmas for Wham! It never rained.

I have no idea what I wrote in that essay. But through it I felt touched, in some small way, by George's magic wand, the generosity of his songwriter's gift. He looked like someone who'd come from nothing and turned himself into something. If he could do it, why couldn't we all? He hid a secret I could sense without being able to spell it out loud.

The burly Scot gave me 20/20 for my homework, making a point of taking me aside for a quiet word. He said, "Paul, you have a talent for this," the first time I'd ever been told I was good at anything. In that moment, I decided I would one day like to be a writer, a notional possibility at such far remove from the lowly employment we were being farmed for as to now feel almost laughable. It is a kindness I've remembered with every pay check received during my working adult life since.

It is 1985. I am 13. And in my own small way, led gently by George's unknowing, distant, guiding hand, I begin the slow, clunky process of accepting that change is afoot, that my *coming out* is less probability, more inevitability. And there is your metamorphosis, right there.

* *

For a while, George Michael turned into my professional default mechanism while interviewing stars, a useful divining rod to organize the good-natured from the ill. Kate Moss loved recounting a story about a party George had thrown in the three-tiered back garden of his Highgate pile after the closing ceremony of the London Olympics, 2012, an event they'd both lent their amazing faces to. Paparazzi parked up outside and she'd escaped by climbing over the back wall in the early hours of the next morning, before legging it to her home across neighboring fences.

In summer 2016, the year George later died, I was dispatched to profile the novelist Jackie Collins in her elegant Bel Air home, a louche dreamscape crafted entirely from marble, mirror, and gold, against which she twinkled mischievously in one of her tailored white trouser suits. Her swimming pool was copied from a Hockney painting. She said she rented the next-door property out to Al Pacino. She, too, wanted to keep her neighbors correct. With the benefit of middle-aged hindsight, if I really wanted to turn into anybody, it was probably her. I can't even sing karaoke and hate cameras. I adored *Rock Star.*

It is 1985. I am 13. And in my own small way, led gently by George's unknowing, distant, guiding hand, I begin the slow, clunky process of accepting that change is afoot, that my *coming out* is less probability, more inevitability. And there is your metamorphosis, right there.

I'd arrived twenty minutes early and wandered the pristine sidewalks of her Los Angeles neighborhood to kill time, happening upon the Will Rogers Memorial Park at the northern end of her boulevard. "Oh, George's park?" she said, when I told her about the walk. No surname, no explanation, just complete cultural ownership of the site of his arrest for soliciting during a police sting in 1998, handed over to one of her absolute favorites. I mentioned the George incident might make a good story line for one of her blockbusters, at which point she scribbled something down longhand in a notebook before sauntering off into a recess of her extravagant parlor to sign a glossy hardback of *The Lucky Santangelo Cookbook* for my mum, another fan.

I heard about George's cottaging arrest while at my first press conference, for the Spice Girls, backstage in a colorless, airless, windowless suite at the then-named Nynex Arena, Manchester. Rumors were rife that one or all of the Girls were about to quit. They were then performing the exact same sleight of hand on the ambitions of suburban girls, on the exact same astronomical global platform that George and Andrew had for boys a generation earlier with Wham! The UK showbiz press, a hardy, journeyman contingent as it turned out, had descended on the event and the quick, excitable rumble of impending world news began to fill the room. In the event, it came from unexpected sources. Mobile phones began buzzing before the girls took to the stage, all playing the same unexceptional ringtone. They were just there to announce extra tour dates, anyway.

One by one, the room emptied as the story filtered through from reporters' respective news desks, of George Michael being caught with his pants down, coming on to an undercover LAPD officer at a latrine in Will Rogers' public lavatories. *Zip Me Up Before You Go Go* had been born, the moment George Michael officially came, or was rather thrown, out of the public closet.

For anyone keeping a close eye on his tale, the fifteen years prior follow the basic public relations' rubric of keeping George's sexuality hiding in plain sight. Decoys were planted in the press. The rumors would go away. Until they came back. Another decoy. Etc. While researching a book on British gay culture, I spoke at length with the former record label impresario Colin Bell, a remarkable gentleman who interconnects most of the dots on the British pink pop map of the early 1980s. He told the story of taking a meeting with George in his office with the head of the label, London Recordings, about the possibility of managing Wham! In the infancy of his career, George asked around about how he should handle his gayness.

Colin Bell was then in the process of transposing a heroically militant, shaven-headed, three-piece synth pop act, Bronski Beat, into the first superpower of open, unashamed, global gay pop. He had watched in joyful admiration as Frankie Goes to Hollywood took an iridescent, propulsive national anthem to gay sex, "Relax," to number one across the world, a historic act of pure gay punk anarchy which rendered most of the earlier provocation of the Sex Pistols the work of shoddy amateurs. Bell suggested George Michael should be similarly direct.

But George was 19 years old, from a Greek Orthodox family at home in Bushey, Hertfordshire, for whom he was vocally expected to marry and sire children. His fan base was bulging with teenage girls to whom he represented a benevolent idyll of approachable manhood, blessed and cursed with the same gently duplicitous sex appeal as Barry Manilow in the 1970s and Cliff Richard during the 1960s. By being the man that might brush their hair, they would reward him with a stage invasion of their knickers, regardless of any practicalities/legalities around their invisible mutual appeal.

George dropped into a complicated socio-political moment, fraught by the thumping dread of one prevailing social certainty, that to be gay was to be somehow morally wrong, physically odd, probably diseased, certainly indecent. Gay bashings were weekend sport for aggravated lads on the piss who'd run out of money from their giros. The same year George Michael scored his first number one single with "Careless Whisper," US Secretary of State for Health Margaret Heckler announced the identification of the HIV virus as the cause of AIDS, a health crisis that would go on to decimate a generation. These were our trenches. The newspapers hated us. Churches told us, repeatedly and without pause for any of their shared doctrinal compassion, that we were bound for hell, while papering over our tacitly approved childhood molestation. An actual law was invented and quickly passed, Clause 28 of the Local Government Act (1988), to stop our existence being acknowledged in any positive way in the British state-school system, lest it "promote" homosexuality, as if the matter of our sexuality could be equated with an offer on the cold shelves at a high-street supermarket. We couldn't serve in the army, foster, or adopt. Legal same-sex relationships were still twenty years away, marriage only an option if conducted against our nature. Whole police units were deployed to punish our intimacy. Gay male sexuality shared between consenting adults was not considered one of the beautiful contours of body and soul. The simple governance of gay attraction was instead deemed a repugnant act of personal weakness, a choice which deserved public damnation by all available establishment bodies and anyone of the passing public who fancied chucking a fist or insult at it.

Manchester's local police chief, James Anderton, summed up this mood of a decade when he instructed a raid on the basement of Rockies nightclub, a hop, skip, and jump away from the house I grew up in, and said on the six o'clock news that gay men "are swirling in a cesspool of their own making." Just because that one statement galvanized and fortified our cause doesn't mean it didn't leave a lasting generational imprint.

So, Boy George told *Smash Hits* he preferred a cup of tea to sex, to shield his ongoing affair with Culture Club's otherwise straight drummer, Jon Moss, a covert love story which contained most of the band's artistic sensitivities. Celibacy turned out to be an infectious calling card in this climate of archaic disapproval. Morrissey and Stephen Fry accounted for their personal lives by claiming it. The fabulously gobby, eye-patched, vampire-of-the-night goth/punk sensation Pete Burns was married to a hairdresser called Lynne. The appearance of John Waters's unlikely leading lady Divine on *Top of the Pops* caused national uproar and a blockage of the complaint lines at the BBC. Ripped to the gills on cocaine and liquor, to cloud a gay shame it took a lifetime of therapy to shed, Elton John married his female sound engineer, Renate Blauel, in Sydney, Australia. Freddie Mercury repeatedly denied rumors of his gayness while singing into a Hoover in barmaid drag and a moustache, recording opera and high-NRG disco hits with Montserrat Caballé and Giorgio Moroder, and only finally officially coming out on his deathbed. Pet Shop Boys folded into their early mythology a story about first meeting one another at an electronics shop on the Kings Road, because that's exactly where two gay men would bump into strangers in the Earl's Court vicinity of the early 1980s, hmm.

George Michael found a different manager in the shape of another garrulous giant of 1980s gay pop, who by coincidence shared half a surname with Colin, Simon Napier-Bell. After leaving the meeting, Colin Bell's secretary, a besotted early fan, casually asked if George was "one of them," to which Bell replied with a nod. Five incidents of this type and a low-level music industry rumor explodes into front-page tabloid gossip.

I never bought into George Michael's beards, the figurative ones at least. Brooke Shields looked like someone fun to go to a fabulous party with, maybe to chat with about frocks and skincare. After George died, his longest-standing tabloid girlfriend, Kathy Jeung, invented a hashtag to talk about their #specialrelationship, a term evoking political bonds whichever way you slice it.

These decoy pictures of George with his girlfriends were all planted during the *Faith* years, when his vaulting commercial ambition played out at its most uncontrolled diaspora. With the record, he became part of an elite 1 percent of worldwide superstars, the kind of symbolic

To be gay was to be somehow morally wrong, physically odd, probably diseased, certainly indecent.

figures on whom a young generation will hang all its hopes and dreams. Icons, even. To watch him elevated to that strata as his compromised self, scared to unsettle or confront the prejudices of the moment, a frightened man projecting complete self-assurance, was the definition of bittersweet, particularly when the opening line of the record is, "Well, I guess it would be nice if I could touch your body." What was stopping you, George?

With his army of six successive US number one singles, masterful stranglehold on MTV's pop video airtime, litter of Grammy Awards, all helmed by George's new styling tropes, borrowing a succession of hackneyed personal signals (leather jacket, aviator sunspecs, quiff, tight denim shot mostly from the rear) to establish him as Bushey's own Elvis, a Home Counties' James Dean, he became part of the literal handful of 1980s stars operating at pop's highest perch: Prince, Michael Jackson, Bruce Springsteen, Madonna, Whitney Houston, George. He was one of our own, fighting on the frontline, dispatching soft-centered balladry watermarked by hard commercial edges.

I not only knew I was gay at this point but had begun testing the water by telling people close to me. With some precise irony, I fully consummated a relationship with a man physically for the first time the same month "I Want Your Sex" was banned by the BBC, noting it in one of the jotters in which I taught myself to write with freedom.

The commercial largesse of *Faith*, or "the beard years" to give them their full gay inscription, was George Michael's most dichotomous. I couldn't listen to the record for years, despite its clear accomplishments, because it was so tied in my mind to the coincidence of my personal liberation with George's continued determination to prize wealth and fame over personal transparency. Then I heard the expertly skilled DJ Andrew Weatherall drop the album's second song, "Father Figure," into one of his roving sets, a kaleidoscopic journey cataloging the outer edges of trippy, low-slung disco to a room full of bearded gays and their friends, woozily ennobled by disinhibiting love drugs at a South London Sunday night nightclub in the mid-00s. Warmed by the comfort of George's voice, that divine instrument, hearing him whip off the purposeful ad lib "I'll be your daddy" in a context Weatherall knew well would cut straight to the communion of the crowd, I forgave *Faith*—and George— everything. He simply couldn't help himself.

With *Faith*, he had reached for the stars, landing on one only to find it covered in dust. To become the epochal, you have to forgo the personal. To write your own banner headlines, you must empty yourself of nuance. And so, in an astonishing artistic about-turn, he disappeared into the abyss to fashion his two undisputed and undiminished masterpieces, *Listen Without Prejudice Vol. 1*, which could not speak any clearer of unleashing himself from the shackles of his hidden sexuality from its title down, then *Older*, in which he candidly chronicled the young death from AIDS of his first real and almost public love, Anselmo Feleppa.

In 1990, when *Listen Without Prejudice Vol. 1* dropped, I would gauge no schoolboy was writing a Kafka-inspired essay titled "The Day I Turned into George Michael" anymore. Post *Faith*, the artist removes his face from public view. He becomes a mystery and an open book. It is the moment he reveals himself to be blessed with free-form artistic genius. Pick a song, any song, from those two records. Pluck it on a guitar. Hum it aloud. Musically, it is The Beatles, The Stones, Sinatra, The Bee Gees, and Stevie Wonder conjoined, punctuated by deferential references to them all. Lyrically, it is the tale of every gay man's transcendence from the man he was taught to be to the man he was meant to be. On "Fastlove" and "Spinning the Wheel" he introduces the cruising lexicon to pop's vocabulary, the former documenting its salacious bodily hit, the latter its multiple panic-button neuroses. These songs are an interior rumination on HIV and the modern man, trying to locate a love that is real and raw in a universe that actively obstacles you from finding it. Nobody has expressed the search for love among the unloved with more pinpoint precision than in the couplet "In the absence of security, I made my way into the night/Stupid Cupid keeps on calling me, but I see nothing in his eyes."

George Michael's liberating wheels of transparency have started to turn. In the video for "Freedom! '90," a leather jacket is burned in a closet, a satisfactory symbolism for those of us tracing the minutiae of his story as that astral musical ascendancy finally takes flight and he allows himself to sing the things he wants to say. His gay story has begun, readying itself for the stoutest response to a police officer's wink in a Los Angeles restroom. George Michael's second metamorphosis, a turning into his true self, has happened.

His public relations rule book has by now been ripped to shreds, burned to the ground. A man of complexity and defiance emerges from their ashes. In the immediate aftermath of his arrest, he conducts his first personal TV interview with the Yorkshire everyman Michael Parkinson, a one-man synonym for Middle England. He refuses to apologize for any of it and numbers some of the institutional phobias that are intertwined with his story. He writes the song "Outside," a wry disco riposte to his arrest, and sets the video at a latrine, with choreographed coppers wielding suggestive truncheons, dancing under mirror-balls to the sound of sirens. We are a cesspool no longer. He conjures the utopian spirit of Fire Island, that nirvana of gay sex and dancing, for four minutes of solid-gold, pop triumph. His work is complete. Wise guys realize, if you'll recall, there's danger in emotional ties.

Pick a song, any song, from those two records. Pluck it on a guitar. Hum it aloud. Musically, it is The Beatles, The Stones, Sinatra, The Bee Gees, and Stevie Wonder conjoined, punctuated by deferential references to them all. Lyrically, it is the tale of every gay man's transcendence from the man he was taught to be to the man he was meant to be.

**

Fame, I have found, from skirting its outside edge during most of the twenty-five years of my professional life, is not a solution to a problem. Even the ones who look like they're good at it only do so because they understand the Faustian core of fame's double bluff. To be loved by strangers may feel like a beautiful thing. But it turns out to be an esoteric oddity which introduces an entire new raft of philosophic, day-to-day impediments. David Beckham once explained to me that to enjoy being hero-worshipped in completion, you must also enjoy the equal measures of hatred that will accompany it.

Fame further means your personal approval is dependent on a withering of your freedoms. The strangely comforting responsibilities of paying a bill, vacuuming a carpet, or understanding a lover's true motivation are hollowed out to become a matter of life laundry deputized to someone else, standing in the ample shadow of your creation.

There is always someone orbiting around that shadowy netherworld, close at hand, with as many narcotics as you might choose to relieve yourself of in this freshly opened space at life's core, for however long you want them to do it. Then there is the question with which everyone who occupies that strange space of the famous asks themselves from time to time. How much of yourself do you give away to save the you that needed validating in the first place?

George did the lot, gave away everything, a gift mailed directly to the tetchy moral guidance counsel at work in the British tabloid press, a place where good and evil are binary constructs, not planets we all flit around on a minute-by-minute basis. He died on Christmas Day 2016, aged 53. A little piece of my heart broke that night. The line "Strange, don't you think I'm looking older?" haunted me for the following fortnight, before realizing that he never would. Because of the temperature his fame fell into, his death carried the heavy weight of a foregone conclusion, part of the stinging narrative of early loss which traces the lives of all who weathered the AIDS pandemic, one which broke every rule of the life cycle. If George Michael were 19 now, when fame has moved from the realms of fantasy to reality and an expectation of anxiety disorders is sewn into the public folio of the famous, who knows? There are many ifs.

George was the glitch in the system between total image management and its reappraisal in a new digital age of transparency. The deaths of Bowie, Prince, and Aretha Franklin felt like the passing of celestial beings, traveling one planet to the next. The death of George Michael felt like a finality, saying farewell to that kindly next-door neighbor who has always been quietly present, signing for your packages and watching out for burglars. Writing, I have found, is the coward's favorite form of fame, one of the few jobs in a public space in which you control your own narrative, silently bending and shaping other people's stories in order to serve your wider purpose. It is a spotlight without glare. Even something you once wrote which you now hate is a handy pointer to the you that existed in the moment you decided not to erase those words. Your name becomes known but not your face. On the arbitrary occasions your picture accompanies your words, it is stuck rigid, immobile, at a flattering angle, lit by studio lights, stubbornly refusing to age for years at a time. I guess that's why we don't make pop or film stars', footballers', or models' money. The only dreams hung on our words, in the end, are our own.

We are allowed to grow old with grace. The whims of the pop machine mean that there will always be a younger, prettier model along to take your place, in whom a new generation can see themselves at their most naked and exposed. Before you know it, another boyband escapee, Robbie Williams, is singing your song, stealing your airtime, taking your drugs, looking to fill his deficit of self-worth with the adoration of strangers. And the beat goes on. Because I can barely touch the physical outline of what it felt like to be 13 and smitten with a pop star now, I would love to read that essay again, to analyze whatever it was that was going through my little head when I scripted "The Day I Turned into George Michael." What keys would it uncover to my unraveling? What story did I use it to begin? Surely, all of it would be between the lines. Whatever fantasy life it was that I imagined he was living turned out to be a more somber business, flecked with moments of absolute clarity and joy, for George, for me, for gay mankind, as we all inched a little closer to our messy selves and the freedom to be accepted as them.

I only ever really wanted to be allowed to be myself, you see. That's the beauty of a true metamorphosis. It is just a chrysalis shedding its skin, turning into something more precious and difficult by a colorful fete of science and nature. We all get there in the end.

I met George Michael once. It was the tenth anniversary party of *Attitude*, the gay magazine I worked at for three years straddling either side of the millennium. There was a time, bored at home, having fulfilled all his wildest artistic and commercial ambitions, George called up the magazine's editor directly from his Highgate home to ask about a story he'd been invigorated by reading. They chatted like old friends. A relationship with the publication began. And so, he came to our party.

That night, in 2004, was the single most glamorous in the magazine's history. Gay culture was going through one of its intermittent, interloping periods of prominence. British politics was catching up and the legislature had begun to iron out our inequalities. Elton John and David Furnish, who would soon become legal husbands, held court in

It is just a chrysalis shedding its skin, turning into something more precious and difficult by a colorful fete of science and nature.

a corner. Boy George caroused through the crowd. Pet Shop Boys made their discreet presence felt in excellent clothes. And the surprise breakout pop stars of the year, Scissor Sisters, a ragbag troupe assembled from the rubble of New York's last stab at defining the world's gay nighttime, performed a jubilant set on a tiny stage in a plush West End bar. Their music seemed to assemble inspirations drawn from the work of each of their gay forebears, honoring them with a fresh camp and candor befitting the composition of a new, more accepting century. I shook George Michael's hand as "Take Your Mama" struck up its first chords. The similarity to one of his best songs, "Freedom! '90," was lost on neither of us in that brief exchange. George Michael raised an eyebrow. High on the moment, I made my way into the night, an unexpected lifetime's mission satisfyingly complete.

Paul Flynn

Paul Flynn is a journalist, editor, and author who has spent the last 25 years documenting pop culture. In 2017, he collated the LGBTQ+ wing of his work in his first book, *Good As You*, a compendium of how British gay equality happened, told through the evolutionary and revolutionary tales of its dance floors, pop songs, magazines, sports stars, hospital wards, television shows, and occasionally, even, its politicians.

Paul was the first writer to profile Elton John in 2000 and David Beckham in 2001 for a gay magazine, *Attitude*, during a four-year stint (1999–2003). With prolific tenures writing for *i-D*, *Pop*, *Love*, *Fantastic Man*, *The Gentlewoman*, and numerous other style titles at the peak of their powers, he has amassed somewhere in the region of 100 cover stories. He is proud to have prioritized minority stories throughout his working life, chipping in to help incubate and maintain a broad, inclusive print media in which LGBTQ+ writers can speak in open, unapologetic, honest voices, telling our stories from the inside.

He has co-written an award-winning play for the National Theatre of Scotland, helped create a piece of art for the Tate, and written liner notes for several of his all-time favorite LPs. Though he has lived in London for most of his professional life, he is staunchly Mancunian, a badge of regional honor he likes to point out to anyone complaining about the hot-button topic of identity politics. His favorite George Michael song is "A Different Corner."

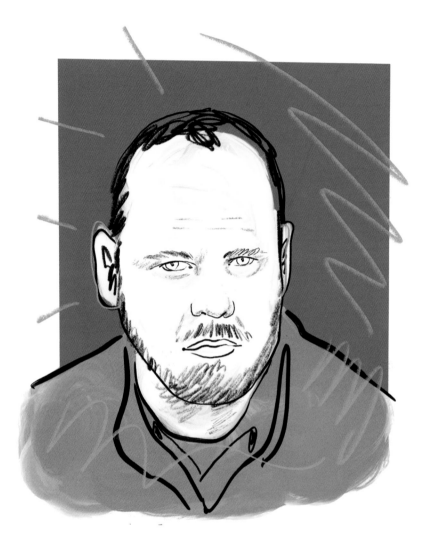

Illustration by Sam Russell Walker

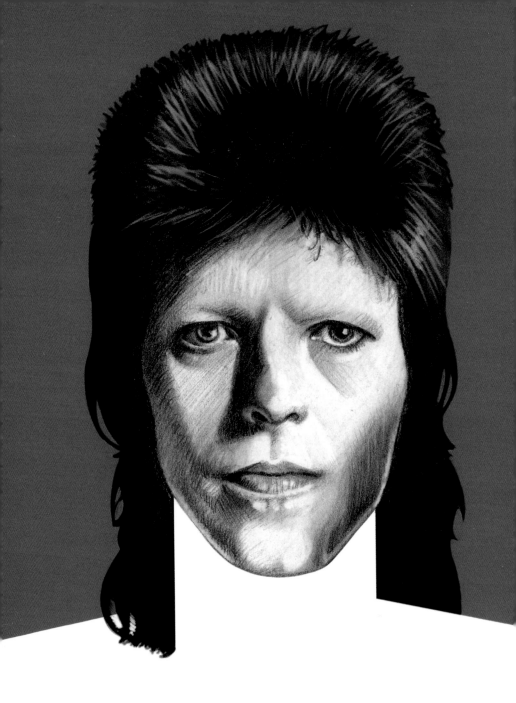

DAVID BOWIE

by Freddy McConnell

Here it is: the Bowie essay. You knew it was coming, right? Would this even be a book about queer icons without someone waxing lyrical about the Thin White Duke? Certainly, the fact of his universally accepted status—as queer icon but also as 140-million-record-selling, 111-single-releasing, 30-movie-appearing, one-knighthood-rejecting music legend—means I feel a certain [read: paralyzing] weight of responsibility.

Because, of course, it's not just us queers who claim Bowie. His chameleonic public personas, much more so than his commercial success, made him eminently claimable. Sure, he is a hero of mine. I am a queer Transgender man, for crying out loud. For years, my mum literally was not sure if I was a boy or a girl. (I still feel the thrill of recognition in that line. It is part of the reason why *Diamond Dogs* is my favorite Bowie album. Also, it is not cool to say *Low* anymore.)

Yet what if you are not queer? What if no one was asking this question when Bowie was becoming and being the biggest songwriting star in the world? These binaries—gay/straight or queer/ally—did not exist in the public imagination of 1960s and 1970s

Illustration by Austin Storie

Britain, at least not in any speakable sense. We have to understand Bowie the queer artist as a product of his time (and then acknowledge our queer times as a product of him, but that is for another essay).

A dearth of options back then meant Ziggy Stardust—Bowie's first all-encompassing stage persona—simply had to be an alien. His spiky copper hair, his sparkly skintight suits, every manifestation, tangible or otherwise, of his gender fluidity, was as new to audiences as it was shocking. In short, the context for reading Ziggy as we do today did not exist then. The next-best thing was outer space and specifically the space race, which Bowie had already culturally trademarked with his first number one hit, "Space Oddity."

Still, his otherworldliness did not make Ziggy *avant-garde*. He (perhaps "they" if the option had occurred) was not even left field. Ziggy was Bowie's first mainstream, global smash. I imagine that for every hysterical young fan at his shows there was an older onlooker—a parent or teacher—unable to look away from the spectacle and yet unable (or too ashamed) to say why.

Of course, back then queer kids latched on to him too, like babies latch on to life-giving teats. The getups, his sinewy sensuality, and his transcendent lyrics would have shone a light in the darkest of closets. But judging by those nostalgic clip shows where celebrities take turns extolling Bowie's brilliance, every straight teen and their mate worshipped him too. Anyone in search of the novel, the scandalous, or just the melodic could justifiably decide that Bowie was for them.

I suspect there are lots of aging, very straight cis men today who quietly resent or are simply confused by the contemporary idea of Bowie as queer icon. In their day, it was all about long hair and loud music. It was about who you weren't (i.e., your parents), not about "exploring" who you were. Then again, those are two ends of the same question, right? We had to start somewhere.

I am not here to criticize the priorities of bygone teens. I happily join their ranks, eager to explain why my special relationship with Bowie is, in fact, the special-est. Indeed, undermining the connection that a straight boy from Maidstone had to Bowie in 1974 feels almost as misguided as a broadsheet columnist deriding Gen Xers for their "wokeness" today.

Even if you just admire Bowie's industrious approach to queering (or glamming, if you prefer) everything he laid eyes on—his more stereotypically masculine, fuck you, rock'n'roll attitude, perhaps—he is yours too. There is enough Bowie for everyone, both in each career chapter and taking his stupendous output as a whole (minus Tin Machine, of course, let's be reasonable). Even better when the artist makes clear, as Bowie did with grace and compassion, that your relationship to their work is no business of theirs.

> Every straight teen and their mate worshipped him too. Anyone in search of the novel, the scandalous, or just the melodic could justifiably decide that Bowie was for them.

* *

Of course, things are different today. By assuming that Bowie is still essential, maybe I am just showing my age. I am aware of this distinct possibility, having recently watched a season of *University Challenge*. When teams made up of undergraduates—average age 19–21—routinely failed to recognize hits by bands like The Cure, The Clash, and The Smiths in the music rounds, the scales of my subjective youth fell from my eyes with a thud.

Do we still need Bowie, now that we have out-and-proud LGBTQ+ stars like Lady Gaga, Frank Ocean, Sam Smith, Olly Alexander, Tegan and Sara, and Janelle Monáe? The question itself is problematic. It implies that Bowie was queer in the contemporary sense and, so, closeted. This theory is only really supported by rumor (unless you count his "coming out" in 1972, which he retracted and expressed regret over a decade later. Perhaps one of his youthful stage personas getting carried away).

For me at least, it is more complicated—more emotional and personal. Bowie is not my queer hero because I think he was queer in the way I am. Sure, I understand him as artistically and politically queer, if not an activist. In terms of queer theory, he ticked every box. He problematized, destabilized, or deconstructed heteronormative ideas of masculinity, gender, and sexuality. He not only challenged but obliterated our notions of who was allowed to be a mainstream pop and rock culture icon.

Without his vision and ambition (and, of course, his pre-watershed turn as a horny, androgynous Starman on *Top of the Pops* in 1972), the push to reclaim "queer" might not have ended in the overwhelming victory we benefit from today. I have no doubt he was an ally, perhaps even one of those slightly too enthusiastic and overbearing ones. Sure, he might have faced accusations of queer appropriation if he did now what he did then, but as *Slate*'s J. Bryan Lowder wrote after Bowie's death in 2016, "you can't appropriate what you help create."[1]

But yes, aside from his credentials as queer hero nonpareil, across infinite space and time, why is he *mine*? Given his god-like stature, how can it possibly feel personal?

**

1987

I am a baby, perhaps a toddler, being serenaded. My father smiles and sings, "Ha ha ha, he he he, I'm the laughing gnome and you can't catch me . . ."

I am less than two years old. We are in our cramped, converted coach house in southeast London. "The Laughing Gnome" was a single by David Bowie, released in 1967. I did not discover this until well into my teens, when my Bowie worship was at its peak. I hear it now as an echo. I thought my dad sang it just for me.

> **He problematized, destabilized, or deconstructed heteronormative ideas of masculinity, gender, and sexuality. He not only challenged but obliterated our notions of who was allowed to be a mainstream pop and rock culture icon.**

1996

I'm in the back seat of my mum's Renault Scenic, driving off on holiday, probably Devon or maybe that trip to Cyprus. I'm listening to a homemade mixtape on my personal cassette player. The foam earpieces and thin, hard plastic band press too hard on my head but I do not care. I am listening to "Heroes" at full volume. The motorway markings and power cables

---

1   J. Bryan Lowder, "Was David Bowie Gay?" (*Slate*, 2016).

undulating past become a music video I am shooting with my eyes. I hear every note of pain and hope in Bowie's voice as if they are my own.

I am eight. My parents recently separated. My dad made me this mixtape.

1998

Dad is recounting an anecdote for the umpteenth time because I love hearing it.

It is the mid-seventies and he is at the train station after school, waiting to go home. He looks down the platform and sees David Bowie. The superstar—his musical hero—is waiting for the boat train. He must be headed to France or off on a European tour! Any fan of Bowie knows he does not like to fly.

"Did you really *not* speak to him?" I ask, incredulous.

"No, I didn't want to bother him. Seeing him was enough."

"Wooooow. So cool."

I go to the same school and reimagine this brief encounter hundreds of times.

2000

I am a solid, if lazy, student and an avid reader. I have a good speaking voice yet my confidence and self-image are starting to buckle under the weight of the wrong puberty. My English teacher tells me I am competing in the school poetry-reading competition.

Reluctant but competitive, I am sheepishly keen to show the world who I am through the music I love. My dad and I decide that my "poem" will be David Bowie's "Future Legend." It opens his camply nihilistic concept album, *Diamond Dogs*:

"Fleas the size of rats sucked on rats the size of cats,
And ten thousand peoploids split into small tribes,
Coveting the highest of the sterile skyscrapers,
Like packs of dogs assaulting the glass fronts of Love-Me Avenue . . ."

. . . I explain to a hundred fellow pupils, all my teachers, and a smattering of parents . . .

"This ain't Rock'n'Roll,
This is Genocide!"

My dad got it. I got it. And, amazingly, so did the audience. I took first prize.

2002

I am of age. It is time to listen to the profound modulations of "Sweet Thing/Candidate/Sweet Thing (Reprise)" in full and uninterrupted. It is my dad's and now my favorite eight and a half minutes of Bowie. We listen in silence and at full volume.

At first, I don't get it. The saxophone is cheesy, the pressure to appreciate is distracting. But I feel entrusted with something, like this is part of an inheritance. So, I persevere, and in my own time, I fall hard for it.

I learn to anticipate the moment Bowie sings *"I'll make you deal, like any other candidate..."* and the syncopated tempo ramps up and *"... if you want it, boys, get it here (thing)..."* and he is talking to me and it is probably the best minute in all of recorded music.

By 16, I do not understand how and I do not have the words but I know I am one of the boys. My dad does not know—no one can know—but that does not matter. Bowie gets me and my dad gets Bowie. We have that.

2004

I read a brick-like paperback biography of Bowie. I want to know everything. I want to escape my anxious, dysphoric self and mounting A-level stress. I want to be in sixties Soho or seventies Berlin. I want to be transported, to escape.

> By 16, I do not understand how and I do not have the words but I know I am one of the boys. My dad does not know—no one can know—but that does not matter. Bowie gets me and my dad gets Bowie. We have that.

I know we both love Bowie's Berlin albums, along with *The Idiot*. So when I have pored over those chapters, I want to talk to my dad about what Bowie and Iggy got up to then—the drugs, the debauchery, the drag.

Almost straightaway, however, I meet resistance. Dad is not interested. For him, he explains, gently yet firm, it is just about the music. This blows my mind. How can it *just* be about the music?

I want to tell him he is missing out, but I hold back. I am old enough to know that this is not how people work. This moment forces me to realize, perhaps later than most teenagers, that my thing with Bowie has to be—should be—just for me. At first, the distance makes me feel wobbly, but soon my stride lengthens.

2008

The vinyl records that have been in my life since the day I was born—*Lodger*, *Low*, *Diamond Dogs*, *Aladdin Sane*, the double *Live* album—suddenly, they are mine. So are the remastered CDs we bought from our local record shop (long gone) in the 1990s. They have all been turned over countless times in our family's hands.

My dad's relationship with Bowie is his own. I do not understand it, but that's OK. I show him how to use iTunes and how to search YouTube for all the famous, and some rare, footage of Bowie et al.

I am at university in Scotland. I take all the music with me.

2013

I am an adult. I am a Transgender man. I am queer. I am very excited for the landmark *David Bowie Is* retrospective at the V&A Museum.

My dad is respectful but we never talk about my transition. Nowadays, we swerve all contentious topics. It is a pact—an ultimately loving one—not uncommon between a parent and the grown-up child they did not anticipate.

For his birthday, I buy us both tickets to the exhibition, which is selling out fast. This will not be *just* about the music, but I feel compelled to share it with him. He is not excited in the way I am excited, but he is game.

On the day, the rooms are hot and busy. Neither of us thrives in crowds but it helps that we move at the same pace, are drawn to the same corners.

Wonderfully, the Berlin-era room is virtually empty. We settle on a box to watch floor-to-ceiling projections of candid footage, interviews, and live performances. Bowie is all big coats and side partings. He looks happy. *Lodger*, which we agree is underrated, fades in and out.

Bowie's ambiguity is everything; it gives us space to connect. He is our difference and our contradictions. He is our musical hero and our shared memories. We sit there for a long time.

Freddy McConnell

Freddy McConnell is a writer and journalist. He gained his degree in Arabic and Islamic Studies living in the West Bank, Syria, and Afghanistan, before beginning his career at *The Guardian*. During a year spent as deputy video editor at *Guardian Australia*, he established their award-winning podcasts team.

In 2018, he returned home to start his family, for which he paused his medical transition to safely carry his own child. Freddy shared this experience in the BIFA-nominated feature documentary *Seahorse*, so called because male seahorses go through pregnancy and birth. It was directed by Jeanie Finlay and produced by the BBC and Grain Media.

After becoming a father, Freddy wanted to help tell the myriad amazing stories of how other queers start their families, which led to the creation of his BBC podcast, *Pride & Joy*. He has also written a forthcoming children's book about a single-parent seahorse family.

Freddy is a committed advocate for LGBTQ+ equality and in particular the rights of Transgender people and their families to safety, dignity, and equality. To this end, he has challenged the government in court on their failure to legally recognize the existence and rights of Transgender parents.

Freddy and his kiddo live in his hometown on the Kent coast, where they enjoy cold swims and bike rides.

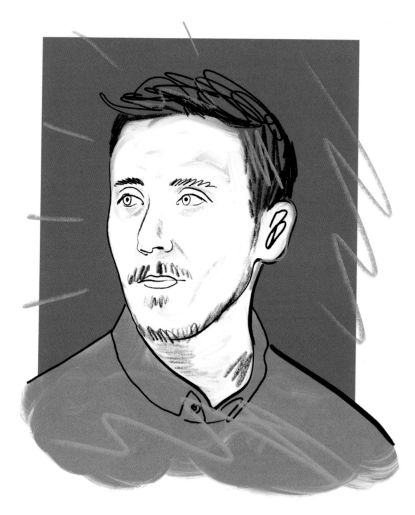

Illustration by Sam Russell Walker

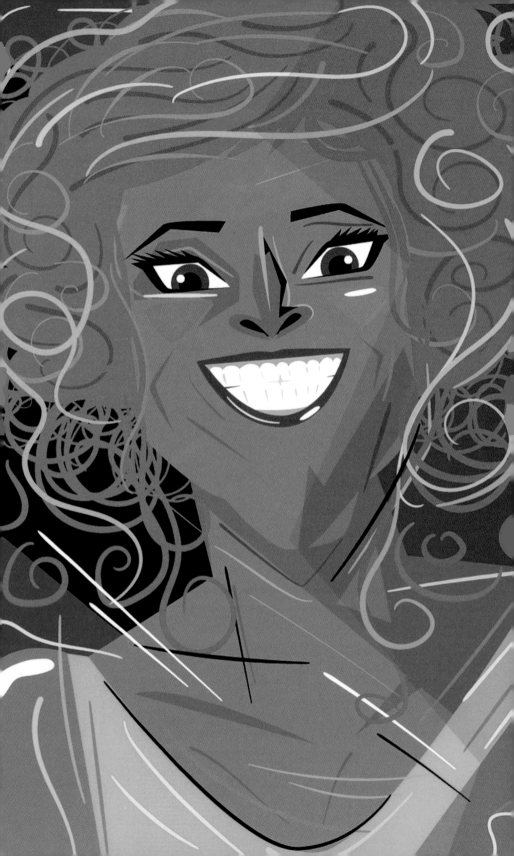

RADICAL GENIUS: THE LASTING INFLUENCE OF ICON VAGINAL DAVIS'S EARLY WORK ON MY LIFE

by Mykki Blanco

How do I begin to articulate my love for Vaginal Davis? You might think I'm being dramatic when I say Vaginal Davis, for me, sits within my being with somewhat of a spiritual force. Because I was only 15 years old the first time I encountered Vaginal's work, and now, writing this love letter, I am 34.

Illustration by Patricio Oliver

Vaginal, for me, is now a hazy forever feeling; more of an emotional geography, more place than actual human being. I think of Vaginal similar to how I think of Jesus Christ—extremely familiar and yet elusive. I was also 15 when I discovered artist Peter Halley's *index Magazine*. Growing up in the rural South in the early 2000s, one of the only places where I could discover the faraway worlds of cosmopolitan arts and culture was my local Barnes & Noble. Barnes & Noble is a chain bookstore and magazine seller usually found in every urban-sprawl, strip-mall complex across the United States. Oh how I remember those rose-colored days fondly, browsing the fashion, art, and culture sections of the magazine racks. My teenage brain turned on, tuned in, and, voraciously hungry, devouring all that seemed "other" somehow to compensate for the "otherness" I felt within. It was in the pages of the *index* that I first set eyes on an interview and feature with Vaginal Creme Davis. To me, Vaginal Davis is an iconoclast, a legend and an art mama; someone who by her sheer existence and artistic will has created universes for generations at the drop of a dime. Vaginal is the guerilla "Terrorist Drag" Goddess of our Black punk mythologies. Vaginal Davis is an internationally known visual artist, whose video pieces, performances, and zines shaped multiple queer-centered cultural movements. Vaginal Davis is a scholar, public intellectual, and teacher. Vaginal is a shape-shifter, birthing timelines, inventing biographies and "her stories," a griot of gutter camp. Springing Venus-like out of the radical West Coast of the 1960s, there is no exact birth date for Ms. Davis—and rightly so. I would not be surprised if Vaginal is immortal.

I remember feeling and innately knowing I was like Vaginal, but not actually understanding how deep or how far our similarities would become. That, I think, is one of the gifts of life bestowed upon us, as you grow into your early teen years. You are still innocent of the many difficult layers of society, and yet you are consciously living in it, aware only of your unique life experience but still further away from any kind of existential awakening. Yet I was close to mine. I saw the close-up portrait on the open magazine page, a handsome Black femme with a straw jaw and a beehive updo akin to Brigitte Bardot, mascara on the lashes and just a touch of lipstick, nothing else. The only other Black femme I had seen up to that point in my life was RuPaul. There is something wild about Vaginal, crazy eyes, something wasn't palatable, not refined and not glamorous. This person was nothing like Ru, this person was ambiguous and nebulous, nefarious even. My 15-year-old brain couldn't really articulate why I was attracted to the raw image of this person, this portrait. Within seconds, I would read the interview, see the editorial photos on the following page, and fall in love with Vaginal Davis forever.

Wait! Dammit! I haven't laid the complete foundation yet. My bad, let me do that for you now. I need to give you a few preliminary details, details about what cosmically led me to an article about Vaginal Davis that particular day at the bookstore and later the email exchange between Vaginal and me that would change my life. So, my darlings, my tale actually begins in a Driver's Education class. Yep, that's right, good old Driver's Ed. Sophomore year of high school, I signed up to learn how to drive, and we (the gym coach who taught the course and his motley crew of underlings) would meet every afternoon in a damp trailer adjacent to the football field. I hated the course. It was optional and I only did it because, well, you know, it's how you learn to operate a car. I eventually dropped out of Driver's Ed because I got a paid offer to play the "Big Mouse" that opens the ballet in a local, but respectable, ballet rendition of Balanchine's *The Nutcracker*. To a 15-year-old queerdo like me, the idea of being paid $600 to dress up in a mouse costume and pretend to know ballet, bouncing around the stage in a tuxedo, was like hitting the lottery, far more cool and interesting than learning to parallel park or use a turn signal. What I did take away, of significant value, from the few classes I attended in that damp trailer was a friendship with a really interesting girl named Jonti.

One of the gifts of life, as you grow into your early teen years, is that you are still innocent of the many difficult layers of society, yet you are consciously living in it, aware only of your unique life experience but still further away from any kind of existential awakening.

Jonti was a petite girl with pale skin, a round face, and princess peach-pink cheeks. Her head was shaved back to front with just a wispy fringe bang falling into her face, wispy hair around her ears. She wore clothing that was more fitting for an old lady rather than a 15-year-old, but she paired her granny fashions with punk elements like combat boots and spiky bracelets—lots and lots of spiky bracelets. Immediately spotting another freak, I attached myself to Jonti. We had seen each other in the hallways, but it was a big high school and there had been no previous time or circumstance allotted for introductions. Jonti and I bonded over many things, but our connection to music was the most precious. She introduced me to a movement that she was a solid and staunch member of, a movement at that point in time that was twenty years our senior but still held tantamount relevance to our lives. This was the "Riot Grrl" movement, and Jonti exposed me and indoctrinated me into all things "Riot Grrl," and I happily joined the militia.

The main band that served as my entry point into "Riot Grrl" was Le Tigre. Le Tigre was an all-girl electronic punk band created in 1998 and fronted by Kathleen Hanna. Hanna was coined as one of the originators of the "Riot Grrl" movement in the early 1990s. The all-girl band consisted of Hanna, artists Johanna Fateman and Sadie Benning, and later JD Samson. I had never heard music like Le Tigre's. It was tinkering agit-pop and dance music with lyrics explicitly about feminism, LGBTQ politics, queer bodies, and queer minds. It was my first time learning about our societal system of patriarchy. My mind exploded! All of the things and themes I had been feeling inside that I could not articulate were now coming to me full throttle. Listening to Le Tigre's music was like a condensed lesson in queer theory, feminist history, art history, and a contemporary, albeit "alternative," take on the current state of the world. It was through Le Tigre's album *Feminist Sweepstakes* that I came upon a track featuring none other than the doyenne of Queercore herself, Lady Vaginal Davis. The song was called "Well, Well, Well" and featured dynamic lyrics that I took to be my clarion call for my newly established alt punk identity. "Raise your hand/Raise your voice/Raise your head/up off the desk/Look who's here/Well well well guess it's time/For show-and-tell." At the end of the song, you hear a voice softly cooing that quickly turns into an orgasmic cackle. It's Vaginal all right, a sound bite that assuredly encapsulates her original brand of magnetic hysteria. So Vaginal's name was mildly familiar that day. I discovered her in the bookshop and she was already dangling somewhere heavy in my subconscious mind.

"Honey, baby doll, I've always been too weird for every scene that I've ever been a part of." "Too weird for the punks, too weird for the gangbangers in Watts." "People just accepted me for what I am; they didn't have a choice exactly." "I'm a big girl." Vaginal Davis is an easy, breezy California girl at heart. Coming of age in the womb of South-Central Los Angeles, Vaginal was a natural-born radical, her name taken from activist, public intellectual, and freedom-fighter Angela Davis. "I feel fortunate that I grew up in a very unique historical moment in the late sixties and early seventies. The Black Panthers just took over my elementary school and the white administration couldn't do a thing to stop them as they were armed and ready to throw down. My inner-city elementary school had Black, Brown, Asian, and some white kids whose parents were too poor for white flight into the suburbs, and here we were all being indoctrinated into spirited Black Nationalism singing protest songs together and learning war chants and solidarity dance routines." A turbulent, utopian age laid the foundation for a young Vaginal Davis to creatively roam free, an imagination unboxed. Davis cites seeing a production of writer and playwright Ntozake Shange's *For Colored Girls Who Have Considered Suicide/ When the Rainbow Is Enuf* as a pivotal moment in their childhood that would go on to inspire their own creations. Shange's play *For Colored Girls* centered on themes of race, gender, sexuality, and class, themes woven into Davis's work throughout her career spanning the last thirty years.

Vaginal was an ingenious youth and the cultivation of their artistic practice began early. Often writing, directing, and producing her own guerilla-style stage and film work, one of the first performance art and musical projects to spring forth from the mind of Davis was a group called The Afro Sisters, formed in 1978. One of the earliest archived works by The Afro Sisters is a video art piece that has now been canonized as a cult classic, *That Fertile Feeling*. A 1982 collaboration between The Afro Sisters and The Amoeba Records Film collective is a low-budget, no-budget, action adventure film. *That Fertile Feeling* is a gritty camp romp of a plot where a baby-faced Davis in a mangled, long, blonde wig and her best friend, Fertile Latoya Jackson, careen around central Los Angeles looking for a place for Fertile to give birth to the eleven babies that have grown in her womb. Turned away from the local hospital for not having health insurance, Fertile and Vaginal then proceed to barge into Fertile's baby daddy's apartment to deliver the babies. Fertile's boyfriend, completely naked and unmoved by the pop-up delivery room created in his kitchenette, proceeds to clean house while Vaginal coaches Fertile through each contraction, screaming and heaving. Absurdly, after Fertile's "eleven-tuplets" are born, she immediately leaves all eleven infants with Vaginal, hops on a skateboard, does a few tricks, and rides off into the sun-drenched afternoon. Whether a comedic comment on living through generations in a welfare state or a tongue-in-cheek take at queer bodies playing at heterosexual normalcy, *That Fertile Feeling* encapsulates the various themes later to be found in so many of Davis's works.

> **Listening to Le Tigre's music was like a condensed lesson in queer theory, feminist history, art history, and a contemporary, albeit "alternative," take on the current state of the world.**

Davis created and carved through her many interdisciplinary projects her own hyperreal version of queerness. Posits on race, class, ridiculousness, and absurdity as a means of societal critique. "Fertile Latoyah Jackson" would also be the name used for one of Vaginal's many art and music fanzines. "Queercore" is the name of an art, music, and social movement that originated in the mid-1980s as an LGBTQIA alternative to the punk rock movement. A 1992 issue of British arts and culture magazine *i-D* describes "Queercore" as a "growing American movement of low-budget punky gay fanzines . . . who reject the gay mainstream and function as self-help network for alienated homos." Vaginal Davis is credited as one of the pioneers and originators of this movement due to the plethora of zines she created throughout the 1980s whose aesthetics mirror the DIY "give no fucks" ethos of the social punk and hard-core scenes while also being a bridge for a certain kind of flamboyant and militant queer ideology. "I was on the punk scene as a drag queen. I had a band called 'The Afro Sisters' and that's where Fertile was born. We handed out copies of Fertile at Afro Sisters' gigs, then shops carried it, then there was this snowballing effect! I found a lot of people were into the consciousness that I was into." "Queercore" was a broad community and zines were significant at the time because they were calling cards to meet and get to know people who had similar ideas, art, and musical tastes as well as perspectives on life in general. Mainstream gay American culture was white, privileged, and homogenous while the punk and hard-core scenes were often homophobic, transphobic, and racist. "I get interviewed a lot because I'm a controversial Black woman. My teachers didn't understand. I was this Black kid that came to school in a dress and they couldn't work out how to teach me. So I did my own thing, taught myself to type and Xerox. I'm a notorious punk rock, retarded whore, six-six with child-bearing hips."

I was lucky to find online, archived and completely intact, one of Vaginal Davis's zines from 1994 called *Yes, Ms. Davis*. Sold at the time for the generous price of two dollars, *Yes, Ms. Davis* draws me closer to understanding Vaginal's vibe at the time, her interests and her inspirations. The opening page of *Yes, Ms. Davis* pictures a vibrant and sexy Vaginal in a bleach-blonde bouffant and tight black bra signing an autograph, side by side with a photo of two butch lesbians in fetish gear on a motorcycle; the photo looks like it was taken at Dyke March. Written on a typewriter, the opening page reads, "Yes, Ms. Davis. That is who I am and always will be. Jodie Foster's army, Sandy Duncan's eye, and now from Arizona, a hardcore all-dyke band named Yes, Ms. Davis—I'm touched and flattered. What is 'Yes, Ms. Davis'? A piece of excrement, that's what it is, necessary excrement. Yes, Ms. Davis loves young, humpy skateboard boys with large penises, so if there are any of you out there who want a piece of Ms. Davis, give her a call at 213-851-7743. Or drop her a line at 7850 Sunset Blvd., penthouse suite, LA, CA 90046 USA and enclose nude photos." The zine is a cornucopia of material ranging from a feature on seminal Black filmmaker Melvin Van Peebles, profiles of "cute and hunky" punk bands, interviews, poetry and beautiful ephemera, the bits and pieces of Davis's life at the time.

I see so much of my alienated, frustrated, and horny younger self reflected in the pages of *Yes, Ms. Davis*. I recognize the queer, punk, misfit brat I was when I read myriad things about Davis's early days, and I wonder how, almost three decades after Davis was first creating this work and creating these worlds, I am drawn into a similar lived experience. I was often one of the only Black kids at the punk and hard-core shows I attended as a teenager, and most certainly was always one of the openly queer. I remember feeling exotic for having these characteristics, for these qualities, while at the same time being excluded. Suburban, middle-class white kids wanting to be anything but suburban and middle-class, reaching to embrace anything or anyone that was deemed alternative or different but failing to truly see me for who I was nonetheless. I relate a lot to the youthful, creative ambition in Davis's many no-budget art actions. When I was 15, I started my own performance art collective. My high-school drama teacher introduced me to performance art. The idea that a medium existed that connected drama, visual art, and physical theater excited the hell out of me. All of the nebulous and strange compositions of life were finally manifesting in a form that I could understand. The vague, unclear meanings, metaphors, and allegories that were feasts for the eyes and the mind, they were all allowed! I was a 15-year-old performance artist in my small town, putting on productions at our local Artspace Gallery, a visual art center that contained artist studios, exhibitions, art residencies, and more. I garnered a bit of attention for my performance art work, and won an "Independent Spirit" award for my "happenings." In an article about me written in 2002, the writer says, "It's tempting to call Quattlebaum a prodigy. At the age of fifteen, the Enloe High School student not only started the Raleigh-based youth theater group Paint In Consciousness Experimental Theatre (P.I.C.E.T.), but he also wrote and directed its first performance piece, Paperdoll Psychology. Performed by seven of his female classmates last November for one night only at Artspace, the play was based on the fictional diary of a girl named Anna who, after experimenting with sex and discovering a humiliating conspiracy among her male partners, commits suicide at age 16. One critic marveled that the piece contained 'more overt class and race critiques than The Vagina Monologues,' calling it 'performance art at its most vital.' But calling Quattlebaum a prodigy—ascribing his talent to something congenital—might discount the years of concerted attention to the arts he's already logged, and the hard work he put into his first major creative work. For Paperdoll Psychology, Quattlebaum read tracts on communist feminism, anarcho-feminism, French feminism, eco-feminism, and womynism, and went on teen girl websites to read the online journals of girls like the protagonist of his piece. Even more impressively, Quattlebaum internalized his research to the point where it informed an original piece of conceptual theater, at an age when many of us were cribbing from the encyclopedia for our class reports."

When reading something like this written about me at such an impressionable age, there is no way that I can neglect to realize this is right around the time I discovered Vaginal Davis. Vaginal's work had blasted my brain open, pushed me headfirst into other universes where I was both foreign and still more right at home, and I needed to know everything and

Vaginal's work had blasted my brain open, pushed me headfirst into other universes where I was both foreign and still more right at home.

anything she knew about performance art. Doing what any clever teenage detective would do, I dug and dug online until I found her personal email and wrote her myself. Since the year 2002, Vaginal Davis's website has not changed; it has been updated frequently to keep up with her whirlwind schedule of lectures, exhibitions, and performances over the years, but it looks exactly as it did when I first went to it in 2002. I remember my old teen email address, blueskytreeboy@hotmail.com, and I remember the excitement I felt the day I logged into my account to find that Vaginal Davis had replied to my message. How I wish I still had access to that account, or that the account existed, because I would love to have factual evidence of the contents of that email exchange. What I remember about our correspondence lingers in me like a Sunday school lesson. I remember asking myriad questions about happenings and installation art and performance art and Vaginal answering me in the distinctive storytelling style that is true to form for Ms. Davis.

What's even more wild to me is, even though Vaginal and my first communication would happen via email, the actual art of physical letter writing is something Davis considers dominant in their own practice. Taken from an interview with Davis in 2014, they say of letter writing, "Letter writing for me is so paramount. I first started writing letters when I was around seven or eight years old. I always thought of myself as being a child of the world confined to the inner city, South-Central Los Angeles. I knew that there was a wider world out there and I wanted to be a part of it, so I actively became involved in letter-writing campaigns, and found pen pals in other countries. I was writing to kids my age behind the Iron Curtain in Russia and East Berlin, and in Japan, in South America, Argentina and Brazil, all the places that I had imagined. And of course in England, because I was an Anglophile at a young age. I was obsessed with castles and all that imagery. It's weird because almost all of those early correspondences from childhood I've still kept going all these years. Those relationships have been really helpful. A lot of them have become prominent people, and these are relationships I've had since we were nine or ten."

Although I don't remember exactly what Vaginal said in our email exchanges, I know she was encouraging, and I remember affirming that if Vaginal Davis is encouraging me to continue my performance art crusade, that is exactly what I should and would do and nothing would stop me! Vaginal Davis fronted numerous art rock bands in the 1980s and 1990s.

Most notably, Pedro, Muriel & Esther with Glen Meadmoore, Chol!ta: The Female Menuedo with punk icon Alice Bag, and Black Fag with Bibbe Hansen. It was around the time of Black Fag that I discovered Davis on YouTube in a grainy VHS performance of a blurred moshpit and what looks to be Davis gesticulating and growling to a crowd on their knees with excitement. "My work was built on punk, its homoeroticism and countercultural position. Amoeba Records, like its sisters Funtone Records in Atlanta and The New Lavender Panthers in Toronto, home of G. B. Jones and Bruce Labruce, later to become my colleagues and collaborators, helped to produce my live shows and films and release my studio musical output. Aside from this anti-corporate ethic, there was another element of the punk world that was significant. The very word 'punk' has its origins in Black southern prison slang, denoting a homosexual or freak. There were so few Black figures in the punk world, we all were automatically seen as uber-freaks."

Listening to a lecture given by Davis in 2013 called "Decolonizing the Cold War," I feel seen in her retelling of being labeled an "uber-freak." Mykki Blanco began as a video art project in 2010, and I see traces of Davis everywhere. In one of the first videos ever created as Mykki Blanco, I speak directly into the camera feigning a Valley Girl accent and explaining away the frivolities of my day with a comedic panache. When I see old performance footage of myself screaming at the top of my lungs in a disheveled wig and in kinder-whore lingerie, I pause, and think how truly unaware I was at the time of the osmosis that had occurred between the legendary Vaginal Davis and myself. Vaginal Davis has worked across disciplines and across mediums, each time breaking the mold of who and what is possible for Black artists, queer folks, and gender-nonconforming punks. I can't imagine my life as Mykki Blanco existing without Davis, without all that Davis lived through and created so that I, and so many like me, could just feel comfortable in our own skin. Vaginal Davis is a living legend and a global treasure whose early works have had a lasting influence on who I am as an artist and the perspectives that I've carried with me from youth into adulthood. I urge anyone and everyone to take a deep dive into the living archive of this matriarch of "terrorist drag," because, like all pioneers, it is society's job to do the catching up to foundations laid by this visionary artist.

Mykki Blanco

Mykki Blanco, the artist persona and stage name of Michael David Quattlebaum Jr., is an internationally renowned musician, performing artist, and LGBTQ+ activist. While their self-titled debut *Mykki* album wasn't released until 2016, they were the creative force behind mixtapes such as *Cosmic Angel* (2012) and *Gay Dog Food* (2014); these groundbreaking mixtapes, along with Blanco's other early releases, defined the "queer rap" genre and paved the way for the possibility of other nonheteronormative and gender-nonconforming artists to break through. Blanco has created cult classic hits, including "Kingpinning," "Haze.Boogie.Life," "Wavvy," "Coke White, Starlight," and "The Initiation." The video for their lead single, "High School Never Ends," from their debut album, was directed by Matt Lambert and won multiple awards on the festival circuit. Blanco has also appeared in other music videos and short films, including a starring role in Madonna's "Dark Ballet" music video, reading Zoe Leonard's "I Want a Dyke for President" poem, appearing in the experimental *No Leash* art film collaboration with Cody Critcheloe for Shayne Oliver's Hood By Air brand, and their multi-character performance in the *Wypipo* short film (as part of their role as guest editor for *Dazed*). Blanco has toured with the likes of Björk, Major Lazer, and Death Grips and worked with diverse musicians, including Kanye West, Devendra Banhart, Amnesia Scanner, Charli XCX, Kathleen Hanna, and Woodkid. As of early 2020, Blanco has completed two albums' worth of new music.

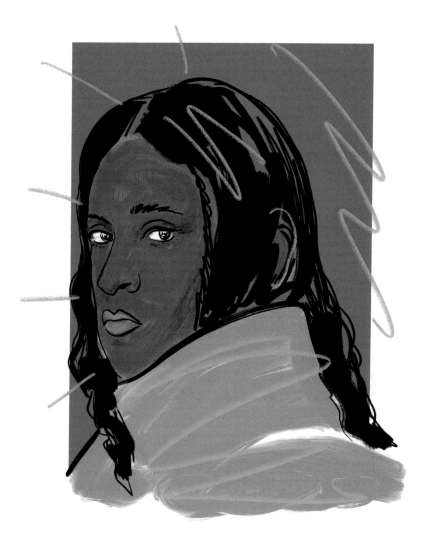

Illustration by Sam Russell Walker

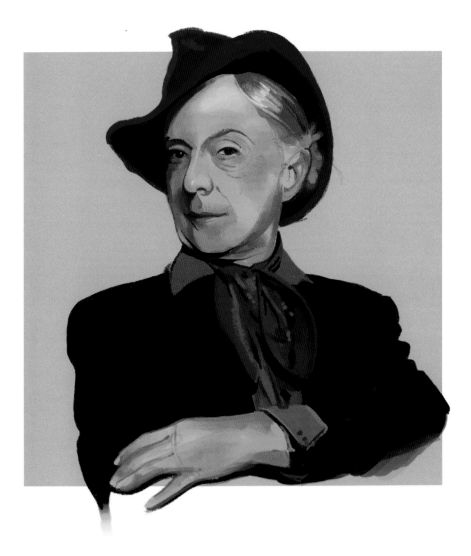

QUENTIN CRISP

by Mark Moore

When *The Naked Civil Servant* was first broadcast on national TV in 1975, it changed everything. The film told the story of Quentin Crisp, exquisitely portrayed by actor John Hurt. We had never quite seen a gay character like this in a film or, for most people, anywhere at all. Previously, gay characters on the telly were effeminate, camp, mincing homosexuals who were shown as a figure of fun and ridicule. Or someone tragic to be pitied. Suddenly we were confronted with an OUT, effeminate homosexual who had such incredible wit and pathos that we laughed *with* him rather than *at* him. We rooted for this underdog who dedicated his life to painting his nails, wearing rouge, lipstick, and mascara, and fearlessly parading around London in the 1930s and onward, all the while trying to avoid the daily queer-bashing and police persecution that were parts of his everyday life. This was a crusade, bringing his "affliction" to the attention of the world, to show that people like him existed. In a word, Mr. Crisp, St. Quentin the Willing Martyr, was an exhibitionist—and exhibitionism was a drug.

Illustration by Fernando Monroy

Before we go on, we must set the scene of those dark and ignorant times. Dirk Bogarde's portrayal of a closeted homosexual being blackmailed in the film *Victim* (1961) paved the way to a modicum of progress. His depiction was so powerful that it helped liberalize the atmosphere around gay people in the buildup to the (partial) decriminalization of gay male sex in 1967. Meanwhile, a comedian like Kenneth Williams, while never officially "out," was so fragrantly queer in his witty movie, radio, and TV performances that he became beloved by the nation. "He's theatrical, not a queer," people would say. However, the radio show *Round the Horne*, on which Williams appeared as one of the Julian and Sandy duo, was rife with gay innuendo and even had parts in spoken Polari (gay slang, for those who are new at this). Soon gay-coded words like "naff" ("not available for fucking") became mainstays of everyday conversation, although the straights never quite figured out their exact meaning.

Other comedians and TV presenters followed in the footsteps of Mr. Williams. Frankie Howerd and the fey campery of Larry Grayson soon became mainstream TV, adored by Middle England. John Inman camped it up delightfully on the TV show *Are You Being Served?* Drag superstar Danny La Rue, the RuPaul of his day, took drag out from the clubs and onto the West End theater and primetime Saturday night TV. He was adored by millions of mums, grannies, and right across the straight public. Danny played it straight, too, for a while. A confirmed bachelor, Danny claimed to be "married to the business." Just don't call it by its name! The mere utterance of a label such as "gay" or "queer" would destroy the whole illusion that these were emasculated, unthreatening poofs and instead turn them into something real and dangerous. Something sexual. Limp wrists and queeny dizziness were otherwise perfectly acceptable. That is, unless you were a gay male who didn't fit into the designated lavender box.

Gay liberation was in its early stages and hit back against this gay stereotyping as well as the mockery and ridicule that came with it. Even when affectionately done, as by Dick Emery's flamboyant and (by the mid-seventies) very much "out" gay character Clarence ("Oh hello, honkytonks!"), for the militant gay man this was just too much. Away with the stereotypes! We will wear leather outfits, checked cowboy shirts, dress as cops and construction workers, and grow handlebar moustaches. We will work out at the gym. We will butch up! Never again will we be stereotypes!

Mr. Crisp, St. Quentin the Willing Martyr, was an exhibitionist—and exhibitionism was a drug.

Around that time Harvey Fierstein (that's Fierstein, not Weinstein)—the magnificent actor/playwright from *The Torch Song Trilogy* (why am I having to tell you this?)—was actually very fond of these stereotypical figures of ridicule. In Vito Russo's *The Celluloid Closet*—the finest book and then documentary ever made on gay, lesbian, bisexual, and Transgender characters in Hollywood and motion pictures—Fierstein says that he always felt that any visibility at that time (in the seventies) was better than no visibility at all. Of course, worse was to come. In the late eighties and nineties the stereotypical portrayal of gays in the movies transformed into those of deranged serial killers, often cross-dressing ones. *The Silence of the Lambs, Dressed to Kill, Basic Instinct, Cruising*. Of course, Alfred Hitchcock had paved the way with a plethora of homicidal queer villains—in *Rebecca, Rope, Strangers on a Train, Psycho*—but somehow, he did it with such style we kind of liked those villains.

Wasn't I talking about Mr. Crisp? So huge was his impact on TV that my father made my brother and me watch the show (we were kids) in the hope that we wouldn't grow up prejudiced against the "afflicted." My dear father, even with his heart in the right place, when joked to by my brother that he was gay, replied, "I hope not. Most homosexuals are very sad and tortured people. 'Gay' really is the most inappropriate name you could give them." And I guess that's just how it was in those days. Or perhaps he just met the wrong kind of gays. He was a lawyer, after all, so if he was just meeting the ones who were in trouble, it's no wonder they were depressed.

Oh yes, Mr. Crisp. Overnight he became the go-to gay for the UK before moving to and conquering America (aged 72) with his *An Audience with Quentin Crisp* live show and his many books, all of which displayed his unique wit and wisdom. He was a sensation and Sting wrote a song about him, "Englishman in New York," but the one you want is Gina X Performance's "No G.D.M. (Dedicated to Quentin Crisp)." However, there was one problem: he was an effeminate homosexual. Yet again, the same stereotype was offered up to, and by, the mainstream, and the gay activists did not like him one little bit. Then it got much, much worse. Mr. Crisp believed that gays were NOT normal people and he didn't believe in gay liberation. "The world would be better without homosexuals," he said. Talk about awkward.

Mr. Crisp came from the early part of the twentieth century, where I'm sure he felt the full brunt of the agony of being queer, so I get why he felt the way he did in his brave, ironic, and self-deprecating way. However, the timing of *The Naked Civil Servant* on TV—just before the punk revolution of 1976—was serendipitous. Mr. Crisp's mix of narcissism and self-loathing, his ability to upset those who wanted him to toe the PC line, the shock tactics and the nihilism, it was all very punk. He attracted people of all sexual persuasions who felt they just didn't fit in with any club that would have them as a member: individuals, freaks, outsiders, and artists. I felt that in spite of the things he said that upset the activists, he was still a shining beacon of hope for anyone who felt different, didn't fit in, who refused to be invisible and for those who wanted the freedom to be themselves without apology. I will always love Mr. Crisp for that.

ME AND MR. CRISP

When I read that Mr. Crisp was in the phone book and that anyone could call him, I couldn't resist. Thus, in the early nineties, began my regular transatlantic phone calls to him. He would always pick up the phone and answer in a long drawl, "Oh yeeeeeeeessssss?" He was used to strangers calling and he knew what they wanted. Basically, they wanted the Quentin Crisp Show via the telephone, and he would happily provide this. I was, of course, thrilled to be getting my own one-man show which resembled his *An Evening with Quentin Crisp* theater performance, where audience members would ask questions that Mr. Crisp would reply to with spontaneous and witty, off-the-cuff answers. I told him that his quote "Never keep up with the Joneses. Drag them down to your level. It's cheaper," was my motto to live by. I also told him that his book *How to Have a Lifestyle* was practically my bible and gushed about how much he had influenced my life. "Oh, I do apologize if my advice made a mess of it," he replied with, I'm guessing, a smile.

As the phone calls progressed, I continued to be charmed and entertained by Mr Crisp, but I would be slightly disappointed when he would go into stock answers and routines during our conversations—things I'd heard in various interviews or read in his books. I could relate to this as I, too, would go into stock answers during interviews when asked a question for the umpteenth time, but, taking advice from John

Waters, I always remembered to answer the question as if it were the first time I had ever been asked it.

The problem was that Quentin Crisp had been asked practically everything and therefore had a stock answer for practically everything. I decided I needed to change tack and not be a journalist or an audience member when we spoke. So I rang him and spoke as if he were my dear old friend Quentin whom I had just called for a natter. And what lovely natters we had. We spoke about mundane things, how his day had been, people he had bumped into on his walk, and we also spoke a lot about the movies, swapping recommendations. He would ask me about being a pop star and a DJ. He found it quite baffling that playing other people's records could be a highly paid job that got you flown around the world. "Don't they have someone there who could buy the record and play it?" he would ask. He also said that young people don't dance anymore. They twitch.

He attracted people of all sexual persuasions who felt they just didn't fit in with any club that would have them as a member: individuals, freaks, outsiders, and artists.

Inevitably, I would find him going into stock answers and into performance mode. One time he told me about a movie he liked, *Down and Out in Beverly Hills*, and he practically read out one of his reviews from his book *How to Go to the Movies*. But some of the time it felt like we were actually having a conversation and during those moments I got a glimpse of a very different Quentin Crisp from the one that he presented as his public persona. A lighter Mr. Crisp. A gossipier and queenier Mr. Crisp. "Queenier? Wasn't Mr Crisp inherently queeny?" you may ask. Well, yes, but this was a different kind of queeny. Less stately and intellectual and a lot more juvenile. But still as witty as ever.

Once I called and he said he couldn't speak long as "they" had mysteriously sent a nurse to his home. Nevertheless, he refused to get off the phone. "I don't know who she is! She just turned up and now she's trying to give me an injection! Get away from me, you terrible woman! You can see the evil in her eyes!" This was followed by screams, after which he scrambled back to the phone to carry on the running commentary. He had turned into a naughty little schoolgirl baiting his nemesis, but laughing here and there during his asides to me at the absurdity of it all. Although sounding genuinely frightened, I think there was a part of him that still felt the need to entertain me.

"Are you okay? Should I call the police? Who sent her?" I asked. "I don't know who she is!" he said again. "Don't look at me like that with those evil eyes! You're a witch!" he screamed across the room. I imagined the carnage taking place in the squalor of his one-room apartment and when he finally relinquished the phone, I decided that one of his celebrity benefactors, who often paid for his hospital bills, must have sent a nurse to look after him.

> His quote "Never keep up with the Joneses. Drag them down to your level. It's cheaper," was my motto to live by.

About a year or so later, *Resident Alien: The New York Diaries*, the last autobiography published while he was alive, came out in 1996. In one of the chapters he tells how the police entered his room and, for no known reason, he was bundled into an ambulance before being dragged to a hospital where a nurse administered an injection. Was this the same event? I guess that this sort of thing happened a lot to Mr. Crisp.

In closing I will mention that for the price of a meal anyone could phone and then meet Mr. Crisp at Cooper's Diner on East Fifth St., New York (chosen for its closeness to his room rather than for the food). They would get his one-man show in the flesh and he, as he put it, would "sing for his supper." This was one of the ways in which the penniless Mr. Crisp managed to eat. The other was by attending what he called "the champagne and peanut circuit" offered by launch parties and opening-night VIP invitations, where he ate any food that was on offer.

I love that when the "all alone in the world" Mr. Crisp died (in 1999), it was found that he had amassed a small fortune (possibly untouched) that was close to half a million dollars, most of which he left to his beloved nieces. Never keep up with the Joneses. Drag them down to your level. It's cheaper.

(PS, Mr. Crisp's preferred pronouns during our calls were Mr. Crisp/Mr. Crisp. Failing that, he/him were acceptable.)

Mark Moore

Mark Moore is a music producer, DJ, and writer. Mark is a respected and loved character who's deeply ingrained in the history of UK club culture and is hugely influential on both dance and pop music. As a regular attendee and occasional DJ at another feted London nightspot—The Wag—Mark even made it into the video for David Bowie's "Blue Jean," which cast London's nocturnal creative elite. Mark also held a residency at Heaven's lauded Asylum night (which later became Pyramid). He was one of the first supporters of Chicago house and Detroit techno in Britain (mixing it with electronic European dance music like Yello, Soft Cell, and Cabaret Voltaire), alongside Colin Favor and Evil Eddie Richards. Being the first night in the UK to play house music, the venue attracted Danny Rampling, Mr. C, Pete Tong, Paul Oakenfold, Pet Shop Boys, and even Liza Minelli. This led to Rampling offering Mark guest spots at the seminal Shoom nights and also a guest set at The Hacienda's Zumbar party. Having played a key part in the UK's house music rise, Mark took things up yet another level. His idea to form S'Express with co-producer Pascal Gabriel was a natural progression from life as a regular on the club scene. Swept along on a huge wave of excitement for acid and rave culture, S'Express had a number one chart smash with "Theme from S-Express." This was their first of several worldwide hit records which helped thrust these new sounds into the world's spotlight and positioned dance music/DJ culture as a viable force. Mark's meteoric rise to fame paved the way for electronic dance music stars to come. He has remixed Prince, Erasure, Malcolm McLaren, Randy Crawford, Divine & Bobby O, Dead or Alive, The B-52s, and Soft Cell, among others. A (surprising) remix/collaboration was on a version of "Hey Music Lover" with Philip Glass, who Mark befriended in London. With Malcolm McLaren, Mark and William Orbit created the seminal Vogue track "Deep in Vogue" (a Billboard Dance Chart number one), which sampled the film *Paris Is Burning* and no doubt influenced the Madonna song "Vogue" a year later. Moore has written and published short stories and interviewed Siouxsie Sioux and John Waters for publications, including *i-D*. He has appeared in various documentaries, including the *Joy of Disco* and guested on a recent news program in tribute to David Bowie (both for the BBC).

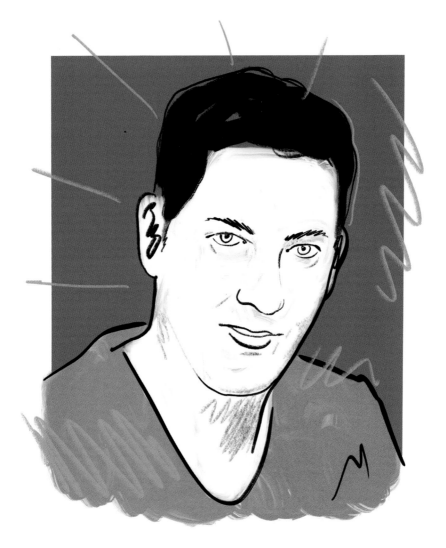

Illustration by Sam Russell Walker

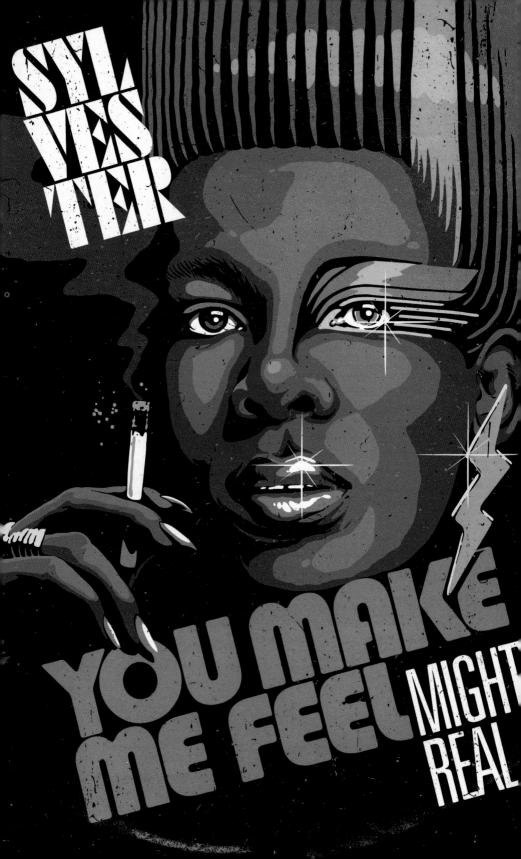

SYLVESTER

by David Furnish

I'll never forget the moment I heard Sylvester for the first time. It was the seventies. Disco mania was sweeping the country. Something drew me to it. I loved it. We were dancing in a friend's rec room. (A "rec room" is that wonderful North American invention, the recreation room. I suppose all fun was to be had there specifically, and nowhere else!) We didn't know it at the time, but those other boys and I all turned out to be gay later in life. Like the magazines and the music, we were drawn to each other, knowing without knowing. Feeling connected in our difference but without the conscious vocabulary to name how or why. Disco connected us. It was the great entrée into this wonderful happy place. A place you could inhabit, lose yourself, and feel free. I first encountered Sylvester just from the music—not visually or from a performance—but from the voice and the beat. What a voice and what a beat! The music was magical. Those first tracks I heard, "You Make Me Feel (Mighty Real)" and "Dance (Disco Heat)" are so firmly part of the seventies zeitgeist now, so ubiquitous and inextricable from the era, that it's hard to convey how revolutionary and fresh they sounded to me that day dancing around my friend's house.

Illustration by Butcher Billy

At the time I didn't understand the person behind the music. The album artwork for 1978's *Step II* was a picture of a 1970s shoe, a falling champagne glass, and a beautiful Black glistening foot, the toes painted with scarlet nail polish. There was one picture on the back of the record sleeve of Sylvester—his look not yet fully developed as when I would eventually see him perform live—tall, imposing, a little softer looking than other male singers of the time, wearing a golden kaftan. I didn't understand the visual language at all. But the voice spoke to me, this beautiful man singing in this glorious falsetto. I just loved the music. I was drawn to the music. They're records that still sound great today. Every summer, Elton and I have a ritual when we're on holiday in France. We sit out at night on the terrace under the stars, and we listen to our favorite records. We always play *Living Proof* from beginning to end, because it's such a superbly crafted live album. It captures an amazing performance, a moment in culture, a moment in our lives.

Sylvester James was born in 1947 in South-Central Los Angeles and brought up primarily by his mother. Church was a huge part of their lives—the glamorous women dressing up for Sunday services and the gospel choir of their Pentecostal congregation clearly made a huge impression on him. Rejected by the church because of his sexuality, he moved to San Francisco, finding a new family and church of sorts in the bustling gay Castro district. He joined the avant-garde psychedelic hippy performance troupe The Cockettes—the very same group that drag queen Divine performed with. Sylvester also got involved in activism, making friends with the unofficial Mayor of Castro Street Harvey Milk, who was the first openly gay man in California to be elected to public office. Through the madness of experimentation and distractions of San Francisco life, Sylvester discovered and joined forces with singers and church ladies Izora Rhodes and Martha Wash—the gospel sound of his childhood brought into the gay world. With these powerful voices behind him, Sylvester was on the way to creating his own church. A house of disco! "You Make Me Feel (Mighty Real)" was his breakthrough hit, taking him around the world, putting him on television and into the homes of America. Sylvester's crowning as the "Queen of Disco" came at his iconic performance at the San Francisco Opera House with the Symphony Orchestra. The first popular act to perform on this stage, Sylvester's show brought together the stuffy tux-wearing opera crowd with the queer kids of the Castro. A representative of the city gave Sylvester the keys to the city and declared it "Sylvester Day"—a culturally significant moment of recognition for the gay community. The show offered a healing moment for the city following Harvey Milk's assassination. Sylvester brought people together in celebration, he slowed down Mighty Real and had the audience sing it together like a hymn.

Sylvester was from another planet. Watching him perform live was nothing short of transformative. When I saw him live, I can honestly say it was probably the most significant, life-changing moment for me in terms of starting to embrace who I was as a gay man. I'd never seen anything like it before. Growing up there was one quasi-mainstream drag character in Canada called Craig Russell who was in a film called *Outrageous* (definitely worth a YouTube!), but that felt a bit too scary for me. I wasn't quite ready to go there yet, whereas Sylvester had mainstream success with the music; it just felt a little bit safer. The gig was at Ontario Place, an exposition-type family-friendly theme park. I've no idea who was in charge of programming, but it was surreal to book Sylvester. He would have made more sense at a downtown bar or disco club, but there was real subversive power in queering that straight space. I was aged about sixteen or seventeen. I went alone because I was slightly nervous about going. I had this sense that Sylvester was not your run-of-the-mill disco artist. He wasn't The Bee Gees, he wasn't Earth, Wind & Fire, he wasn't Chic. I went on my own because I didn't really feel safe going with anyone else. It was an instinct. Personally I was fearless with regard to seeking these types of things out, but I didn't have too many people that I could share this with. The crazy thing is, out of the four of us who made friends in our High School Drama Program, three of us turned out to be gay and the fourth one turned out to be Eric McCormack, who played Will in *Will & Grace*. On second thought, perhaps that's not as statistically unlikely as I led myself to believe! So while we were all as gay or gay-friendly as it got, we never discussed or explored the possibility with each other that we might be gay. It was a thing that remained unspoken and unsaid.

Sylvester was a vision—he appeared on the stage, this super-tall, very broad-shouldered Black man wearing the beaded skull cap, the Syreeta headpiece style (Stevie Wonder's first wife!), and this oversized glitter-sequined tunic with stirrup pants and a flat kitten heel. Backed up by Izora Rhodes and Martha Wash, whom he called "Two Tons O' Fun," before they became The Weather Girls, they combined, with the band, to become an overwhelmingly joyous force of nature. To see the evocation of that, backed up with that amazing musicality was just euphoric for me. I had only ever seen pop stars on TV shows like *Solid Gold*, which was the equivalent of *Top of the Pops,* where people stood on stage with a bunch of kids dancing in the audience and then lip-synced to their records. But Sylvester was live and alive. That voice was real, the backup singers were unbelievable, the band was incredible. The authenticity of the culture lifting up the music buoyed by Sylvester's otherworldly energy was just heaven. I remember dancing and singing ecstatically. He had just brought out a second album, the follow-up album to *Step II*, featuring the singles "Stars" and "Body Strong." They opened the show with "Body Strong," the opening whirls and spins like a spaceship landing, the vocals dropping in, repeating, "You make, you make, you make my body strong," a magic spell echoing over that tinny beat—it drove us all mad. I wanted it to go on forever. It was that exact same show that he did at the San Francisco Opera House—the same set list, same production, and the same amazingly tight band. Listen to the live album *Living Proof.* That energy, the humor, the excitement, it is all still there.

> The voice spoke to me, this beautiful man singing in this glorious falsetto. I loved the music. I was drawn to the music.

Something unlocked within me that night. Sylvester's ease with himself, his enjoyment in being himself, his love of music, and sharing that unapologetically with us was a gift, his message to us. It was freedom of expression and in such a celebratory way. It was life-affirming. It was the greatest party in the world and everybody was invited. Everybody was welcome. *Living Proof* was a service, we were his congregation, and he was in the pulpit, preaching truth, love, and acceptance. You can take the singer out of the church, but you'll never take church out of the singer. Sylvester adopts many of the preacher's maneuvers—the call and the response, the direct address of the congregation, the whipping up of the audience. The vocal arrangements with Wash and Rhodes are infused with gospel.

The sum of these parts moves beyond party and approaches an inclusive irresistible religious experience that takes over body and soul.

I remember everyone in the audience looking around—and there were a lot of gay men there—but it was also incredibly diverse, made up of people that loved the music. Gay culture operated in the darkness, in nightclubs, in parks, society projecting stigma and shame onto us. Now here we were, with straight people, celebrating life, simply enjoying the music together. Sylvester brought us together in the light. For me personally, I knew gay culture existed, I knew there was a part of Toronto where it really flourished, but I kind of skirted around the perimeter of it, getting more and more courageous as I dipped in. But the gay scene remained separate, and here was this mixed audience with Sylvester being 100 percent himself in full, I don't wanna call it drag, in full Sylvester! There's no other word for it, it was Sylvester, it was his identity, it was his gender fluidity. He was a proud Black queer man who had broken through into the mainstream. Seeing that celebrated in this family-friendly environment in Ontario Place was very incongruous, but also felt right and natural. That moment was in a sense twenty or thirty years ahead of its time. It wasn't until later you saw things like Boy George picking up a big music award and saying to the camera, "Thank you America, you know a good drag queen when you see one." Nobody said things like that on television. In that regard, Sylvester was way ahead of the curve. Pop stars continued to play with gender. Grace Jones on the *Nightclubbing* album sleeve wearing her Armani blazer—that amazing aerodynamic blue color with the wedge haircut. Annie Lennox subverting gender norms and female stereotypes exploring gender fluidity. Recently there was a huge furor about Harry Styles wearing a dress on the cover of American *Vogue*. It's fantastic to see someone in his position playing with gender, but also surprising there was such an outcry when Sylvester was doing it decades before.

When gay culture went from something you felt you had to hide to something you could share that was more accepted in the mainstream, it was incredibly powerful. When subcultures move into the mainstream, we perhaps lose some things. We should protect our culture, but we also shouldn't be afraid of it growing and evolving. In my sexuality and identity, I've never been into isolating or segregation. The friends that I have in life are a cross section of people. The people that I mix with and draw inspiration from come from all walks of life, just like that audience watching Sylvester. He tapped into that profound truth, that this coming together in celebration, this "Sharing Something Perfect Between Ourselves," made it OK to be himself—and that meant I was included too.

> When I saw him live, I can honestly say
> it was probably the most significant,
> life-changing moment for me.

I love the idea of queer culture as a Trojan horse. It's similar to Elton's impact. People buy into the music first. Then they sense his unabashed way—this is who I am and I'm proud of it. When those two things come together, that's when culture changes, that's when mainstream society changes and becomes more broad-minded and more inclusive. It's never a continuous spectrum of improvement. Progress occurs in fits and starts. I remember when I was working in a job for this redneck Canadian processed meats company, in their marketing department. I was a student intern and Boy George and Culture Club were all over the radio, and I remember this one secretary working for the really gruff corner office guy and she said, "I don't care how fucking gay he is, I just love his voice, he's got amazing soul and the records are brilliant." When I heard things like that, it made me realize the power of music to change hearts and minds. Loving the song leads to tolerating the person, which can grow to acceptance and then blossoms into love for the person, in their entirety.

The decline of disco coincided with the arrival of AIDS. I was in my early twenties. I was just about to come out. People were saying this is God's retribution: "Gays are getting what they deserve." American Republican senator Jesse Helms on the US Senate floor talked about how this was God's justice. Helms said, "We have got to call a spade a spade, and a perverted human being a perverted human being." Statements like this had a huge impact on what was then mainstream gay disco culture—because disco came from the gay clubs, it came from the gay world. Gay sexuality and disco became entwined in many people's minds, and identifying one as morally repugnant led to the rejection of both. Disco, dance music, started in the Black gay world and it got pushed back underground. Sylvester kept putting out records and making great music, but it just wasn't on the radio or charts like it had been. It was there if you sought it out, and the magazines that I continued to read and follow—*i-D* magazine was added to the menu, in addition to *The Face*—they kept reporting and covering it. *The Advocate* in America was another important gay title for many as it emerged and became more and more accessible and available. Disco and AIDS were simultaneously identified as something shameful that people wanted to hide.

AIDS and disco collided in the real world when the "Queen of Disco" himself contracted the disease. In 1987, Sylvester's boyfriend, Rick Cranmer, died from an AIDS-related illness and soon after Sylvester was also diagnosed with AIDS. His health failing, Sylvester appeared in a wheelchair at the Castro's Gay Freedom Parade in front of a banner emblazoned "People Living with AIDS." To see such a recognized name being so open about his diagnosis was revolutionary. It was amazingly brave and it stirred within me a combination of admiration and fear, because he wasn't well. When I saw this person that was so larger than life and so vibrant and so life-affirming, to see him suffering was terrifying. At that point there were no antiviral drugs like AZT. You got AIDS, you died. On the one hand it was great to see him publicly, supporting his community; on the other it was a reminder that this was something that most gay people were at risk of contracting and dying from. It pushed me back in the closet. It's why I ran away to Britain when I was 27. I really tried to come out when I was 21, in 1982/83 and that's when Rock Hudson was on the cover of *People* magazine, kissing Linda Evans in *Dynasty*. The fear and lack of knowledge was huge: "Oh my god, he's given her AIDS, kissing her on television." News crews hounded him, helicopters circling over his house. Hudson flew off to France to the Pasteur Institute to get experimental HIV treatment. AIDS was a very shameful thing at that time. It was terrifying. It was utterly terrifying. Seeing Sylvester in the parade no matter what, even in a wheelchair, was a testament to his commitment but also a reminder that we were living through bleak times.

I cannot overemphasize how terrifying that period was. We lost a generation of vibrant beautiful human beings. Sex and death became enmeshed. Freedom turned into hideous suffering. Happiness crumbled into fear. Hope degraded to loss. A generation of young men stepping out of the closet full of excitement and being met with this merciless pandemic. I still deal with it to this day. The PTSD-like trauma stays with you forever. Like grief, you just get used to carrying it around with you. It's a bit like you're going through life walking on trap doors, thinking that at any moment you are gonna hit that trap door that swings open and swallows you up. Either you're going to get sick and die or you're going to be rejected and judged and cast aside. I wanted the same things in life that everyone else wanted. I wanted a happy relationship. I wanted to start a family. I wanted to have a career that I enjoyed and that fulfilled me, that I was successful at. Being gay got in the way of all of those things; as an aspiring gay businessman, there were no role models. It is bizarre when you go from a situation like that to being in a relationship with Elton, and the way we live our life together demonstrates to a lot of people that it is possible. Those things are within everyone's reach and they should be within everyone's reach. But something lingers, some doubt—in a way you never quite get rid of that trap-door syndrome. I've been to therapy to deal with it. In our work with the Elton John AIDS Foundation I travel the world and put my arms around people and tell them to be themselves and tell them that we support and love them, but there's always that thing in the back of your mind, that you're not safe as a gay man, which is strange for someone who's had the acceptance and support that I've had in my relationship with Elton. It scars your psyche, it scars your soul. It leaves an imprint that I don't think you ever completely shake off. I still work on it. I work on it every day. It's not like a horrible hair shirt that I have to wear all the time, but there are still moments where I go into the occasional situation where I just think, oh maybe this won't go my way, or maybe I won't get the result I want because I'm gay. That it's going to hold me back somehow. But that is what the internalized shame, trauma, and societal homophobia do to us. They scar us. Books like Matthew Todd's *Straight Jacket* explain the situation so clearly: if you live every day in a society which tells you, you can't get married, you can't be in the military, of course those messages are going to stunt the development of a healthy sense of self. When you look at Vito Russo's work *The Celluloid Closet,* and you look at the depictions of gays and lesbians in films, the message is clear—there is no happy ending for LGBTQ+ people. Even in old episodes of *Dynasty* from the eighties the only gay character, Steven Carrington, ends up . . . well, straight. We are presented with this handsome man of extraordinary privilege, and his father rejects his sexuality, rejects him, his lover dies, he ends up in court testifying against his father, and then he runs into the arms of a woman and finds happiness. Again, the message is clear, even in this glamorous fantasy world of light entertainment—being gay results in suffering, death, and families torn apart. For gay people, there is no escapism. Where's the redemption in that? If there's no hope for Steven Carrington, what hope is there for us?!

When gay culture went from something you felt you had to hide to something you could share that was more accepted in the mainstream, it was incredibly powerful.

My children give me hope. Our sons have grown up in an environment where they live with a same-sex couple and see love and support, and they get real happiness and strength from that. To them there isn't a reason in the world for anyone from the outside to look at that and find it strange or odd. It makes no sense to them. We are incredibly privileged and fortunate that in the community that we circulate in, our local school and the parents, everyone's been brilliant, everyone's been accepting. When my nine-year-old son overhears me talking about *Rocketman* being censored in Russia, he asks, "Papa, why do they censor your film in Russia?" And I sit down and explain to him that there are parts of the world that aren't as accepting as this part of the world, they think it's wrong to see two men kissing on screen. He doesn't comprehend why they think like that. "They're wrong, Papa, they're just wrong." It's all he's ever seen. It's all he's ever known. To him it's completely normal and fine and happy. That's the point we want to get to for all members of the LGBTQ+ community. Fighting for the safety, protection, and rights of Trans and non-binary people is our next battle. Trans people have to deal with so much, they're vilified in the press just as gay people were in the eighties. Our hard-won rights are constantly under threat. Trump walked back Obama-era healthcare protections for Trans people. Then the Supreme Court ruled that the 1964 Civil Rights Act protects LGBT employees from discrimination based on sex. Two steps forward and one step back. But generally, it feels as though awareness of these issues is

His music was life-affirming. That's what makes him powerful. That's his legacy, his freedom.

growing. I'm excited about the world my sons are growing up in. I am excited about how differently they think. They don't judge.

Hope for me comes in seeing the next generation of LGBTQ+ performers breaking down barriers and bringing people together through music. Hope comes through the work we do with the Elton John AIDS Foundation bringing education, awareness, increased testing, and effective treatments to people all around the world. Sylvester turned on a light inside me; his life and death changed mine forever. Like Elton, Sylvester was the first openly gay person a lot of people came into contact with. Whatever people's learned prejudices, or lack of understanding, the love of music is universal; it is beyond morality or religion or intellectual judgment (no matter how misguided). If you love the music, it is harder for you to hate the person. If Sylvester brings you joy, there's less room for fear. That is the power of being visible and proudly out. That is the power of culture and art. It connects people through our shared experiences, our shared emotions, and just like Sylvester, in honoring our uniqueness, we can also focus on what we share in common. He presented this alternative way of looking at and celebrating life. The music was just so good that it made it easy for other people to take it into their hearts. It wasn't threatening, it wasn't intimidating, it was life-affirming. And that's what makes him such a powerful, powerful figure in cultural terms. That's Sylvester's legacy, his freedom.

Sylvester died in 1988. In his will, Sylvester bequeathed all future musical royalties to two HIV/AIDS charities, Project Open Hand and the AIDS Emergency Fund.

David Furnish

As CEO of Rocket Entertainment and chairman of the Elton John AIDS Foundation, David Furnish is an entrepreneur with a global and strategic outlook occupying a unique intersection of philanthropy, film, music, and theater. As Elton's manager, David is the architect and leader for: the recent extraordinary success of the *Farewell Yellow Brick Road* tour worldwide; producer of *Rocketman*, the fantasy musical motion picture of Elton John's life, which won a Golden Globe for Best Actor and Best Original Song, an Academy Award for Best Original Song, and four British Academy Film Award nominations; Elton's autobiography, *Me*; and executive producer of the widely acclaimed theatrical show *Billy Elliot: The Musical*.

A tireless campaigner, David Furnish is a leading voice in the worldwide fight against HIV and AIDS. He has led the Elton John AIDS Foundation for over 20 years and travels across the globe to meet people at risk and living with HIV firsthand, as well as community groups, doctors, and activists, to raise the attention of this epidemic and build partnerships with major companies to fund innovative programming and involve the mass public in support of the foundation. He has spearheaded numerous fundraisers for the foundation, including the memorable White Tie & Tiara, the Academy Awards Viewing Party, and Midsummer Party, and took on the physical challenge of climbing Mount Kilimanjaro, in Tanzania, to raise funds and awareness as he reached the summit on World AIDS Day. David has met with global political figures to influence policy shifts and global financing for the AIDS epidemic by sharing the personal stories and challenges that he witnesses on his global travels with the foundation. David recently led the strategic amalgamation of two separate foundations into one global powerhouse for more impact to end the AIDS epidemic. He and Elton were awarded the British LGBT Global Impact Award in 2020 for their life-changing work with the foundation. To date, the Elton John AIDS Foundation is the sixth-largest independent AIDS funder globally, has saved the lives of over 5 million of the most marginalized groups infected with HIV, and has raised awareness of HIV among more than 100 million people.

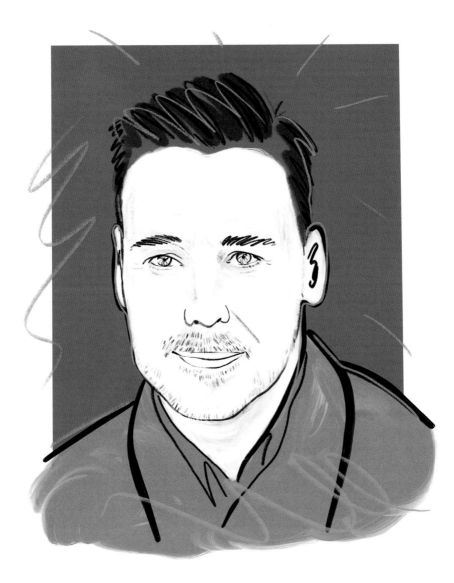

Illustration by Sam Russell Walker

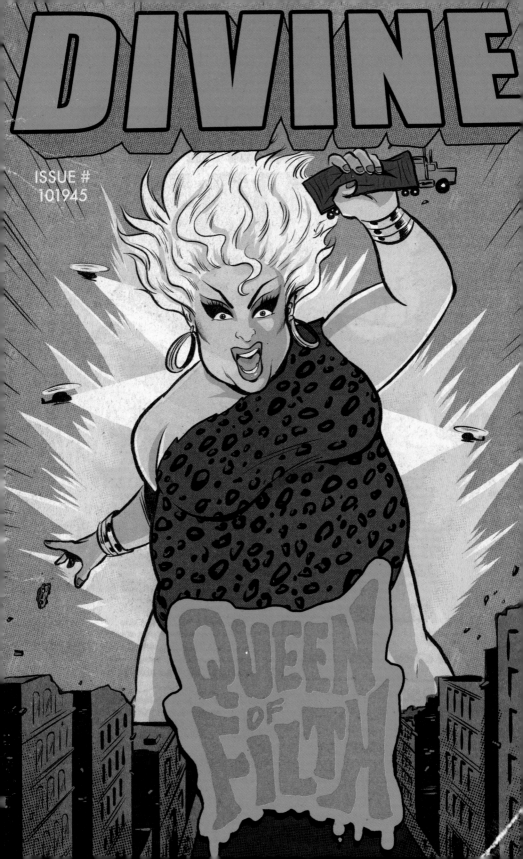

DIVINE

by Elton John

The very first time I saw *Pink Flamingos*, I fell for Divine. The film opens on a shot of her mobile home, surrounded by kitsch garden ornaments. Divine's in hiding with her misfit family because the tabloids have christened her the "Filthiest Person Alive." Her look is instantly iconic: hairline shaved right back, a shock of tangerine hair, and pointed high eyebrows. I felt an immediate connection. Firstly, because she was so funny. Secondly, there aren't many human beings like Divine, a quintessential, true punk rebel.

Divine was christened Harris Glenn Milstead but was better known as Glenn. He grew up in Baltimore in the fifties, came of age in the sixties, and made friends with fellow upstart John Waters, with whom he developed his drag persona, a larger-than-life Queen of Filth, Divine. They collaborated on numerous guerilla-style films shot in Baltimore with a cast of local characters, the freaks who lived on the outskirts of a society which explicitly rejected them, the grist to their artistic mill. *They* were the people your parents warned you about.

Illustration by Cheyne

Pink Flamingos was an exercise in deliberate, exquisite poor taste. It purposefully revolted audiences everywhere, dotted with cannibalism, bestiality, and foot fetishism. It climaxes with the still supremely shocking scene of Divine's character eating dog shit, set with an auteur's perfection to the children's nursery rhyme "How Much Is That Doggy in the Window?" The world and I had never seen anything like it. It was banned in numerous countries, so of course gained instant cult classic status. Divine mutated into an international star, continuing to make films with Waters. Glenn took his beautiful, uproarious, divine creation and fashioned out of all its extremity a pop career. Just prior to his death, he even threatened proper commercial crossover with his iconic turn as Edna Turnblad, mother of the heroine in the fabulous movie *Hairspray*. Glenn played the exasperated, all-American housewife to perfection. Gone were the foul antics of *Pink Flamingos*. It seemed as if Glenn would leave the dog shit behind and embark on a respected acting career. Perhaps he would even take male roles, too. One is left wanting from the career of Divine. There are so many what-ifs . . .

In spite of these, perhaps because of them, his legend is set in stone.

The very first time I saw *Pink Flamingos*, I fell for Divine. I felt an immediate connection.

＊＊

My relationship with drag has been a life-long love affair. The first time I ever saw anyone in drag was the early seventies. My manager, John Reid—also the first person I ever slept with—took me to Danny La Rue's club in London. I was a very sheltered gay man back then and I didn't know much about this sort of thing. But schooled on the kind of campness sequestered away on Radio 4, like Kenneth Williams, I was hungry for it all. I had no idea real drag queens existed until that visit started the ball rolling.

I quickly developed favorites. Lee Sutton at the Vauxhall Tavern; Regina Fong at the Black Cap in Camden, who I would, incidentally, later get to appear with at a Stonewall benefit. The glamour of drag connected with something deep inside me. I can't remember the first time I dressed in drag privately, but it soon transpired into a public habit and to this day comprises some of my happiest memories.

If there was a chance to drag up, I would take it. I'd rented a house in Saint-Tropez on holiday with my friend Tony King, who's looked after me throughout my career. The first time I met John Lennon— another of Tony's designated charges—was on a video shoot for the *Mind Games* album where Tony was in full drag as the Queen. So, Tony and I decided to throw a drag party in Saint-Tropez. The next day I took some of the other people out in drag and had pictures taken privately by the swimming pool on the diving board. Unbeknownst to us, there were paparazzi in the bushes and the photos ended up plastered all over *Paris Match* the next week. Another time, in Hawaii, I came down to dinner at the Four Seasons in full drag, looking like Audrey Hepburn. I appeared on the front of Richard Avedon's *Versace* book in a sequined dress. I can make reasonable claims to being an actual cover girl, darling. I have paid my drag dues.

When I came out as gay and met John Reid, he had so many gay friends and employees it felt natural to give each other drag names. In a way, designating someone with a drag name was my way of telling them I loved them: drag is a communal sport—I like to get everyone involved. Tony became "Joy" and I became "Sharon," because I was so common. Rod Stewart was always "Phyllis." Freddie Mercury became "Melina" after Melina Mercouri, the Greek actress and singer. He was a real Melina, I can assure you. John Lennon became "Carol Dakota" after his New York building, the Dakota. If you can't think of the correct name, you go to the surname first and work it out from there. Not everyone gets a drag name. But all of my dearest friends are bequeathed with one.

✴ ✴

Glenn was the actor, the performer; Divine, the character that evolved over the years in partnership with Waters. I lovingly called him Divvy. For Glenn, pronouns were interchangeable. In gay culture that's how we spoke to one another back then, by switching genders and nicknames. Divine and Glenn were always inextricably linked. Separate but the same. Two sides of the same coin. The stage persona and the person are interdependent yet share a strange symbiotic relationship. Glenn eventually wanted to move forward as a "serious" actor but owed his fame to his alter-ego.

It's a rare joy when you love the art, get to meet the artist, and love them, too. And that's what happened when I met Divine—a friendship blossomed. Nights out on the town with Freddie Mercury and Divvy followed a certain rhythm. Divine would call, his raspy, lilting voice almost running his words together, "Can I come over to smoke a joint?" He would, then we'd go out to dinner. Divvy was so lovely to be with. He was a very gentle character, nothing like as flamboyant as his film persona. Then again, a lot of performers aren't. I'm not either. It was onstage and onscreen that he expressed himself, his alter-ego screaming to get out. He just wanted to be himself.

That is exactly who I was when I started wearing the costumes and flamboyant stage-wear that would become synonymous with "Elton John." In my shows I'm forever stuck behind a piano, so the outfits had to count. I looked to people like Liberace, to anyone who had that essence of glamour within them and weren't scared to let it out. Drag artists perform gender in exaggerated expressions, which was exactly what I wanted to do. I lived my life so playfully and excessively in my twenties and thirties because I had never had the courage to live it in my teenage years. Like Divvy, I grew up in the fifties, a conservative era. I knew nothing about sex and wasn't allowed to wear the clothes I wanted to. Glenn's childhood had been similar in that respect, and I could see that Divine's spirit was very close to mine. For both of us, as soon as we could, we just burst onto the scene. Boy, did we make up for lost time.

> I can't remember the first time I dressed in drag privately, but it soon transpired into a public habit and to this day comprises some of my happiest memories.

In 1976, I invited Divvy onstage to perform with me for an encore at Madison Square Garden. In hindsight, perhaps I should have warned my band first. Still a cult star under Waters's direction, confined to the arthouse extremes, they had no idea who Divine was. I sat at my piano and watched in awe as she climbed up the stairs to the stage in an amazing foil dress. One of her heels snapped on the stairs, but of course she styled it out, screaming, into her mic, "Oh fuck, my heel's just broken!" She rolled onstage and you could visibly read "Who the fuck is this?" on the band's faces. They had absolutely no idea. That night was just me and Divvy having fun onstage in front of thousands of people.

Divvy set something of a precedent at that show. On a later night of my tour, I came onstage in drag as Tina Turner, in full "What's Love Got to Do with It" regalia. Skirt, wig, everything. I didn't tell my band about that either—just arrived onstage, sat down, and nobody knew who the fuck I was until I started playing.

The New York club scene in the seventies was incredible. It was all about the music. Crisco Disco, Le Jardin, and 12 West were fabulous, even though one night Crisco Disco refused Divvy and me entry. We'd gone out for a lovely dinner and had both stolen ashtrays from the restaurant. We turned up at Crisco Disco, Divine in a kaftan, me in some colorful, outrageous outfit. The doorman shouted, "What do you think this is? Fucking Halloween? You ain't comin' in here like this." And Divine yelled, "Fuck you," exactly in the manner of Dawn Davenport in *Female Trouble*, and we both threw and smashed our ashtrays and hotfooted it off to 12 West to dance the night away.

Another time, in Hawaii, I came down to dinner at the Four Seasons in full drag, looking like Audrey Hepburn.

Divine and I certainly shared compulsive behaviors. I completely understand where Divvy ended up. I was just as ravenous for my addictions as he was for his. Luckily they didn't kill me because I saw the light. For Divvy, eating got so out of control that he became very unhealthy. I didn't do drugs all the time and was lucky in the sense that I worked, frequently on the road. If drugs had kept me from touring, I'd be dead by now. There were periods where I got and stayed clean, but I always went back to the drugs. I finally got clean for good in 1990. It's different for everyone. As much as I loved Divvy, I can't tell you what was going on inside him.

Divine passed away from a heart attack in 1988, just after the triumphant *Hairspray* premiere. It was the night before shooting was to begin on a role in the sitcom, *Married . . . with Children*. Divvy was about to finally fulfill his dream of performing as Glenn, as himself, out of drag in a major role on television.

For me, Glenn's death will always feel tied up with the height of the AIDS epidemic. It isn't just the coincidence of the timing, at the height of the pandemic. His life and career were cut short just as he was breaking into the mainstream, on the eve of his acceptance as Glenn. That feeling of lives being cut short, abbreviated at the precise moment they were blossoming, was commonplace. It was simultaneously heart-breaking. In the eighties we lost an entire generation of young gay men in their prime. It was a period of intense loss, horrific both for me personally and for the gay community as a whole. I was losing two or three people a week and it was all so overwhelming. The press called AIDS the "gay plague," as if we had caused it.

No one cared about what was happening. It was fucking frightening. I didn't do enough. You had to get your hands dirty. You had to be there on the frontline. Eventually, the incredible ACT-UP! activist Larry Kramer became a good friend and ally, but I should've been there for him years before I was. I started the Elton John AIDS Foundation to try to make up for lost time.

> **We lost an entire generation of young gay men in their prime. It was a period of intense loss, horrific both for me personally and for the gay community as a whole.**

I'm not particularly religious, but I built a little chapel in my house, full of plaques of people who died of AIDS, the names of people I loved. I go there to remind myself that there's still a lot more work to be done. We've made some incredible advances medically, of course. We now have PREP and antiviral drugs, but we still have to address the stigma and fear which prevent people from getting tested, and the lack of education that prevents people from understanding that being HIV positive isn't the death sentence it once was. There's still a lot of work to do, but it is not insurmountable. As a community, we can stand together to face it.

Divine was the best of us. He was so brave, unique, and fearless. He laughed in the face of a conservative society which ridiculed and rejected him. But Divvy internalized a lot of that trauma and pain and that certainly led to his premature death. That's why we need to protect the next generation of LGBTQ+ people—especially those challenging gender norms—so that they can go on to have long, happy, brilliant lives, living however they want to, saying "fuck you" to all the hypocrisy, fear, and shame built into so much of mainstream society.

I rewatched *Female Trouble* about a month ago with my husband, David, and was utterly overwhelmed by how ahead of its time it was. Divine was a ray of sunshine. And today I see so many drag queens performing, and non-binary and Transgender activists doing the most incredibly brave things. They are the trailblazers, and we must applaud and support them. That's what the Elton John AIDS Foundation does.

We want the people pushed out by society, the people John Waters loved and championed, to know what they are worth. "No one gets left behind" is our motto, and that's what my life is all about. Whatever you've been through, whatever you've done, everyone deserves redemption. Divine's fearlessness inspires me to this day. Divvy's spirit will linger forever. Glenn was a lesson to us all.

Elton John

Sir Elton John is one of the top-selling solo artists of all time, with 26 gold, 38 platinum or multi-platinum, and one diamond albums, and over 50 Top 40 hits, and he has sold more than 300 million records worldwide. He holds the record for the biggest-selling single of all time, "Candle in the Wind 1997," which sold over 33 million copies. After more than 50 years on the road, Elton announced the *Farewell Yellow Brick Road* tour, encompassing five continents and over 350 dates. To date, Elton has delivered more than 4,000 performances in over 80 countries since launching his first tour in 1970. In 2019, a fantasy musical motion picture of Elton's life, *Rocketman*, was released to high acclaim, and his first and only autobiography, *Me*, was published and instantly became a *New York Times* bestseller. Among the many awards and honors bestowed upon him are six Grammys, including a Grammy Legend award, a Tony and two Academy Awards, a Best British Male Artist Brit Award, induction into the Rock and Roll Hall of Fame and the Songwriters Hall of Fame, the Kennedy Center Honor, Legend of Live Award, and 13 Ivor Novello Awards between 1973 and 2001.

Elton has been acknowledged for his philanthropic and music contributions with a knighthood from HM Queen Elizabeth II, and most recently Elton received the Légion d'honneur from President Macron, the Companion of Honour in the UK, and won a Golden Globe and an Academy Award for the Best Original Song in *Rocketman*. In 1992, Elton established the Elton John AIDS Foundation after losing many friends and loved ones to the AIDS epidemic. Today, after years of fundraising, advocacy, and funding innovative grants, the foundation is the sixth-largest independent AIDS funder globally. Crucially, Elton and the foundation are committed to breaking down the barriers that prevent people—mainly gay men, people who inject drugs, Transgender women, and adolescents—from accessing the life-saving treatment and prevention available around the world and to fight the AIDS epidemic with love and kindness so people feel accepted, involved, and loved. Elton has traveled to South Africa, Ukraine, and Armenia; across the US; and to many other countries. He has spoken at many international AIDS conferences to use his platform and influence to push, persuade, and demand change and care for people at risk or living with HIV, and he is committed to not leaving anyone behind in the AIDS epidemic.

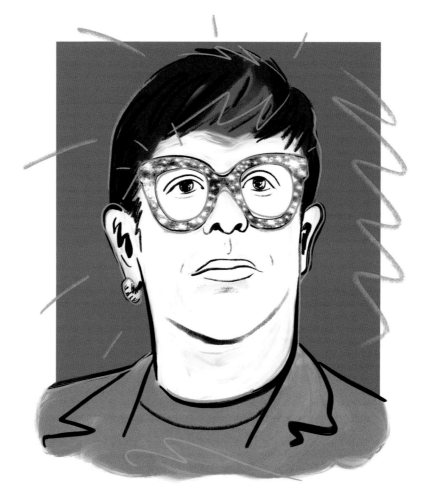

Illustration by Sam Russell Walker

Lesbians and Gays Support the Miners was run out of the backroom of Gay's The Word, a pioneering queer bookshop. The campaign, in support of the 1984-85 Miners' Strike, forged historic alliances between LGBT rights campaigners and the labour movement

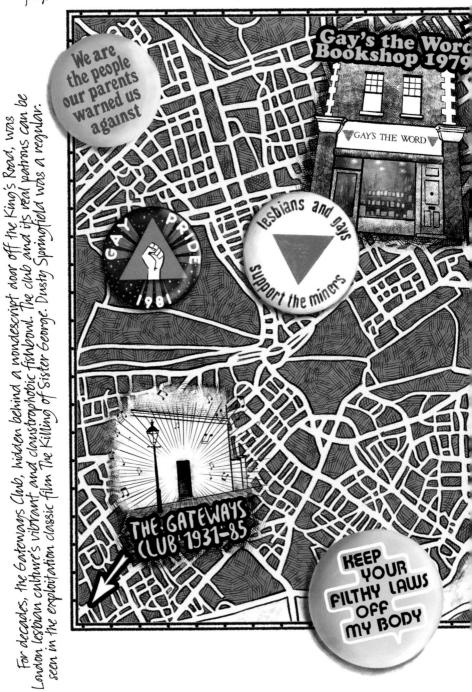

For decades, the Gateways Club, hidden behind a nondescript door off the King's Road, was London lesbian culture's vibrant and claustrophobic fishbowl. The club and its real patrons can be seen in the exploitation classic film The Killing of Sister George. Dusty Springfield was a regular.

We are the people our parents warned us against

Gay's the Word Bookshop 1979

GAY'S THE WORD

GAY PRIDE 1981

lesbians and gays support the miners

THE GATEWAYS CLUB 1931-85

KEEP YOUR FILTHY LAWS OFF MY BODY

'n century Molly houses provided a space for feminine gender expression and male sexual and romantic ...counters, even hosting Molly weddings. Mollies anticipated many modern queer identities from gay men to ...ns lesbians. Plump Nelly, a molly, ran this house with her cis wife before their arrest and trial in 1726. ...lly culture declined later in the 18th century, as public sexuality and morality became increasingly regulated.

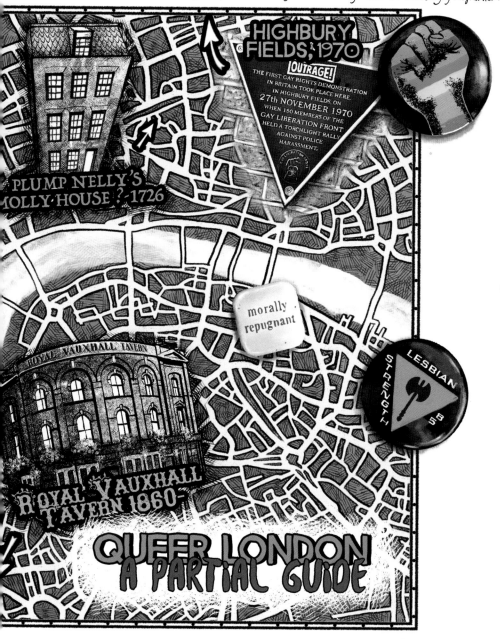

...e Royal Vauxhall Tavern is one of London's oldest surviving gay venues. Starting life as a Victorian music hall, by the late 1940s the RVT had become a drag venue and ...y meeting place. It remains a mainstay of the London drag and queer cabaret scene, with legendary cabaret night Duckie still going strong at twenty-four years.

Words of Joy

02

There are different types of joy. There are spontaneous fireworks of hysterical shoulder-shaking laughter with friends, like when you get the giggles in school assembly and nearly wet yourself. Then there are those deep cosmic moments, approaching a fervent spiritual awakening, where everything seems to make sense—a cosmic joy, like when you hold your newborn baby for the first time, or a rescue dog chooses you with pleading puppy-dog eyes (neither of these things has happened to me, but I picture them being quite moving). These essays will hopefully engender both types of joy—they'll make you laugh, and make you cry—but in that nice cathartic happy way, like *Titanic* or *The Notebook*.

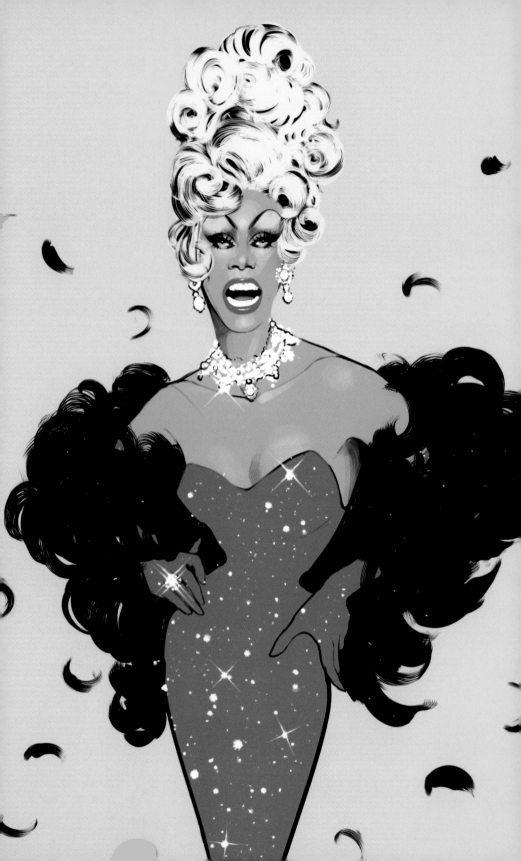

RUPAUL

by Jack Guinness

"Let me get this straight. You publicly came out, did a ton of interviews, launched a queer website, and spent all your money commissioning pieces JUST SO YOU COULD MEET RUPAUL?!" What kind of maniac-stalker-weirdo would do something like that? I replied to my boyfriend's wild accusation. We both knew without saying a word that I was exactly the type of maniac-stalker-weirdo that would do something like that. My life had been a never-ending series of long cons. First as a lonely child, and then as a painfully isolated teen, I retreated into a fantasy world. I imagined one day I'd have an impossibly glamorous life feted as a male supermodel with a pile of celebrity(ish) friends and a fabulous wardrobe of designer clothes. I looked around my dreary life and pined for something more. My early life in South London in the eighties was impossibly beige (perhaps a hangover from the hand-me-down seventies clothes and furniture that filled our flat): the food, our family Volvo . . . my pallid skin. I wanted hot pink, gold, and a tan! I'd caught a flash of something sparkly in the corner of my eye and I have spent the rest of my life chasing it, while it's remained frustratingly on the periphery,

---

Illustration by Adam Johannesson

always out of reach. This is the chase for fame. The promise of escape. To make the fantasy real. And now I have fashioned a rather fabulous life for myself. But something nags. There's a snag. A thread has caught and I'm unraveling. I need more. I need meaning. Inside of me, in the pit of my being, I am still that daydreaming little boy lost, and the more glamorous everything outside gets, the bigger, wider, and more painful the chasm between who I know I am and who everyone else thinks I am becomes. There's a breach at the core. That is the irony of glamour, of shimmer—it simply isn't real. But what was the spark that set me on this course? What shooting star caught me magpie-eyed and ruined my life? It was RuPaul, of course. Covering a Kiki Dee song, of course. With Elton John . . . of course.

Glamour offers a tempting and dangerous allure for many queer people. As we internalize society's disapproval of our identity—our sexuality and gender expression, which is such a core essential part of ourselves—we get caught up in a spiral of shame and a sense of worthlessness. Our parents and society often shame us, and then we continue to shame ourselves. My generation, in pre–social media times, then set off into the night, to clubs that we were too young to be in, sometimes in dangerous situations, so much of it fun but ultimately unsatisfying. Too many of us lose ourselves in the unholy trinity of sex, drugs, and alcohol addiction, co-dependency, and toxic relationships or patterns of behavior. Ironically, we lose ourselves in the very places where we're searching for meaning and identity. This emptiness springing from an impoverished sense of self-worth (a poison tree planted by a disapproving and oppressive culture, which we then ourselves feed and water through self-destructive thinking and behavior) leads us to seek out status-giving armor—designer clothes, glamorous friends, high-powered jobs, or perfect bodies. Through this mechanism we tell ourselves and show others that we have worth, we are important, we are valid. We're shapeshifters, adapting to people, places, and things, changing ourselves to be liked or to stay physically safe, but this all comes at a price. That fixed inner sense of self can become stunted and undeveloped. When we feel worthless on the inside, no wonder we're drawn to external objects that give a sense of worth.

Then we enter the gay community and find it inevitably infected with much of the toxicity of "straight cis" society, namely the two pillars of colonial patriarchy—money and power, with racism and misogyny (which reveals itself as effeminacy shaming) as the methods of keeping those pillars in place. White gay men have a special responsibility to unpack and challenge these concepts. Our Black, Brown, Trans, and lesbian family fought so hard for our rights, and in this ongoing and seemingly worsening climate of violence and oppression directed at Trans people, in the unchecked power of institutional racism and misogyny, we must now show up and fight on their behalf. Never before have there been more resources for white gay men (and white people in general) to educate ourselves about our privilege, our history as colonial oppressors that have created the systems that we benefit from, and face our "whiteness" and the politics of race, which, as Reni Eddo-Lodge writes, "operates on its inherent invisibility." Our challenge now, as individuals and as a global queer community, is to develop a strong and consistent identity imbued with a sense of self that is internally generated, not externally signaled.

Glamour offers a tempting and dangerous allure for many queer people. As we internalize society's disapproval of our identity—our sexuality and gender expression, which is such a core essential part of ourselves—we get caught up in a spiral of shame and a sense of worthlessness.

Through years of therapy (thank you to my therapists who have saved my life and given it meaning) I have further developed this inner, unchanging core self. I believe the power of community—of seeing ourselves mirrored in each other, feeling seen, connected, and loved—also develops this authentic self. Intersectionality—the interconnectedness of different marginalized social groups and our overlapping interests and rights—is the LGBTQ+ community's greatest strength. We are woven together not just through our oppression but by the wonderful difference and uniqueness that make us targets of hatred in the first place. Through telling our stories and listening to the stories of others, we develop a healthy, boundaried connectedness that reinforces us on a deeper level, moving us away from external status signifiers and identity masks, allowing us to move into maturity and wholeness.

I spent years as a male model selling a certain type of performative masculinity. I was told by agents to "butch" it up, whatever that means. I policed my mannerisms, trying not to appear too feminine. I adopted what Matthew Todd refers to in his fantastic book of the same name as a "straight jacket." I was performing oppressive drag, the opposite of everything real drag stands for. I wasn't challenging, exploring, or playing with gender, I was hiding behind its most restrictive socially acceptable forms. I was complicit in my own imprisonment, trapped in toxic masculinity. What a miserable existence. After coming out publicly—or rather, "breaking out"—I felt able to be my true, full self. I stopped internalizing a sense of shame that others were projecting onto me. I am trying to stop self-shaming. Our inheritance as queer people is not shame. It is hope and love. Having to question, explore, and claim your sexuality and gender (and often be oppressed for it) can create empathic, thoughtful, and inspiring human beings. We are descended from a long line of pioneers, our history stretching back through human civilization across endless cultures. We must walk tall in that legacy, knowing that in spite of and because of our suffering, we are brave, awesome, and powerful individuals. We are a family.

Our Trans and lesbian family fought so hard for our rights, and in this ongoing and seemingly worsening climate of violence and oppression of Trans people, in the unchecked power of institutional racism and misogyny, we must now show up and fight on their behalf.

**

I was twelve. The year was 1994. In a music video playing on a Saturday morning music television show (was it *Going Live!* or *CD:UK*?), there she was. All fifty feet of her. Palpable sexual chemistry sparked between her and confirmed bachelor (and suspected serial womanizer) Elton John. She was probably his new girlfriend—that's how an unknown model had managed to snag such a great gig (she was so tall she had to be a supermodel because that's what tall people did for a living, unless they were employed as giants). Something deep down inside me knew she wasn't simply a woman. She was beyond the binary. She wasn't simply a man either. She was something more. More than the sum of her parts.

A magical forbidden taboo creature sent to tempt, inspire, and drive us mad. Somehow deep down I knew Elton didn't really fancy women either, but together, as they dressed up as famous lovers from history, the illusion was irresistible.

I suppose I knew there was something different about Elton John before I really understood what being "gay" meant. He was rebellious, boundary-crossing, and didn't care what you thought of him. Before we know, we know. Gay people are drawn to each other before we understand our sexuality: as outsiders, as breakers of norms, as the rejected. We sense a shared secret revealing itself through pain or wild abandon—clues, glances, and nods pull like magnets. The dejected John, desperate for his father's love in James Baldwin's *Go Tell It on the Mountain*, drew me in long before I read *Giovanni's Room* or discovered James's homosexuality. George Michael's rebellious anti-establishment streak, cheeky wink, and camper than camp videos lit a fire in me. A boy crying alone on a train in Bronski Beat's "Smalltown Boy" climaxed into falsetto, bringing tears to my eyes, without me knowing why. The lyrics called to me: a mother who doesn't understand; knowing you have to escape where you came from; desperately seeking love. And so RuPaul burst through my television in an off-the-shoulder Breton top, a 6.5-foot-tall Black siren in a ginormous blonde wig, calling me out from my miserable beige life and promising to take me away to somewhere fabulous.

Our inheritance as queer people is not shame. It is hope and love. Having to question, explore, and claim your sexuality and gender (and often be oppressed for it) can create empathic, thoughtful, and inspiring human beings.

Born RuPaul Andre Charles on 17 November 1960 in San Diego, RuPaul moved to Atlanta to study performing arts, then headed to NYC and became a celebrated fixture on the party scene, employed by nightlife legends like Susanne Bartsch. Female impersonation happened by happy/gay accident. Performing in a gender-fuck punk band, one night Ru dragged-up and the crowd went wild. RuPaul listened to the Universe's stage direction and didn't look back. This is one of Ru's greatest lessons for us; we all have neat, fixed ideas about who we are and what we want to do in life. In the moments where I've relinquished control and expanded my narrow view of myself, I have found joy and success. Read the clues. Ru didn't necessarily grow up wanting to be a female impersonator, but when he smelled a hit, he seized the moment, making it his own. He became an international pop star with the single "Supermodel," won a trailblazing MAC Cosmetics campaign, and as their spokesperson, raised funds for the MAC AIDS Fund.

After a few years in the wilderness (though he never stopped gigging around the world) RuPaul returned with *Drag Race*—a simultaneous pastiche and celebration of reality TV shows such as *Project Runway* and *America's Next Top Model*. It was turned down by every major network and eventually found a home on gay-centric cable channel Logo TV. Now the show calls the very mainstream VH1 home, with past seasons streaming on the international digital monster Netflix.

Drag Race is a global phenomenon, spawning spin-offs, tours, live shows, and events, as well as international versions in the UK, Thailand, and Holland. It relaunched RuPaul on the global stage and ironically allowed him to appear as RuPaul out of drag for the first time (though still wearing some fabulous outfits). What a strange, wild journey. Rupaul took a risk and detoured into drag while remaining true to his punk values. He acts and hosts, both in and out of drag, celebrated as the powerful human that he is. RuPaul sees his work as a challenge to identity stereotypes and politics, telling *Vogue*, "We live in such an egocentric world where identity is king, and we've elected the poster child for the ego in the USA . . . Drag is the perfect balance to that mentality. Ego is all about saying 'I'm better than you are' and drag says 'you are not your clothes, you are not what it says you are on your birth certificate. You are a creation of your own imagination.'"

This is one of Ru's greatest lessons for us; we all have neat fixed ideas about who we are and what we want to do in life. In the moments where I've relinquished control and expanded my narrow view of myself, I have found success and joy.

I simply cannot overstate how much joy *Drag Race* brings to my life, and into the lives of millions of people around the world. I am never

We must walk tall in that legacy, knowing that in spite of and because of our suffering, we are brave, awesome, and powerful individuals.

happier than when I'm watching *Drag Race*. Watching the show I feel like I've come home. I'm with my chosen family. It creates a connectedness with the global queer community that hasn't existed before, set firmly in the mainstream. When I was a teenager I had to desperately seek out any literature, films, or television shows that made me feel less alone. I could never have imagined that our community could come out of the shadows, and not just be tolerated, but celebrated. It is legacy making, shaping our culture.

Now, through the global popularity of *Drag Race*, RuPaul sets the agenda for his legion of fans, subverting the mainstream by inspiring a generation of queer (and straight) youth. Ru rightfully remains a poster child for misfits and generation queer. He is not here to make us feel safe, he wants to challenge and destroy. Burn it all down and start again! His punk impulses are seemingly at odds with his mainstream success and engagement with consumerist culture—one in-joke of *Drag Race* is that Ru also seems to have a new product to peddle—the joke resonates because it is true! We are all full of tensions and contradictions. Ultimately Ru's work is about ripping off the illusions we cloak ourselves in, questioning our very "identity"—"We're all born naked and the rest is drag."

RuPaul's hosting style references the catchphrases and performances of iconic film stars and performers, from Joan Crawford to Liza to Blaxploitation films. It was these references (some obvious, some frustratingly obscure) that inspired me to create *The Queer Bible* website in the first place. I wanted a place to go where I could immerse myself in the same culture landmarks that RuPaul had been exposed to. The AIDS epidemic robbed us of an entire generation who would now be our elders— queer people who could educate us, show us the films, play us the music, and let us in on the jokes that make up queer culture. *Drag Race* is a gateway drug into queer culture. You want to know why "reading is fundamental"? Watch *Paris Is Burning*. Who owns "51% of this company?" Watch Faye Dunaway as Joan Crawford in *Mommie Dearest*. "My girls" are Maggie Smith's in *The Prime of Miss Jean Brodie*. And Ru's catchphrases themselves have entered the popular lexicon. As depicted in the iconic film about the New York drag ball scene, *Paris Is Burning*, we need "Drag Mothers" to initiate us into our mysterious, wonderful and subversive birthright.

Now everyone has access to a Drag Mother. In turn, RuPaul inspired me to create *The Queer Bible*; to create something beyond myself, something real. A platform for others to tell their stories in their own voices. A space and community for the next generation, who can joyously celebrate our culture and educate us about evolving concepts of gender and politics. By looking back we are empowered to look forward. As a child, the shallow and bombastic caught my eye; now I'm reaching toward something deep and solid. Ru has claimed, passing through the glamour and lure of New York nightlife and Hollywood, a meaningful path. Now RuPaul inspires a generation to seek out those fierce humans who bravely stomped before us and celebrate who they are.

RuPaul inspired me to create *The Queer Bible*; to create something beyond myself, something real. A platform for others to tell their stories in their own voices. A space and community for the next generation, who can joyously celebrate our culture and educate us about evolving concepts of gender and politics.

I think back to that little boy watching RuPaul on television. Ru appeared as a Fairy Godmother, traveling by my side. I think of all the confusion, bullying, and suffering that was to come for me. So many times I wanted to give up, but I'm so glad I carried on. On the other side of that pain was a beautiful life: little Jack would accept himself, repair relationships with his biological family, and would find an additional chosen family in the queer community. He would eventually be happy, be proud, and love who he is. I thank RuPaul for showing me that is possible. As Ru says, "If you can't love yourself, how in the hell you gonna love somebody else? Can I get an Amen!"

Jack Guinness

In a recent profile, *British GQ* described Jack Guinness as the "Coolest Man in Britain." Cambridge-educated Jack Guinness began his career as a model, starring in global campaigns for brands such as L'Oréal, Dunhill, and Dolce & Gabbana.

As a writer, style, and fashion commentator, he has contributed to *Sunday Times Style*, *Vogue Italia*, *The Guardian* (London), *British GQ*, *Gentleman's Journal*, and *Tatler*.

In digital, Jack has developed and starred in content for Gucci, Ralph Lauren, *Vogue*, *VICE*, and *GQ*, traveled to Japan to star in Channel 4's anarchic *World of Weird* series, and hosted live social media takeovers for brands such as Alexa Chung and Hugo Boss. Guinness is proud to be on the British Fashion Council's advisory Style Council for London Fashion Week Men's and passionately champions young designers and British manufacturing. Jack was recently announced as a contributing editor for *British GQ* magazine.

Jack publicly "came out" in an interview with the *The Guardian* newspaper and launched the LGBTQ+ community The Queer Bible, which celebrates the works and lives of the global queer community. Jack's new project is *The Queer Bible* podcast with guests including Sir Ian McKellen, activist Munroe Bergdorf, and *Drag Race*'s Courtney Act.

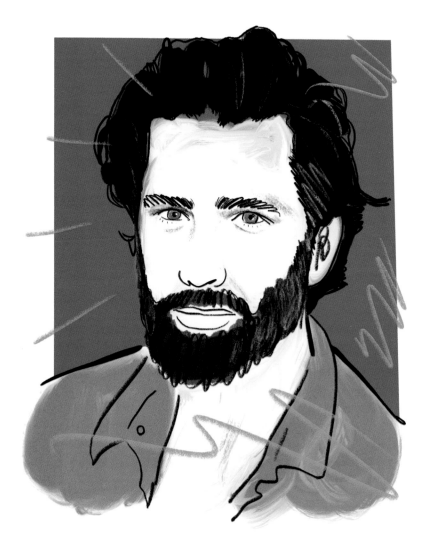

Illustration by Sam Russell Walker

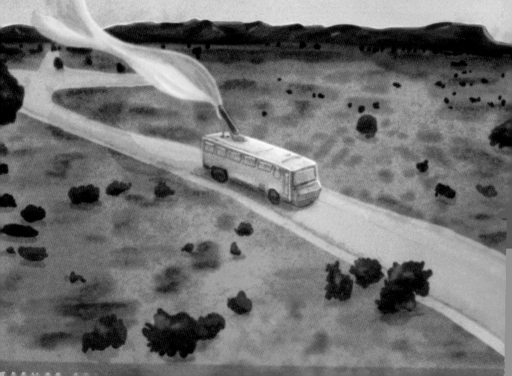

THE ADVENTURES OF

PRISCILLA

QUEEN OF THE DESERT

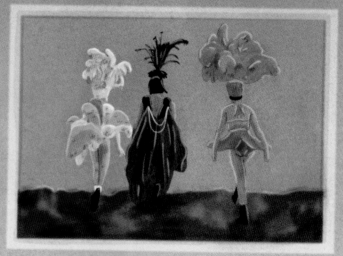

STEPHAN ELLIOTT

THE ADVENTURES OF PRISCILLA, QUEEN OF THE DESERT

by Courtney Act

Priscilla, queen of the mother-fucking desert! What a movie. What a lifeline. A glimmer of hope growing up in the queer-barren desert of working-class suburban Australia in the mid-nineties! I was 12 at the time and by no means living a life as queer—loud and proud as I am now—nor was the world at large. *Priscilla* was a cultural anomaly that was the highest-grossing Australian film of 1994. It won an Academy Award and a BAFTA. It was celebrated at the Sydney 2000 Olympics closing ceremony, when a parade

---

Illustration by Jamie Elder

of drag queens re-created a scene from the film in what was the first open involvement of queer people in an Olympic event. It was also turned into a musical that has been performed around the world, including in the West End in London and on Broadway, where it won a Tony. This wasn't a niche, underground, queer delight; families put on their Sunday best and set off to the flicks to see the movie that everyone was talking about, a movie about three Sydney drag queens driving a bus they had named "Priscilla, Queen of the Desert" into the center of Australia.

My dad remembers our family sitting down to watch *Priscilla* on VHS in our very nineties black-and-white living room. White-wool Berber carpet, black leather couches, black-and-white damask pleated balloon curtains, even a big black-and-white print of that Michael Ochs photo of Marilyn Monroe leaning over a high-rise ledge with the New York City skyline in the background. But the real prized possession was our big black (keep your minds out of the gutter, please) wood-veneer entertainment unit which housed our giant 56cm cathode-ray tube television. I felt like I was sitting in Kansas staring into the technicolor dream-world fantasy of Oz. On the screen I saw a glittery rainbow that ranged from the holographic green sequins on Hugo Weaving's dress to the stunning sunburnt landscape of the Australian outback. My dad particularly recalls, when the credits rolled, me belting out opera and mimicking Guy Pearce's iconic scene lip-syncing to *La Traviata*. His character, Felicia, was wearing a silver fish-scale sequin jumpsuit, sparkly silver and black makeup, and a glittering silver turban. He was sitting on a giant silver high heel, strapped to the top of a silver bus hurtling through the desert with giant lengths of silver lamé billowing behind. In my rudimentary homage I ran up and down the house high on my tiptoes, from room to room, across wooden floorboards, to linoleum, to the aforementioned wool Berber with one of Mum's silk scarves trailing behind me. I'm sure across the country many young drag apprentices were doing the same.

The inspiration didn't stop there. Later that year I was on a bus tour of my own, but instead of three drag queens it was forty high-school-aged kids (though at least three of us did turn out to be drag queens). We all went to the same theater school, the Fame Theatre Company, in Brisbane, and just like in the film, we drove from regional town to regional town; from Bundaberg to Biloela and to Gladstone performing a show called *The Spirit of Christmas*. We performed this semi-educational show for other school-aged kids in non-air-conditioned theaters, wearing mostly synthetic fibers on 40-degree tropical summer days across the great south-east of my home state, Queensland. (Yes, I was aptly born in "Queens"land.) On the 14-hour drive to Rockhampton someone slipped the *Priscilla* soundtrack into the cassette player and I, gingerly perched over the back of a bus seat, began lip-syncing "I Don't Care if the Sun Don't Shine" by Patti Page—just like Felicia.

On the last night of the tour in Toowoomba, after we had bumped out the set and packed up the costumes, we had a wrap party, which was a talent show for our fellow cast members. We were teenagers so it wasn't your traditional cocaine and hookers kinda shindig (that came later). My friend Scotty and I decided to do a number together. For some reason he had brought wigs from his costume box at home and we borrowed some wardrobe from the girls. There we were in curly pussycat wigs, a smear of lipstick, a lick of mascara, and me in an itsy bitsy, teeny weeny, mambo-pink-and-blue bikini. Inspired by my prior scene-stealing performance, we encored "I Don't Care if the Sun Don't Shine" and it brought the house down! One of those things that people who were there still talk about today, it was a memorable moment and my first time in drag.

But *Priscilla* didn't just inspire camp moments, it humanized queer people in a way that hadn't been done before in Australia. It cut through with sensational drag that demanded to be looked at, then connected on a much deeper level with heart, storytelling, and humor. Audiences saw behind and inside the lives of these three heroic misfits who were on their journey to Alice Springs. Hugo Weaving's character, Tick, aka Mitzi Del Bra, gets a call out of the blue from his ex-wife calling in a favor—she needs an act to perform at Lasseters Hotel Casino, which she manages. Omitting the part about the wife, Tick asks Felicia to join him, along with older Trans woman and drag performer Bernadet, played by Terence Stamp. As the movie sets off we see the girls at each other's throats and bitching about their lives in Sydney, and it's revealed that not only does Tick have a wife but also a child.

The girls arrive at the first town, Broken Hill, and after losing a card game Tick reluctantly agrees to do "one lap of the main drag, in drag." Tick, dressed as Mitzi, is wearing the now-infamous "thong dress" made of pink and orange flip-flops, and Felicia is wearing a magnificent wig made of blue and purple plastic tubing. These are just two of the many magnificent costumes inspired by the creativity of Sydney drag queens, created by Tim Chappel and Lizzy Gardiner, who won the Oscar for Best Costume Design. The girls wander into the Palace Hotel, which couldn't be further from a gay bar. The place is packed with working-class men and one woman who aggressively approaches the girls as Bernadette is placing her drink order.

"We've got nothing here for people like you. Nothing!"

"Now listen here, you mullet. Why don't you just light your tampon, and blow your box apart? Because it's the only bang you're ever gonna get, sweetheart!"

After an uncomfortable silence the crowd burst out in laughter, the library is closed, and the girls are welcomed even if they don't necessarily fit in.

The next morning they emerge from their hotel to find Priscilla (the bus) vandalized with the words "AIDS FUCKERS GO HOME" painted across the side in big red letters. It's a very sobering moment after the jubilation of last night's bonding, and a humbling reminder about queer acceptance during this era. Bernadette comforts Adam with: "It's funny. We all sit around mindlessly slagging off that vile stink-hole of a city. But in its own strange way, it takes care of us. I don't know if that ugly wall of suburbia's been put there to stop them getting in, or us getting out. Come on. Don't let it drag you down. Let it toughen you up. I can only fight because I've learnt to. Being a man one day and a woman the next isn't an easy thing to do."

Our trio is bonded together in the realization that their gay bubble in Sydney that they were all so eager to get away from might not be as bad as they thought. This moment gives the film an honesty and depth; the girls played jester all night entertaining the crowd and leaving the audience on a high, then are slapped in the face with the cold harsh reality of morning.

The obligatory bus breakdown occurs and Felicia paints over the graffiti, turning their bus purple ("It's not purple. It's lavender"). My loins were captivated by hunky Guy Pearce in plaid overalls; it was a sexual awakening for 12-year-old me. I liked his muscles, the way his face looked, and was fascinated with how he appeared masculine but didn't act or dress it. I hadn't seen a man depicted as sexy and camp before; usually a camp character was the butt of the joke, not one of the hot male leads. I wouldn't consciously understand I liked boys for six more years, but I was definitely aware there was something about Felicia that stirred an unusual feeling in me.

> But *Priscilla* didn't just inspire camp moments, it humanized queer people in a way that hadn't been done before in Australia. It cut through with sensational drag that demanded to be looked at, then connected on a much deeper level with heart, storytelling, and humor.

Bernadette wanders the desert in search of help while Tick starts choreographing the show. Bernadette returns with help, an older white couple, who just as soon leave them for dead when they realize what these three are—drag queens. There is a lovely moment of cultural awareness, though, when they are rescued by an Aboriginal man called Alan, played wonderfully by indigenous Australian musician Alan Dargin. He invites them to an outback gathering of indigenous folk, where they listen to music and the girls decide to put on a show. There is a gorgeous exchange of cultures when they put Alan in drag and he joins the girls in a performance of "I Will Survive" by Gloria Gaynor, mixed with sounds of the didgeridoo and indigenous chanting.

As an adjacent aside, in Aboriginal culture the Trans women are called "sistergirls" and the Trans men are called "brotherboys." The Tiwi Islands, a few hours north of Darwin, up at the top end of Australia, have the largest population per capita of indigenous Trans folk. Miriam Margolyes recently did a TV series where she traveled around the country exploring what it means to be Australian. On her travels she meets a group of sistergirls, and while she's not intending on being confrontational, she says all the wrong things. Pointing out facial hair on one of the girls, Miriam says, "To be a woman you're going to have to get rid of all that stuff . . . because that's what women do."

Thankfully, one of the girls, Crystal, is there to school Miriam:

"In our culture we respect that person regardless of their look. So me telling you to shave is stupid of me. I should know it's not what you look like outside, it's who you are and how you feel."

It's a moment that reveals the wisdom and nuances of indigenous culture that we could all learn from.

Priscilla's tone is uniquely Australian because it doesn't take itself too seriously. In the context of the time, that felt necessary, because its self-deprecating comedy created a crack in the otherwise hard exterior of Australian machismo and allowed the storytelling to penetrate and connect on a human level. In her smash-hit 2018 show *Nanette*, Australian comedian Hannah Gadsby has shown how far we have come when she speaks about self-deprecating humor:

"Do you understand what self-deprecation means when it comes from somebody who already exists in the margins? It's not humility, it's humiliation. I put myself down in order to speak, in order to seek permission to speak, and I simply will not do that anymore, not to myself or anybody who identifies with me."

It's really fascinating when it comes to social movements, whether it be queer folk, people of color, disabled people, or women, how we've changed our approach to things now. Back then all we had was comedy, all we had was humor. We couldn't demand respect. We weren't even afforded the right to be respected, so we had to self-deprecate in order to create a place for ourselves. It was a means to an end, and it is so beautifully observed when watching *Priscilla* now.

The film tenderly explores a romance between Bernadette and her unlikely love interest: Bob. He's the mechanic the girls meet when Priscilla breaks down. Bob remembers going to see Les Girls in Sydney when he was a "young bloke" and it's revealed that Bernadette is one of the most famous Les Girls ever produced. Les Girls was a showgirl review that ran in the heart of Sydney's red-light district, Kings Cross, from 1963–94, featuring Trans performers and drag queens alike in a sit-down-dinner cabaret show that was a hit with locals and international guests. My mum and dad even went to Les Girls back in the seventies; the show was a must-see tourist attraction of its day. After Bob's wife, Cynthia, leaves him, Bob joins the girls on their journey to Alice and we get to witness the blossoming of their fine romance. This portrayal of a Trans woman and the man courting her is so unique even today. It's wholesome and heartwarming, and we get to see the simplicity of two people exploring the beginning of a love story rather than the often-politicized context of a Trans woman dating a straight-identifying man. Bob's sexuality is never questioned by himself or others, which would so often be the case even today.

Another beautiful way in which *Priscilla* defies tropes and uses fiction to deliver truth comes in Coober Pedy, a rough mining town where Guy Pearce's character gets attacked by Frank, a misogynistic, homophobic bloke who gets spooked when he realizes that Felicia is a man in drag. In an aggressive fight scene that is all too triggering for many queer people, Felicia is held down and beaten, but before the final blow is dealt Bernadette appears to save the day. Frank, grabbing his crotch aggressively, yells, "Come on, Bernadette, fuck me," and, using her years of experience in dealing with the fragile straight male identity, she approaches Frank as he continues to taunt her. The confidence in her approach only confuses the threats of Frank and as she gets face to face, using the element of surprise, she delivers two swift knees to Frank's crotch. We are reminded that despite Bernadette being an older woman she has survived because she has learned to fight. Frank falls to the ground as Bernadette flicks her hair and delivers the iconic line: "Now you're fucked!"

> **Back then all we had was comedy, all we had was humor. We couldn't demand respect. We weren't even afforded the right to be respected, so we had to self-deprecate in order to create a place for ourselves.**

Priscilla is full of iconic lines that have been woven into the Australian lexicon as well as attitudes that have shaped the Australian psyche. When the film came out in 1994, Sydney was being ravaged by the AIDS crisis. Death notices no longer fit on the front page of the *Sydney Star Observer* and were moved to a pull-out section in the middle. But *Priscilla* was a streak of hope among the decimation.

Writer and director Stephan Elliott was a gay man who was inspired by his local community to make this film, a beautiful example of queer people telling queer stories and getting it so right. The film was a worldwide hit, and went on to influence and inform so many with its positive and heartfelt portrayals of LGBT people. For 12-year-old me running through the house on my tiptoes with Mum's silk scarf trailing behind me, it created a space for the life that I would one day lead. I can't say that watching *Priscilla* made me want to be a drag queen—that process unfolded when I was 18 and moved to Sydney—but I know *Priscilla* created a world where that was possible.

When I arrived in Sydney in the year 2000, I was so enraptured with the drag queens of The Albury Hotel. I was living in a post-*Priscilla* world before smartphones, social media, reality TV, and location-based dating apps, and I stood at the bar enamored by the glamazons before me. I was so inspired by their freedom, color, and irreverence. I craved a mainstream entertainment career inspired by The Spice Girls, and at the time being a drag queen was the furthest from a mainstream entertainment career one could get. But drag spoke to me, and when I picked it up on New Year's Eve at 18 years old, I was never able to put it down.

> I can't say that watching *Priscilla* made me want to be a drag queen—that process unfolded when I was 18 and moved to Sydney—but I know *Priscilla* created a world where that was possible.

Despite my better judgment and the recommendations of those around me at the time to quit, drag has given me the career and life of my dreams; I have traveled around the world performing for amazing audiences and lost more competition reality shows than I can remember. I've never had to hide or compromise who I am in a world that so often has told me otherwise. I always carry in my heart the Sydney drag scene that helped shape me into the performer I am today. A drag scene that inspired *The Adventures of Priscilla, Queen of the Desert*, a movie that in return inspired that drag scene.

I've never had to hide or compromise who I am in a world that so often has told me otherwise.

Courtney Act

Boy. Girl. Artist. Advocate. Courtney Act is more than just the sum of her parts. She is a contemporary artist who embodies the zeitgeist of an era. One of the first artists to show their gender fluidity, Courtney broke out of the box in 2003 to make it through to the semi-finals of the premiere season of *Australian Idol*, then signed to Sony/BMG.

In 2014, she returned to the television arena as one of the Top 3 in Season 6 of the Emmy Award–winning *RuPaul's Drag Race*, with a legion of new fans around the world. Courtney then released her debut EP, *Kaleidoscope*, featuring mainstream pop beats and lux music videos. Her videos online have been viewed over 40 million times. 2017 marked the international tour of her original show: *The Girl from Oz*. This sold-out world tour culminated in her debut at the Edinburgh Festival Fringe with five-star reviews. 2018 saw Courtney Act and Shane Jenek plow full steam ahead as winner of *Celebrity Big Brother* UK—educating viewers on queer issues such as gender identity and fluidity, sexuality, same-sex marriage, and much more. After her successful world tour, *Courtney Act: Under the Covers*, she made television history as the host of UK's first bisexual dating show on E!'s *The Bi Life* to wrap up an extraordinary year in her very own Christmas special, *The Courtney Act Show*, for Channel 4 UK and Peach (Australia).

Not one for resting on her stilettoed laurels, Courtney Act competed in last year's inaugural *Eurovision—Australia Decides*, launching her smash-hit single "Fight for Love." Making television history again, this time as one-half of the world's first same-sex pairing, Courtney Act and Shane Jenek danced their way into the heart of the nation and as a runner-up in Network Ten's *Dancing with the Stars*.

In the past year, Courtney has made numerous guest appearances on shows such as BBC's *Blind Election Dates*, MTV's *Served! With Jade Thirwall*, and recently on ITV's *Celebrity Karaoke Club*. This year has also marked Shane Jenek's debut as songwriter and composer for Courtney Act's new show *FLUID*, featuring all original material and songs. In *FLUID*, Courtney shares her experience with gender fluidity with a blend of exposition, song, dance, and costume evolution. *FLUID* made its world premiere at Darlinghurst Theatre for Mardi Gras Festival to standing ovations.

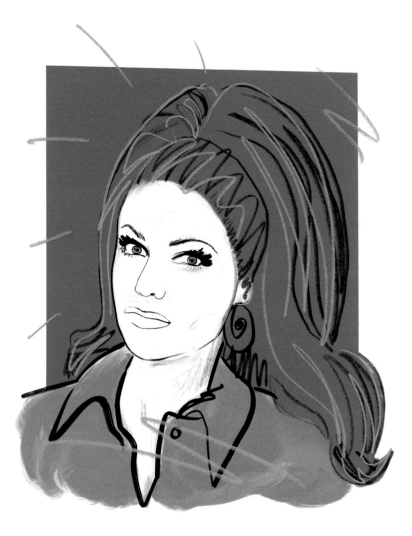

Illustration by Sam Russell Walker

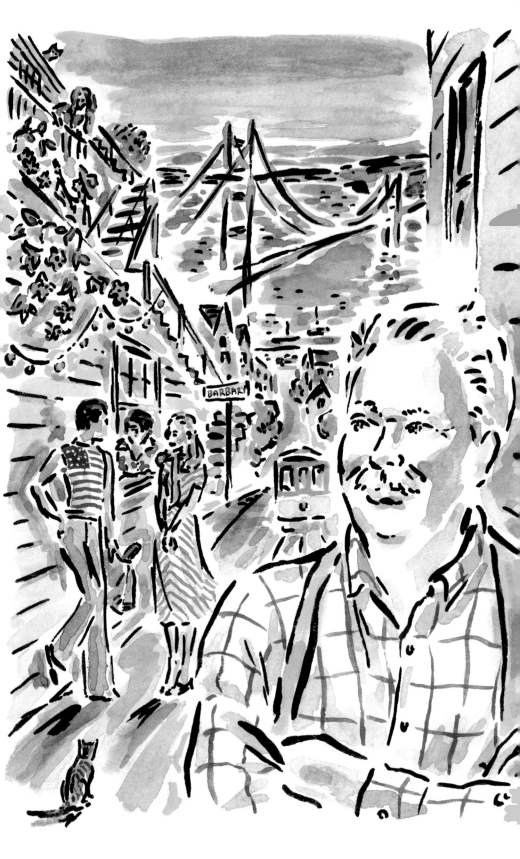

ARMISTEAD MAUPIN

by Graham Norton

I never came out. It didn't seem practical. Living in a small town in rural Ireland in the early eighties there was no context for me to be gay in, so why tell anyone? I would just have been gay watching afternoon TV or riding my bike into town. With no prospect of being gay in the very important *boy meets boy* scenario, I felt it would just have upset everyone without any real benefit. Instead, I resolved to go to where the boys were.

My plan was to take my J1 visa from university and travel to Los Angeles for the summer. I had a pen pal there, David Villapando, who had revealed in his letters that not only was he gay but that he was doing something about it. In fact, he was doing quite a lot about it. Every month or so I would receive what was essentially handwritten porn on thin blue airmail paper. It seemed that David would be the perfect person to show me the ropes. I know it seems ridiculous that the closest gay person I could find was five thousand miles away, but subconsciously, that was probably how I wanted it.

What was harder to understand was my chosen route to LA. I bought a plane ticket to New York and then decided to use a pre-paid seven-day rambler ticket on the Trailways

---

Illustration by Clym Evernden

bus network to get me across the continent and into the experienced arms of my pen pal. This plan might have worked except that my twenty-year-old self felt that a map of any kind seemed simply too prosaic and middle-aged to even consider. I was going from one coast to the other. How hard could it be?

Well, given that my week-long rambler ticket ran out as the bus came to a shuddering halt at the San Francisco bus station, it seems it was more challenging than I'd thought. The journey should really only take four days. In retrospect, perhaps my diversion to Boulder, Colorado, to see where *Mork and Mindy* was set had been an error. Another day had been lost for a pointless layover in Little Rock because of the song that Marilyn Monroe and Jane Russell sing in the movie *Gentlemen Prefer Blondes*. Did I mention I was not actually out at this point in my life?

Like a scene from a bad movie about a young man arriving in San Francisco, as I stepped bleary and aching from the bus with my backpack weighing heavily, a flatbed truck came around the corner with three drag queens waving and screaming on the back of it. Obviously, I knew that the city had a reputation for being gay, but nonetheless, this seemed a little overstated.

It transpired that I had arrived on the day of Gay Pride. I walked up to Market Street and watched the parade go by. Actual Grace Jones was on a float singing to me. My Irish head and heart were close to bursting. In among the drag queens, leather daddies, and gray-haired proud parents marching in solidarity with their children, I remember seeing some placards with the initials AIDS on them. When asked, the pleasant woman standing beside me on the sidewalk explained happily, "Oh, it's a bad disease they get." I had a vague recollection of reading something about it deep inside the *Cork Examiner*. A type of cancer, I thought. Other groups on the parade were angry that the city had forced the bath houses to shut their doors. The day had slowly turned from being a celebration of pride to a closing-down party.

Short of money and with no more ticket to ride, I never did get to LA. Within days I had found a job doing the breakfast shift in a new faux-French café in the financial district and I was renting a room in a hippie commune. At work I was surrounded by a young hip crowd, interested in movies, clubbing, and cocktails. They were precisely the type of Americans I imagined I would be hanging out with. Back home in the commune I was surrounded by well-meaning, often earnest people, who were focused on building a better future. The precocious, faux-world-weary young man I had been back in Ireland would have wasted no time in mocking these hippies and their impossible dreams, but now, actually living among them, I found there was something about their sincerity that was infectious. The way they accepted me with no questions asked was humbling. I knew that I was just a sarcastic little cynic, only interested in their extremely affordable rent, but the manner in which they approached me, assuming I was a better, bigger person than that, made me want to be the man they thought I was. I sometimes wonder who I would have become and what direction my life might have taken if I had never met those hippies.

> **Like a scene from a bad movie about a young man arriving in San Francisco, as I stepped bleary and aching from the bus with my backpack weighing heavily, a flatbed truck came around the corner with three drag queens waving and screaming on the back of it.**

Despite life in the commune feeling quite removed from the rest of the city, every morning the *San Francisco Chronicle* was delivered with a satisfying thud onto the steps that led from the street up to the front door. The various sections got handed around as we breakfasted on bowls of something so healthy it wasn't immediately identifiable as fit for human consumption.

There was one column I had noticed but never read. It was called "Tales of the City" and was, as far as I could tell, a continuing fiction series. I assumed it must be awful. If a writer was any good, why would they be penning a daily soap opera in the newspaper? This particular morning, however, it caught my eye. A character, Michael, was visiting London and noticing the differences between leather bars in San Francisco and the ones in Earl's Court. It was funny and frank and didn't seem like the sort of thing that should be appearing in a daily newspaper. The next morning, I went back for more. I was hooked.

So much has been written about Armistead Maupin and the extraordinary success of the world he created in "Tales of the City." Mary Anne, Michael, Mrs. Madrigal, all living and loving in the ramshackle splendor of 28 Barbary Lane, an address as real to me as any that have ever been my actual home. People quite rightly focus on his storytelling, the characterizations, the humor, and the huge amount of heart in his work. For me there was also something else, something life-changing and important. He wrote about gay men and women, but that wasn't their defining feature. Their sexuality wasn't a problem or a secret, it was simply an unapologetic part of their lives that also had room for friends and jobs and many, many twists and turns. For me this was revolutionary. These were gay people that were hedonistic at the same time as being domestic, political as well as playful, happy, and heartbroken. Being gay hadn't crushed them or forced them to live in a constricted box. It was only through reading "Tales of the City" that I slowly realized that previously, I hadn't thought that possible.

I had read stories featuring gay characters before. In Ireland I had nervously bought a book called *The Other Persuasion*. It was an anthology of stories exploring the theme of homosexuality in fiction. Reluctantly, I had permitted myself to buy it and bring it home because it contained work by such luminaries as Marcel Proust, E. M. Forster, Gertrude Stein, and Gore Vidal. My mother mightn't have welcomed it into the house, but she couldn't forbid me from owning literature. One might assume that reading so many stories featuring gay characters might have helped me accept my own sexuality, but when the tales are a litany of rape, incest, suicides, and blackmail, all they do is shut the closet door just a little tighter. In "Tales of the City," Armistead Maupin allowed his characters to live in the light. The shadows of the night in his world were reserved for criminal activity and subterfuge, not people finding their truth in love and sex.

People quite rightly focus on his storytelling, the characterizations, the humor, and the huge amount of heart in his work. For me there was also something else, something life-changing and important.

After my time in San Francisco, I moved to London and the next phase of my life, trying to be an actor and living as an out gay man much closer to home. Memory fails me as to why I didn't know that Armistead's columns had been collected into novel form. In fact, the stories I had been reading in the morning paper went on to form the fourth novel, *Babycakes*. I think it was a fellow waiter who turned me on to the books and I devoured them. It was like going back to the San Francisco I had loved, spending time with his characters who were every bit as real to me as the friends I had made in that city. Normally after finishing a book there is a sense of accomplishment or satisfaction, but not with the end of these novels. It's far closer to a sense of loss. As you turn the final page you are being served an eviction notice from 28 Barbary Lane. The book closes, a door slams. I really can't think of any other fiction that has made me feel this way.

Happily, Armistead continues to create. There are nine books in the series all together. The final one, *The Days of Anna Madrigal*, was published in 2014 and was the perfect conclusion to the series. Now he is busy going back to the stories I read with a mouthful of funky granola in 1983, as he explores that period of Mona Ramsey's life. I can't wait.

Having interviewed many authors over the years, I have regretfully come to the conclusion that quite a few are best encountered between the covers of their books. That is where they are at their best. Not so Armistead Maupin. He is that rarest of birds, a writer who is as engaging, entertaining, and inspiring as his work.

> **Armistead Maupin allowed his characters to live in the light. The shadows of the night in his world were reserved for criminal activity and subterfuge, not people finding their truth in love and sex.**

I first met Armistead in 2004. It was Gay Pride in San Francisco, almost twenty years since I had stumbled upon the parade, and I was now one of the grand marshals, along with Alan Cumming and Bruce Vilanch. Late one night, we ended up in Armistead Maupin's house. It was like being wrapped in the pages of his books. Transformed into a sort of Mr. Madrigal, Armistead played host to the great and the good, the waifs and the strays, in his beautiful, tall, thin house looking over the lights of the city he had made so many readers fall in love with. The distinctive aroma of weed mingled with the damp summer evening air. Too often in life we aren't aware of the moments we should be savoring, but this was different. We felt like we had been awarded the keys to the city.

In so many ways, Armistead and San Francisco seem as one. The man and the city are so intertwined. He was the introduction or the memory of that place for so many people. Then in 2012, he left.

It was such a bold and unexpected move. He was sixty-eight, and wildly successful. For most people that would signal a time to settle down and enjoy a retirement of sorts. For Armistead it was instead a moment to walk away from his life, the world he had created, and start again in New Mexico with his husband, the photographer Chris Turner, and Philo, their labradoodle. People took it personally. How dare he turn his back on the city that he had mythologized more than any other contemporary author? If he was leaving, it was as if Barbary Lane was being shuttered up and an ugly For Sale sign being stuck to the gate. It was irrational, but I could, if not understand, then at least sympathize with those feelings. How was it possible that the presence or absence of one man could alter an entire city and why did the location of an author dictate what he could write about it?

Of course, there were more books and the Golden Gate Bridge still stands tall. I began to wonder if what had really unsettled us all was that Armistead had shown a courage and a daring that the rest of us lacked. At 57, I'm shocked at how resistant I am to change. When I consider how upset I am if I can't find my preferred brand of deodorant, I really doubt that I could cope with just walking away from my house and friends and beginning again.

How was it possible that the presence or absence of one man could alter an entire city?

What Armistead has taught me is that the trappings of success can be just that. Traps. We work so hard to get them but then they hold us in their grip. Sitting still, remaining the same, may feel comfortable but as I grow older, I ask myself if it is just giving in? Perhaps the secret to a full and happy life is having as many fresh starts as possible?

Now Armistead, Chris, and Philo have done it again and are currently residing in London. This has meant I've got to spend some more time with them and get to know them better. Armistead sits, manspreading in his uniform of jeans, braces, and work shirt, and his eyes twinkle as he weaves stories from his past. Names are dropped, gossip shared, confessions made. As he speaks it is hard to appreciate the change he has helped bring about, but make no mistake, his soft voice is that of a radical, his gentle manner belongs to a revolutionary. He doesn't preach; instead he communicates. And that message he shares with the world is that gay men and women are just people trying to muddle their way through this life the same as everyone else.

What Armistead has taught me is that the trappings of success can be just that. Traps. We work so hard to get them but then they hold us in their grip.

Armistead began writing his stories in the seventies and yet I am certain they still speak to young queer folk today. Imagine how much more daunting things seem now that you can hide in your bedroom and use Google and porn to discover what your gay future may hold. What Armistead Maupin can still teach us is that the results of a search engine are only a tiny fraction of who we will be and what our lives might be like. Barbary Lane will always be a place where we can feel safe and seen, and ultimately isn't that what everyone wants? Thank you, Mr. Madrigal.

Graham Norton

Graham Norton is one of the UK's best-loved presenters, and he has picked up almost every TV award going, including numerous BAFTAs, National Television Awards, and International Emmys. His tenure as the UK's premiere chat-show host started on Channel 4 in the late 1990s with *So Graham Norton* and *V Graham Norton*, and continues now on BBC One with *The Graham Norton Show*. Since moving to the BBC, he has hosted numerous hit shows including the BAFTA Film Awards, the BAFTA Television Awards, *Elton John: Uncensored*, *Adele at the BBC*, *How Do You Solve a Problem Like Maria?*, *Any Dream Will Do*, *I'd Do Anything*, and *Let It Shine*. He's been hosting the iconic *Eurovision Song Contest* for over a decade and hosts his own Saturday morning show on BBC Radio 2, now the highest-rated single radio show in Europe. Most recently, Graham appeared as a judge on the smash hit *RuPaul's Drag Race UK* (BBC). As a writer, Graham has written two hugely successful memoirs. His debut novel, *Holding*, was released to critical acclaim and huge commercial success in 2016, and his second, *A Keeper*, was a *Sunday Times* bestseller and was shortlisted for the National Book Awards. In 2020, he published his third novel, *Home Stretch*.

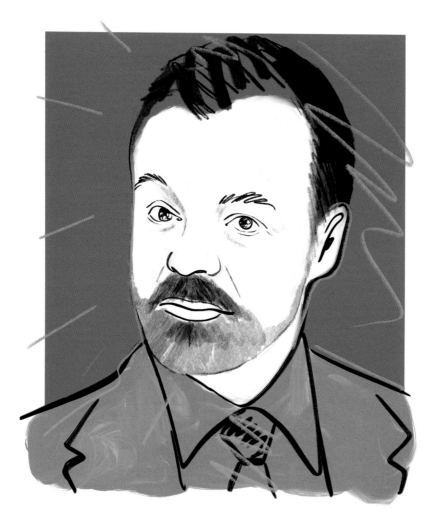

Illustration by Sam Russell Walker

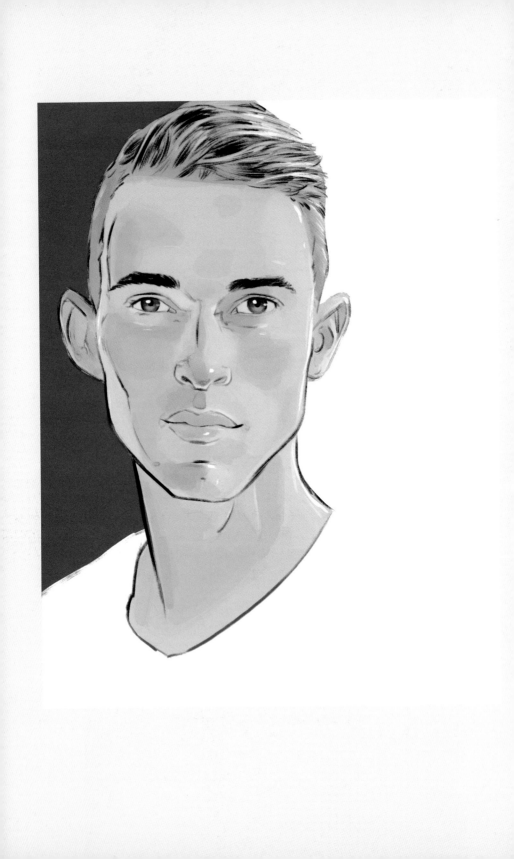

ADAM RIPPON

by Gus Kenworthy

I was aware of Adam before we actually ever met. We were both on the qualification journey to the 2018 Winter Olympics, trying to earn spots in our respective sports and we were getting a bit of media attention because we were the only two openly gay men trying to make the team. When I began following his journey, I knew almost nothing about him or about figure skating in general, but as a fellow gay man I was rooting for him. It seemed he was rooting for me, too, because on 12 December 2017 he messaged me saying, "I think you're so awesome and I SO admire you for being yourself. You also have my dream teeth. I hope we get the chance to meet in Korea! Until then . . ." It was such a kind and wholesome message and it came in the midst of my selection events when I truly needed it. I wrote him back asking him about his qualification process and letting him know that I was cheering him on, too. He earned his spot first—the figure skating and free-skiing events don't line up on the same dates—and I earned mine about a week and a half after him, and we knew that we would both be going to the Games as the first two openly gay men in Winter Olympics' history. It was very exciting.

Illustration by Ego Rodriguez

My first Olympics in 2014 I was in the closet, and although I won a silver medal, I don't think I really enjoyed my time there, and the subsequent media tour that followed caused me tremendous turmoil because I felt like a fraud. I knew that getting to go back to a second Games as my honest, authentic self was going to be a much different experience, but I had no idea how much better it was going to be and how important Adam would be in that experience. There was an interview before the Games where NBC asked Adam what it was like to be a gay athlete, to which he responded, "It's just like being a straight athlete, but with better eyebrows." I howled when I saw the quote. Adam being so boldly himself in turn gave me the permission to be more myself. I feel like I came into my own when I came out. Until that point I had kept my cards so close to my chest that I had really stifled my sense of humor and a lot of the things that make me, me. Even though I was now being myself, I found myself falling into old tendencies and seeing Adam be so blatantly, well . . . Adam, gave me permission to do the same. To really let my guard down.

Even though I didn't win a medal in 2018, I felt proud showcasing my authentic self to the world. My family and my boyfriend at the time, Matt, were there cheering me on, and it was incredible to have their support. Before I went up to take my run in the final round of our competition, I hugged my family and kissed my boyfriend—a very casual, normal, insignificant kiss. I didn't really think anything of it at the time but unbeknownst to me the whole thing was being filmed and broadcast around the world. After the competition everybody was asking me about "that kiss"! At first I didn't even know what they were talking about. In a way that kiss, that moment, was kind of my legacy for those Games. And even though it was an "insignificant" kiss it was actually probably one of the most significant kisses of my life. That kiss was beamed into televisions around the world, into living rooms in countries where homosexuality is still not accepted or where it's still illegal. That kiss was seen by parents who have struggled to accept their gay sons and by young gay athletes who have feared there might not be a future for them in sports. Gay representation—whether it's on TV, in pop culture, in sports, or just in our daily lives—is what has helped normalize and destigmatize homosexuality in society and I think that kiss did a lot in terms of normalization. That kiss was my purpose in Korea, whether I knew it or not, and getting to be myself, out and proud alongside Adam Rippon, was one of the greatest privileges of my career.

For the upcoming 2022 Winter Olympics I'll be competing for Team Great Britain. I was born in Essex and my mum's English. My dad's American but he was working in London when he met my mum. They fell in love and had three boys, the last of which was me. We moved to the States when I was three, so I grew up in the States and have always thought of myself as American, but I hold dual citizenship. There were a lot of factors in my decision to switch teams, but the biggest was to honor my mum. For two full Olympic cycles she's come to World Cups and qualifying events, dressed in stars and stripes and waving an American flag, cheering me and my teammates on even though she's not American. This time, I want to pay tribute to her and hold up the Union Jack to let her know that I'm as proud of my English mum as she is of her half-English son.

That kiss was beamed into televisions around the world, into living rooms in countries where homosexuality is still not accepted or where it's still illegal. That kiss was seen by parents who have struggled to accept their gay sons and by young gay athletes who have feared there might not be a future for them in sports.

Adam is funny and brazen and bold and self-deprecating, all while oozing confidence. He's almost impossible not to like and within minutes of meeting him I knew we were going to be friends for life. Unlike the Summer Olympics where all the athletes are housed together, in the Winter Olympics the villages are spread out over two or more locations. In Korea there was a coastal village and a mountain village that were about an hour and a half from one another. Adam was in the coastal village and I was in the mountain village, so we hadn't met prior to the opening ceremony. That night I was looking for him everywhere because it was the first time that the athletes from all the different sports had been in the same place at once. As I was looking for him I was filming it on my Instagram story, going up to each and every person asking, "Adam? Adam? Is that you?" It started as kind of a joke because there were literally hundreds of people and everyone's wearing the exact same outfit, but then I worried I may not actually find him in this sea of stars and stripes. I did, though. And when I did, he screamed at the top of his lungs, threw his hands up, and jumped on me, wrapping his legs around my waist. Everybody, athletes and coaches from other countries, turned to see what was happening and Adam just hugged me, not caring how extra and dramatic it was. He is truly unapologetically himself and it's one of my favorite things about him.

At the opening ceremony you end up waiting for hours in the staging area before actually getting to walk out into the arena, so I plopped down beside him, surrounded by figure skaters I'd never met, and we did what we do best: talk. We talked and talked and really just became instant friends. I know it's a bit cliché but I truly felt like I had known him for my whole life. Normally when you walk out you're kind of expected to stick with the people from your sport, but I willingly abandoned the skiers without hesitation to walk with Adam and the figure skaters. As we took our first few steps into the stadium, with lights flashing everywhere and thousands of people screaming and cheering, Adam grabbed my hand and quickly squeezed it tightly, then he let go and we both started waving to the crowd and the cameras. It was a moment I'll never forget for the rest of my life. The first time an openly gay man walked into a Winter Olympics opening ceremony—and it was not just a man, it was two. Holding hands. It's so surreal to think back on.

Now, three years later, he is one of my closest friends and I wouldn't think to walk in the parade of nations next to anybody else. At that moment, though, it just happened. We didn't plan it. I could have just as easily seen him and said "hi" and given him a hug and gone back to the ski people, and he could have stayed with the figure-skating people and each of us just done our own thing. That "hello" could have been the only interaction that we ever had. But instead we stayed beside each other for hours. When my family got to Korea, we all went together to watch him compete. We did interviews together following the Games. When we were flying home, we arranged to be on the same flight and changed our seats so we could sit next to each other. And in the years since, we've gone on trips together, gone on double dates, shared countless meals, poured our hearts out to one another over drinks, and stayed in one another's guest rooms when we couldn't drive home afterward. It is so weird to think if anyone asks us, "How did you guys meet," we'd be like, oh, it was the opening ceremony of the Olympics! We were the only two openly gay US athletes and we bonded over *RuPaul's Drag Race*.

I think it's quite common for people, especially athletes, to bond over sports and talking about players and teams and stats. That's pretty much what Adam and I connected over, except the athletes we were gabbing about were Trixie Mattel and Shangela and the cast of *RuPaul's Drag Race All Stars* Season 3, which was about midway through its season the night of the opening ceremony. This may sound strange considering that I'm a professional athlete, but I've never really been a huge sports fan. I always liked playing sports, but I never really cared too much to watch them. Some of my best friends, past roommates, and my brothers watch their teams play religiously and I never understood the die-hard commitment to it until I discovered *Drag Race*! In the same way many Americans have Sunday night football parties and make a social event out of watching their team, I too host viewing parties. A handful of friends, Adam included, come over whenever a new season of *Drag Race* is airing and we'll have drinks and food and it's very social—except that no one is allowed to talk during the show. This is a cardinal rule. People will still scream and laugh and stuff, but talking and commentary is reserved for the commercial breaks. And nobody argues because everybody feels the same respect is owed and nobody wants to miss the jokes. It really is our "beautiful game."

> It was a moment I'll never forget for the rest of my life. The first time an openly gay man walked into a Winter Olympics opening ceremony—and it was not just a man, it was two.

Drag Race is my connective tissue to much of the gay community. It introduced me to an art form that I have the utmost respect for and it's often an easy conversation starter. I felt pretty isolated as a kid. I grew up in a tiny town of 2,000 people, with only 47 others in my graduating class, and there was virtually no gay representation or sense of a gay community. Or if there had been, I wasn't seeing it. I was keeping myself so deeply in the closet, so entrenched in denial, that most of the time I think I was actually avoiding anything that might confirm my gayness. I remember *Brokeback Mountain* playing at the little movie theater in town and secretly yearning to see it, but saying no when my mum asked if I wanted to go. And so when I finally found *Drag Race* it was like a whole new world had been exposed to me. There is a magical moment in The Werk Room when the queens are getting ready. They're gluing down their eyebrows, contouring their faces, and putting on their makeup, and for a second they look truly horrendous and it feels like there's no coming back from whatever they've just done to their faces. Then, suddenly, they make a complete transformation and come out the other side looking absolutely stunning. Anyway, during this time they end up pouring their hearts out to their sisters beside them and it really just makes you fall in love with each of them and their stories. They are brave and bold and they live their truths so fiercely and visibly that in turn it enables others to do the same. Just like Adam did for me at the 2018 Olympics. Even though I've never done drag (well, not properly, at least) and it's obviously completely different to skiing, I find myself connecting to the experience of many of the queens more so than I ever did to any of my fellow skiers. I see a lot of hope in them and I want others to see that same hope in me and my story. That's why it was a dream come true when, shortly following the 2018 Games, I got to be a guest judge on the show. Oh, and Adam did too.

Adam is a trailblazer, for the LGBTQ+ community, for gay kids in sports, and for me. I think, to use snow as an analogy, it's a lot easier to walk across a field of snow when someone else has done it first. So in my sport I certainly feel like I did that for other people and I certainly feel I was the first one out in my sport and any action sport. I set that trail to make it easier for someone else. For my post-ski career? I think Adam has set the trail for me. He's made a path in the snow, so hopefully it will be a smoother walk.

I think, to use snow as an analogy, it's a lot easier to walk across a field of snow when someone else has done it first.

Gus Kenworthy

Gus Kenworthy is a British-American freestyle skier, actor, and YouTuber. Born in Chelmsford, Essex, UK, Gus's family moved to Telluride, Colorado, when he was 2 and he began skiing shortly after. He picked up his first sponsor at the age of 16, and at 29 years old he continues to push the sport and establish new boundaries. His dedication to his craft established him as one of the top park skiers in the world, and one of a select few athletes that consistently makes the podium in slopestyle, halfpipe, and big air events. At the age of 23, Gus earned the privilege of representing the United States at the 2014 Olympic Games in Sochi, Russia, proudly bringing home the silver medal in slopestyle.

In 2015, Gus made the bold and courageous decision to come out as an openly gay man. Never one to shy away from the camera or his fans, he chose the cover of ESPN magazine as the vehicle to deliver the news, and received widespread support, love, and praise for the choice to reveal his true self. He then went on to make history as one of only two openly gay men to compete for the United States at the Winter Olympics in Pyeongchang, South Korea, in 2018. Prior to his qualifying run for slopestyle, Gus kissed his boyfriend on camera, immortalizing it as the "kiss seen round the world," an iconic moment for the global LGBTQ+ and sport communities alike. Gus transitioned into his new role seamlessly, using his fame to bring to light issues he is passionate about. No stranger to activism, Gus announced in 2019 that he would be participating in the AIDS/LifeCycle ride, a 545-mile bike ride from San Francisco to Los Angeles, pledging to raise $1 million for the organization. In 2019, he made his acting debut on *American Horror Story: 1984*, the wildly popular horror show that's in its ninth season. Beyond his athletic prowess, Gus has become a symbol of hope and acceptance, transcending boundaries and overcoming obstacles, proving to be a one-of-a-kind icon. Gus's talent has no bounds; through his success as an Olympic medalist in skiing, his efforts in activism, and overall star power, Gus Kenworthy has established himself as a global icon.

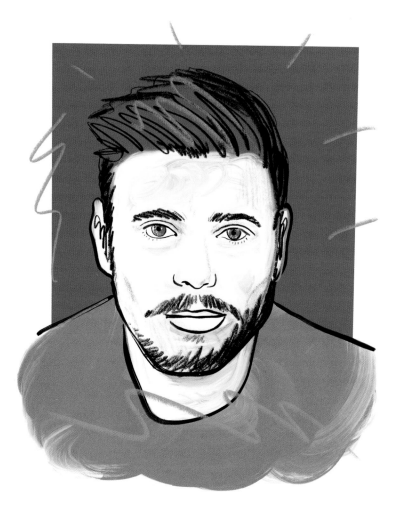

Illustration by Sam Russell Walker

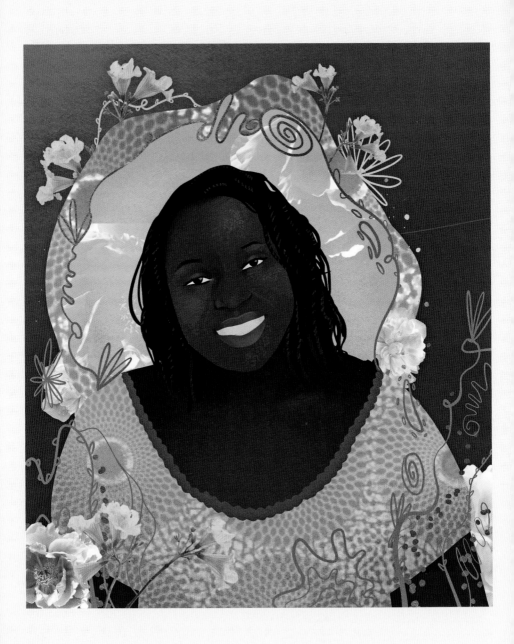

MOUD GOBA: MY SISTER'S KEEPER

by Lady Phyll

I've long had a fascination with the night sky. I'm not unique in staring up at the inky blue, often orange-washed cosmos when I can't sleep; and whether by a window or al fresco, the depth of the sky at night offers an escape hatch from the myriad, tussling, nagging, important priorities that so animate a life like mine—a life of junctures and activism, of never-ending and always important acts of defiance, kindness, and care. My daughter, my work, my communities, all the people and things I've filled my life with. All important, all worthy, all mine. This life I've built, fought for, and defended is not one I want to escape, but one that requires—by defiant design—moments for me to reflect and remember, imagine and dream. I often wonder who else looks up at the night sky without longing for something different, but for a breath, a moment, a pause. Who else is looking with me?

Illustration by Amir Khadar

When I was younger, before I knew my purpose or my drive, my grandmother would watch me searching the night sky, as if for answers, or a sign. She'd remind me that up there our Ancestors play and scheme and connect, using the stars as chess pieces and our lives and our spirits as the connective tissue between generations, movements, and time. And if the night sky was ever magical before then, it became so electric in its potential after. It is this numinous wonder that I know connects me to people like me around the world. And not just like me—busy, tired, curious, determined—but Black, lesbian, warrior woman. For to who else does the night sky offer itself up as a spiritual or existential plunge pool? Who else can dive into the cool, expansive, foreverness of the night sky and feel themselves held, understood, and comforted?

I think immediately of my sister, friend, and comrade Moud Goba. She came, near-broken, to England many years ago and forever transformed my life. It was by chance—or divine intervention—that I first heard her name. She was seeking asylum in the UK, escaping a life in Zimbabwe from which she deserved much more, and she encountered here, in a place that sells itself as some sort of bastion of freedom, democracy, and equality, nothing but disbelief and doubt. She was treated as if she didn't have a right to claim asylum, to pursue her human rights of freedom, happiness, and safety. Like me, she's a Black African lesbian. She's a mother, a sister, someone's child. I could cry thinking about the first time we met and we embraced. It was her eyes more than anything that captivated me. The cosmos and everything the Ancestors fought for and believe in shine in her eyes.

We became fast friends. I did what I could to help her asylum process along and to be for her what so many people had been for me: a strong, consistent, dependable, and generous friend. There is something that we do as friends of people we see as our chosen family, "those in our communities," where we buy things for ourselves but not really needing them in the end, or quietly topping up their Oyster card or SIM card, and when we carry out acts of kindness, they are unspoken or very silent. It often meant listening, trying to help make sense of the new world she had emerged into, and trying to show her that despite the double-standards, the racism, the misogyny, a life could be built here— and a good one at that. I won't get into the particularities of Moud's asylum-seeking, or what brought her to England; that is her story to tell. But what I can speak of is what Moud taught me about our life together.

I doubt she intended to change my life and I could never have imagined how, but if the cosmos, as my grandmother always suggested, is the playground of the Ancestors, then we were brought together to transform each other and in turn the world.

It is only by looking at the course of somebody's life that we truly begin to understand the potential for our own. In a world that often reduces us to the most groundbreaking or controversial thing we've done, diving into lives beyond their surface impact and value can often feel radical. Radical because we're all so time-poor. Radical because we've been taught to forget. Radical because in doing so we remember someone's humanity, their aching longing and working for a future that is denied them and denied us all. And if history is written by the victors and if definitions belong to the definers, to echo Toni Morrison, then by us examining, writing, and bringing up out of the depths the lives of our community, we can begin to understand victory as something else altogether. Victory, for queer Black people, manifests in ways we can never imagine because we never hear our victories told. From the small, quotidian victories that so energize a life to the grandiose wins that forever alter the course of the future, our stories matter. It is precisely because they matter that people work so hard to keep us silent. In our stories are blueprints, hard-earned knowledge, and wisdom of wins forged in struggle.

> I could cry thinking about the first time
> we met and we embraced. It was her eyes
> more than anything that captivated me.
> The cosmos and everything the Ancestors
> fought for and believe in shine in her eyes.

And Moud, for me, is the manifestation of a heavenly grace that is deeply rooted in both struggle and victory. She is a warrior woman molded from the clay of the motherland, baked hard in battle and tender to the touch. As we've shared this life together, each bearing witness to the triumphs of the other, I remain so guided by what appears to be her unalterable internal gauge toward social justice. Unlike so many, her work is not for accolades or ego, rather for the sanctity of life. We all deserve the wealth

It is only by looking at the course of somebody's life that we truly begin to understand the potential for our own.

of the world, the cosmos, each other. Moud has taught me that in giving myself to others, to see myself in the life, struggles, and victories of others, I become more me, more whole, more ancestral. We are connected in our fights for equality, for life, and for joy. My sword is sharpened, my hips made more full, in battle with her.

Moud, for me, is the manifestation of a heavenly grace that is deeply rooted in both struggle and victory. She is a warrior woman molded from the clay of the motherland, baked hard in battle and tender to the touch.

I am my sister's keeper, and she mine. None of us is born knowing how to heal wounds or catch tears, none already born woven tough with the resilience that this life so demands, but we learn by doing. We each learn by the example set by those who stepped forward, arms out, uncertain, unsteady but determined to be for others what we so desperately needed ourselves. Moud's fail-safe barometer of social justice is not gassed by the cloying pressure of an ego, rather the atmosphere-shifting cries of injustice. And together we have learned that the future we deserve to live in is not only possible, but here. That the future we need starts as immediately as now. That we begin and continue this work side by side, sweating, offering each other hugs and water and looking up into the night sky for that shooting-star wink from the Ancestors.

In dedication to a friend, a sister, a confidant, and part of my chosen family, Moud Goba, thank you.

Lady Phyll

Phyll Opoku-Gyimah is the nucleus of the award-winning celebration and protest that is UK Black Pride. Widely known as Lady Phyll—partly due to her decision to reject an MBE in the New Year's Honours' list to protest Britain's role in formulating anti-LGBTQ+ penal codes across its empire—she is also the executive director of Kaleidoscope Trust, an organization working toward the liberation of LGBTQ people around the world; a community builder and organizer; an Albert Kennedy Trust patron; and a public speaker focusing on race, gender, sexuality, and class. She's regularly called upon to advise nascent LGBTQ+ organizations around the world to help leaders create cogent organizing strategies, establish robust partnership networks, and work effectively in service of the LGBTQ community.

Founded in 2005, UK Black Pride is Europe's largest celebration for LGBTQ+ people of African, Asian, Caribbean, Middle Eastern, and Latin American descent, and is a safe space to celebrate diverse sexualities, gender identities, gender expressions, and cultures. UK Black Pride organizes an annual celebration during pride month, as well as a variety of activities throughout the year, which promote and advocate for the spiritual, emotional, and intellectual health and well-being of the communities we represent.

Established in 2011, Kaleidoscope Trust works to uphold the human rights of lesbian, gay, bisexual, and Transgender (LGBTQ+) people in countries around the world where they are discriminated against or marginalized due to their sexual orientation, gender identity, and/or gender expression.

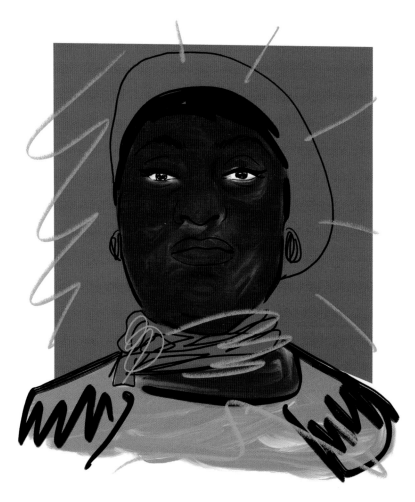

Illustration by Sam Russell Walker

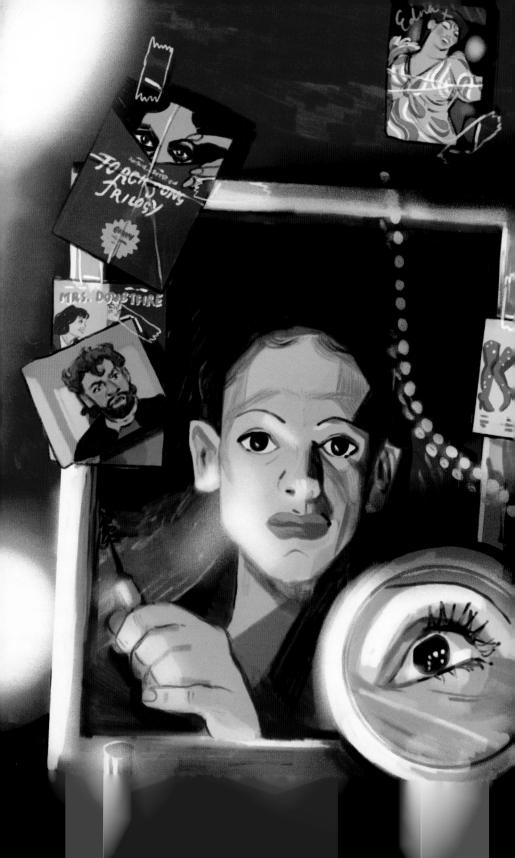

HARVEY FIERSTEIN

by Matthew Todd

"There's nothing I need from anyone except love and respect. And anyone who can't give me those two things has no place in my life."

—ARNOLD BECKOFF IN *TORCH SONG TRILOGY*, BY HARVEY FIERSTEIN (1982)

One Sunday evening in the early eighties, when I was around eight or nine, as I rushed downstairs for a glass of squash, my mum stopped me and said, "Matthew, there's a film on BBC2 that I think you would really like."

"Oh . . . Mum," I said, looking at her dramatically. "I'm already watching it."

In fact, I was glued. The story of a young woman gently asserting her unconventional views and burgeoning sexuality onto a strait-laced family, all set to pretty, perky songs,

Illustration by Brogan Bertie

was right up my alley. It was *The Sound of Music*. Mum might not have known I was gay at that point, but she definitely knew I was queer.

As a kid I was obsessive about films and TV. *Wonder Woman*, *Superman*, and *The Wizard of Oz* were particular favorites, and trips with Mum to the local puppet theater and pantomimes soon followed.

At the age of eleven, my parents took me and my brother to our first big stage musical, Andrew Lloyd Webber's *Starlight Express*. The high I got from this ridiculously camp story of lovesore singing trains was off the chart. The Day-Glo insanity was as strong as any drug my peers would soon be taking and, with AIDS-related homo-hysteria raging outside the theater doors, the escape of entertainment was as real to me as an emergency chute from a burning plane. If I'd been forced to stay in reality, I would have suffocated.

And it was a terrible reality. As the eighties progressed, gay people were constantly portrayed in the media as perverts who molested children and spread disease. I was of the Section 28 generation—the hated 1988 law that Mrs. Thatcher's government brought in, after Rupert Murdoch's *Sun* newspaper convinced the country that left-wing schools were intent on turning the nation's kids queer. Section 28's wording stated that schools shall not "promote the teaching in any maintained school of the acceptability of homosexuality as a pretended family relationship." The message I received from the state when I was fourteen years old was not only that gay people were dangerous but that their relationships weren't real. Gay people didn't love. They had pretend relationships. It was as if they were pretend people.

Two years later, at sixteen, I came out, and my passion for theater becoming more serious, I saw my first straight play (in both senses of the word) at the National Theatre. The more I saw the more I wondered where stories about people like me were. Despite the theater being full of gay people, backstage, onstage, and in the audience, I wouldn't see a piece of theater with gay central characters until 1994, when I saw *My Night with Reg* by Kevin Elyot, a hilarious but tragic tale of self-destruction. I absolutely love it still, but it also depressed me.

What I had needed to see to counter Section 28's hateful message were films and plays that showed men in love with men, women in love with women, gay people exploring lives together and not just suffering, apologizing, or dying. Derek Jarman's groundbreaking work-of-art film *Sebastiane* is "sex positive" but hard to relate to for a lovesick teen.

Philadelphia was an amazing cinematic step forward but was about dying. The Joe Orton biopic *Prick Up Your Ears* is brilliant but even before Joe is bludgeoned to death by his boyfriend, it is beyond bleak.

But then one day in the early nineties I saw the first gay film that really touched my heart. My Jewish gay best friend shared my love of drama, in the arts and in life, and told me about this gay film he'd taped, which was funny and painful but, actually, about love. Ironically, I'd seen it advertised in teen fave *Sky* magazine in 1988 in an ad showing a line-up of men's feet with one wearing pink fluffy bunny rabbit slippers and the subtitle "It takes a lot of guts and a helluva sense of humour to live life in Arnold's shoes." But because it wasn't hateful, I didn't really understand what it was.

I was of the Section 28 generation—the hated 1988 law that Mrs. Thatcher's government brought in, after Rupert Murdoch's *Sun* newspaper convinced the country that left-wing schools were intent on turning the nation's kids queer.

But that Saturday afternoon, with my friend chain-smoking in case his mum came back and caught us, watching *Torch Song Trilogy* on a crackly VHS tape changed my life. As Arnold Beckoff owned his sexuality, his effeminacy, his right to love and to have a family, something changed in me. It was truly the first time I heard anyone on screen talk of gay love. The first time a film with gay characters didn't depress the hell out of me. The first time I realized that maybe some famous heterosexual people (Matthew Broderick and Anne Bancroft star in the movie) perhaps did not hate gay people.

It was also the first time I was introduced to one of the most important gay men in modern American entertainment history and someone who to this day is a huge inspiration and hero to me.

Torch Song Trilogy (1988, directed by Paul Bogart) is about a Jewish American named Arnold Beckoff, in his twenties living in Brooklyn, a drag performer, who longs for a lover and family of his own. The trilogy refers to the character's three loves—a bisexual man struggling to come to terms with his sexuality, his younger boyfriend (portrayed in the film by then teen fave Matthew Broderick), and his adopted son, as well as his fiery mother, played by Anne Bancroft. It's full of brilliantly stagey wit, is emotional, unapologetic, and addresses the concept of gay parenting long before it became mainstream. It is, at its core, an expression of the heart and passion of its writer and star, Harvey Fierstein.

Born in 1954 in Brooklyn, New York, to Jewish European immigrants, Harvey Fierstein got his big break as a teenager playing an asthmatic lesbian in Andy Warhol's only play, *Pork*, performed in 1971 at an experimental off-Broadway theater called La MaMa in Manhattan's East Village. When the play transferred to London, too young to go with it, Harvey stayed in New York and trained as an artist, making a living in his twenties as a drag performer. A distinct talent, with incredible vibrancy and an unmistakable gravelly voice (yes, the penny's probably dropping now, yes, *him*), local writers were falling over themselves to work with the young performer, so much so that a producer suggested he might try to write his own work. Not able to spell, Harvey thought it a bad idea, but reassured he could pay someone a couple of bucks to fix the spelling, he set about doing just that.

> **What I had needed to see to counter Section 28's hateful message were films and plays that showed men in love with men, women in love with women, gay people exploring lives together and not just suffering, apologizing, or dying.**

His first works were not commercial. *Flatbush Tosca* was a drag musical version of the opera set in a suburb of Brooklyn which saw Harvey singing in Italian. *Cannibals Just Don't Know No Better* was about a world of gay people who ate anyone who came out as straight. (I'm still totally down for seeing that.) Then, in February 1978, aged twenty-four, he presented two weeks of performances of his latest play, *The International Stud*, about a drag queen's frustration with the anonymous sex scene trying to make a love life work. Harvey later recounted that it was panned by *The Village Voice* paper, who apparently referred to him as "the devil come to Earth for writing this horrible thing," which only spurred him on. The team at the theater, La MaMa, too, saw something in the writing and encouraged him to develop Arnold's story. He got to work, and La MaMa produced two further plays with Arnold Beckoff at their center the following year—*Fugue in a Nursery* and *Widows and Children First!*, addressing the character's adoption of a son and his relationship with his mother. A group called The Glines, which existed to further gay writing, financially supported Harvey while he edited the three plays into one, and in October 1981, *Torch Song Trilogy* premiered at the Richard Allen Center in the Upper West Side. It was due to play for eight weeks but at four hours long was not doing great business until a glowing *New York Times* review brought audiences flooding in. Word spread and in early 1982 the production transferred to the Actors' Playhouse, with Estelle Getty, latterly seen in *The Golden Girls*, as Arnold's mother and a young Matthew Broderick as his son, and was an even bigger hit, playing for five months and securing—incredibly—a Broadway run. In June of that year it transferred to the Little Theatre on Broadway, where it became a bona fide sensation.

No one had seen a play on Broadway that celebrated gay love and, frankly, told homophobes where to stick it. Gay audiences were overwhelmed to see themselves fairly portrayed and straight audiences were handed a way to relate to people they'd been led to believe they could not. While the brilliant *The Boys in the Band* in 1968, more than ten years before, had been the first Broadway play to focus on gay lives, *Torch Song*, with its heart and humor and relatable characters, was the first to make a significant amount of money. There was some dissension. Some gay people felt that in showing a gay man wanting to settle down the play was "aping heterosexuality." Others said that in showing Arnold visiting a famous backroom he had damaged our reputation. But most gay people, like everyone else, absolutely loved it and *Torch Song Trilogy* was the hit of the season. Harvey was visited backstage by superstars such as Barbra Streisand and Carol Channing and won interviews on *The Late Show with Joan Rivers*, and a clutch of awards including two Tony and Drama Desk Awards each for Best Play and Best Actor. A new star was born, and gay love was finally out of the theatrical closet. *Torch Song Trilogy* ran on Broadway for nearly three years, notching up 1,300 performances, with two other actors eventually playing Arnold Beckoff during its run.

Harvey was the most wanted man on Broadway. Film producer Allan Carr had made a cinematic hit out of *Grease* and wanted to create a musical of the hit French film, *La Cage aux Folles*, about two gay men and their son. Having engaged Broadway legend Jerry Herman (*Hello, Dolly!*, *Mack & Mabel*) to write the music, Harvey was the obvious choice to write the book. In the notes accompanying the soundtrack, Herman recalled that Fierstein turned up at a meeting with a scene to end Act 1 where the main character, rejected by his family for being too flamboyant, declares, "I am what I am!" Herman recalls overnight writing the defining gay anthem of all time. *La Cage* opened in 1983 and earned Harvey a third Tony award for Best Book of a Musical. Just as AIDS was cutting New York down, Harvey had produced two smash-hit pieces of theater that demanded acceptance by straight people and allowed gay people to feel good about themselves, a resource which was in short supply.

> As Arnold Beckoff owned his sexuality, his effeminacy, his right to love and to have a family, something changed in me. It was truly the first time I heard anyone on screen talk of gay love.

As the first out leading man on Broadway, not being "discreet" but honest, defiant, and standing up for his brothers and sisters, Harvey became a face of homosexuality. Appearing across TV patiently answering basic questions, such as in 1983 by an albeit supportive TV legend Barbara Walters who asked, "What's it like to be gay?" he politely told her off for not interviewing any out gay men years before.

Not everything he touched turned to gold, though. His 1988 musical with singer Peter Allen, *Legs Diamond*, a job he's since said he took for the money, didn't work and taught him a valuable lesson. His plays after *Torch Song*—*Safe Sex*, *Spookhouse*, and *Forget Him*—did not make the same impact. But no matter, in demand as an actor, he became that rarest of beasts, an out gay man in Hollywood.

In films, he appeared in Woody Allen's smash hit *Bullets over Broadway* as Dianne Wiest's exasperated agent, *Elmo Saves Christmas*, *Death to Smoochy*, and in the sci-fi blockbuster *Independence Day*, directed by gay director Roland Emmerich. Appearing as Rebecca's lover in top-rated TV show *Cheers* earned him an Emmy nomination and he made appearances in *Miami Vice*, *Murder She Wrote*, and the *Larry Sanders Show*, among many others. His unique vocals were heard in Disney's *Mulan*, *Family Guy*, and *The Simpsons*, where he played a gay office worker in an episode geniusly entitled "Homer's Phobia."

A new star was born, and gay love was finally out of the theatrical closet. *Torch Song Trilogy* ran on Broadway for nearly three years, notching up 1,300 performances.

Asked in the nineties if he knew which Hollywood actors were in the closet, he laughed and said those would be the ones avoiding him in public, but in 1993 he himself made more gay cinematic history. Good friends with Robin Williams, Harvey was cast in a project he and his then wife were producing about a divorced man who dresses as a nanny to get access to his children. Harvey played Williams's brother, Uncle Frank, a makeup artist living with his boyfriend, "Aunt" Jack (played by comedian Scott Capurro), who turns Daniel Hillard into Mrs. Doubtfire. The movie made more than $400 million at the box office, second only, in 1993, to *Jurassic Park*. For the first time, huge Hollywood audiences laughed along with gay characters rather than at them. This was a seismic change and pre-dated the similar dynamic of *Will & Grace* that came six years later. I was working as a cinema usher when *Mrs. Doubtfire* was released, and I watched Harvey, Scott, and Robin's triple act disarming audiences over and over again. Just to see that, aged nineteen, for me, was another life-changing moment.

Without fan-boying too excessively, Harvey's integrity has been one of his defining characteristics. An activist as much as an artist, as one of the most famous gay actors in the world he refused roles if there was any risk of defaming his community.

"I was offered the role as the monster in Stephen King's *It*—a clown who ate children," he said in an interview with *Watermark* in 2004. "I wouldn't do it. Even though it was a great role, I felt that I didn't want to be perceived in that way because of the horrible lie that gay people want children. I wasn't even going to put that in the back of people's minds."

Instead he has twice appeared on kids' TV staple *Sesame Street* and also in the TV film *Elmo Saves Christmas*. He also did not throw his gender non-conforming brothers under the bus. In the great 1996 documentary

The Celluloid Closet, about the lack of representation in films, in a section criticising the effeminate "Sissy" stereotype of early Hollywood, Harvey says, "I like the sissy. My view has always been visibility at any costs. I'd rather have negative than nothing. That's just my particular view. And also, because I am a sissy." He followed this up by writing a kids' film and book, *The Sissy Duckling*, which he voiced.

Harvey's integrity has been one of his defining characteristics. An activist as much as an artist, as one of the most famous gay actors in the world he refused roles if there was any risk of defaming his community.

In 2002, Harvey had his biggest career high since *Torch Song Trilogy*, when producers of a stage musical of John Waters's cult film *Hairspray* cast him—who else?—as Edna Turnblad, the role made famous by Divine. The show was the White Ways hit of the year and earned him his fourth Tony award for Best Actor in a Musical.

Hairspray solidified him as a bona fide show-business legend. Entered into the American Theater Hall of Fame in 2007, the same year he was embraced as one of theater's most heterosexual characters, Tevye in *Fiddler on the Roof*. He wrote and performed in a small new musical about the family isolation of a gay man, *A Catered Affair* (2008), appeared as Albin in a revival of *La Cage aux Folles* on Broadway in 2011, and the following year had a hit with the Disney musical *Newsies*. He then had a huge hit writing the book of the Cyndi Lauper musical *Kinky Boots* (2013), about a cross-dressing gay man saving a family business, which continues to play across the world. His play *Casa Valentina* (2014), the true story of a group of men in the 1950s who visited a hotel in the Catskills to dress as women, further confirmed him as one of the foremost LGBTQ writers, and to me is up there with his finest work.

Latterly he got to portray Edna on screen, in the live NBC *Hairspray* broadcast alongside Ariana Grande and Jennifer Hudson, after losing out to John Travolta in the 2007 film. In 2017, he shaved off ninety minutes of the play that made him famous for a new Broadway production, starring Michael Urie, simply retitled *Torch Song*, entertaining and moving a new generation of theatergoers.

I myself have been lucky enough to meet him, albeit briefly. In 1999, before his *Hairspray* resurgence, he toured a one-man show, *This Isn't Going to Be Pretty* (which you can buy on CD). He played one appearance at London's Adelphi Theatre in the summer of that year. He's not as well known here as he is in the States and you can get the feeling he hasn't always been keen to work here. There wasn't a huge amount of publicity about his appearance, but I did hear about it on the radio on the day. I remember as I walked up to the theater finding a huge crowd of people queuing around the block to buy tickets, forcing the managers to open the roped-off Dress Circle to accommodate them. When he walked on stage the crowd erupted, jumping to their feet, like they were welcoming a war hero, which in a way, they were. I've rarely seen a reaction like it. Harvey was hilarious, doing skits and monologues, even performing an old-school drag skit which harked back to his teenage years. Finishing the show with a rendition of, "I Am What I Am," Harvey himself seemed genuinely shaken at the thunderous standing ovation and, like the rest of us, was in tears as he took his curtain call. I had sent a bunch of flowers to the theater to express my gratitude and to ask for an interview with *Attitude*, then stalked him at the stage door after. I remember him saying "Are you from the magazine?" with that voice and Brooklyn accent that I knew so well and giving him a kiss on the cheek. It was an evening of pure love.

It may sound corny but, to me, it's love and honesty that has defined Harvey's career. A man who did not hide when people were hidden, a man who did not apologize when many did, a man who spoke without hesitation of gay love when they told us it didn't exist.

Our culture is saturated by sex. Sex should be celebrated, but an equal celebration of gay love hasn't happened in the arts anywhere nearly enough. People who hate us have told themselves as they've killed us that sex is all that defines us and, sometimes, we've believed them. As Arnold says in one of the most powerful scenes in *Torch Song Trilogy*, when his mother dismisses his feelings about a murder of a character, he screams:

"That's right, Ma! Killed by children; children taught by people like you because everybody knows that queers don't matter, queers don't love and those that do deserve what they get!"

For millions of people like me, Harvey Fierstein showed that we could believe love might be part of our lives, too. He is a pioneer and a visionary.

For me, a soft-spoken teen in Croydon, south London, so far away from a gravelly voiced Jewish drag queen from Brooklyn, his work allowed me the first connection with another gay man. For the first time I felt I had a gay role model who was like me. For the first time I had hope.

> **It's love and honesty that has defined Harvey's career. A man who did not hide when people were hidden, a man who did not apologize when many did, a man who spoke without hesitation of gay love when they told us it didn't exist.**

In 1988, as Section 28 was making me feel like life wasn't worth living, unbeknownst to me there were people fighting—LGBTQ people marching in London and Manchester, lesbians abseiling into the House of Commons, and that same year a film of his play *Torch Song Trilogy* was being released in cinemas. Harvey's uncompromising demand that gay people be treated with the same respect as our heterosexual brothers and sisters is summed up by his interview with Barbara Walters, filmed on the Broadway set of Arnold Beckoff's home in 1983 as *La Cage aux Folles* opened. When Ms. Walters suggests that some audiences watching a play about gay men might believe such things as love and commitment to be only "heterosexual property," Harvey calmly, firmly stated something that really needed stating and so often still does.

"Those are not heterosexual experiences," he said calmly. "And those are not heterosexual words. Those are human words. Love, commitment, family . . . belong to all people."

Thank you, for everything, Harvey.

For the first time I felt I had a gay role model who was like me. For the first time I had hope.

Matthew Todd

Matthew Todd was editor in chief of the UK's bestselling gay magazine, *Attitude*, for eight years where he interviewed countless celebrities, including Madonna, Lady Gaga, and Daniel Radcliffe, as well as Prince William, who made history as the first member of the Royal Family to speak out against homo-, bi-, and transphobic bullying. His acclaimed book on LGBTQ+ mental health, *Straight Jacket: Overcoming Society's Legacy of Gay Shame*, was described as "an essential read for every gay person on the planet" by Sir Elton John, "utterly brilliant" by Owen Jones in *The Guardian*, and as "game changing" and "life saving" by readers. It was shortlisted for the Polari Prize and was voted Boyz Best LGBTQ+ Book of the Year 2017. His play, *Blowing Whistles*, has been performed in the West End, the US, and Australia, and was described as "the brightest gay play in ages" by Whatsonstage.com. His second book, *Pride: The Story of the LGBTQ Equality Movement*, is out now and his work appears in *This Is Not a Drill* and *Letters to the Earth*. He has appeared on TV's *Lorraine* and BBC News, has presented two films for *Newsnight*, and gives talks on LGBTQ+ and mental health issues. He is the recipient of the Stonewall Journalist of the Year, three British Society of Magazine Editors Editor of the Year Awards and an *Attitude* Pride Award, and was awarded the Freedom of the City of London for services to the LGBTQ+ community.

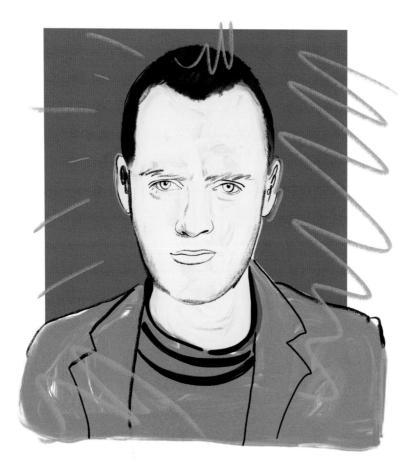

Illustration by Sam Russell Walker

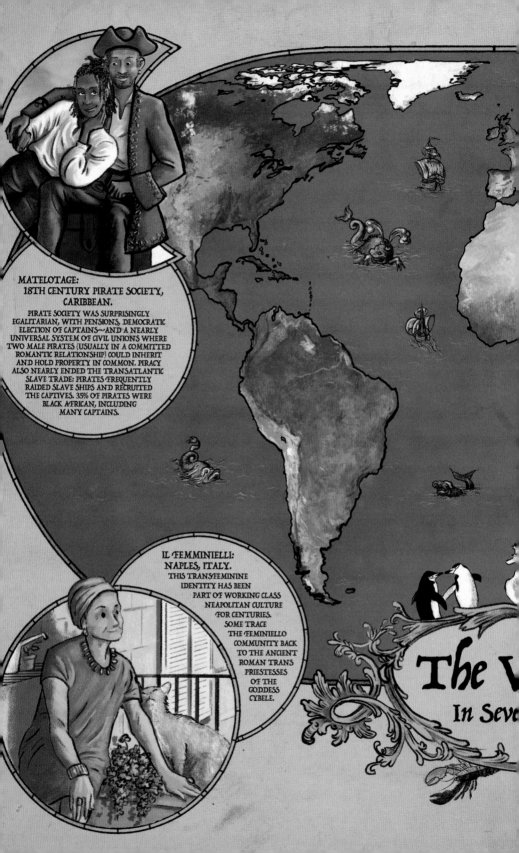

MATELOTAGE:
18TH CENTURY PIRATE SOCIETY, CARIBBEAN.

PIRATE SOCIETY WAS SURPRISINGLY EGALITARIAN, WITH PENSIONS, DEMOCRATIC ELECTION OF CAPTAINS~AND A NEARLY UNIVERSAL SYSTEM OF CIVIL UNIONS WHERE TWO MALE PIRATES (USUALLY IN A COMMITTED ROMANTIC RELATIONSHIP) COULD INHERIT AND HOLD PROPERTY IN COMMON. PIRACY ALSO NEARLY ENDED THE TRANSATLANTIC SLAVE TRADE: PIRATES FREQUENTLY RAIDED SLAVE SHIPS AND RECRUITED THE CAPTIVES. 35% OF PIRATES WERE BLACK AFRICAN, INCLUDING MANY CAPTAINS.

IL FEMMINIELLI:
NAPLES, ITALY.
THIS TRANSFEMININE IDENTITY HAS BEEN PART OF WORKING CLASS NEAPOLITAN CULTURE FOR CENTURIES. SOME TRACE THE FEMINIELLO COMMUNITY BACK TO THE ANCIENT ROMAN TRANS PRIESTESSES OF THE GODDESS CYBELE.

The W
In Seve

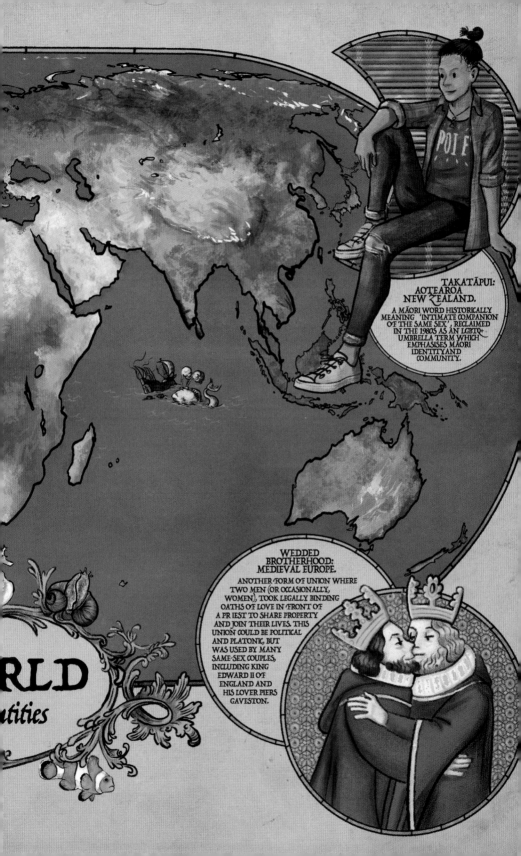

TAKATĀPUI: AOTEAROA NEW ZEALAND.

A MĀORI WORD HISTORICALLY MEANING 'INTIMATE COMPANION OF THE SAME SEX', RECLAIMED IN THE 1980S AS AN LGBTQ+ UMBRELLA TERM WHICH EMPHASISES MĀORI IDENTITY AND COMMUNITY.

WEDDED BROTHERHOOD: MEDIEVAL EUROPE.

ANOTHER FORM OF UNION WHERE TWO MEN (OR OCCASIONALLY, WOMEN), TOOK LEGALLY BINDING OATHS OF LOVE IN FRONT OF A PRIEST TO SHARE PROPERTY AND JOIN THEIR LIVES. THIS UNION COULD BE POLITICAL AND PLATONIC, BUT WAS USED BY MANY SAME-SEX COUPLES, INCLUDING KING EDWARD II OF ENGLAND AND HIS LOVER PIERS GAVESTON.

RLD

atities

Words
to
Inspire
Change

These essays are about the changemakers, the rabble-rousers, the pioneers forging ahead for others. It's hard to be the first. To set out on a path that few or none have trod before. The LGBTQ+ community is rich with these individuals and movements. For example, without our Black and Brown Trans and lesbian family, gay cis men like myself wouldn't enjoy so many of the rights and freedoms we have here in the UK. Without the cultural contribution of the following queer heroes, the world would not be so beautiful, weird, or inspiring. These pieces explain the importance of identity, and also how revolutionary it is when individuals reject narrow societal labeling. I've learned so much from these essays, I've been challenged, educated, and motivated to action by these powerful words, and I hope you are, too.

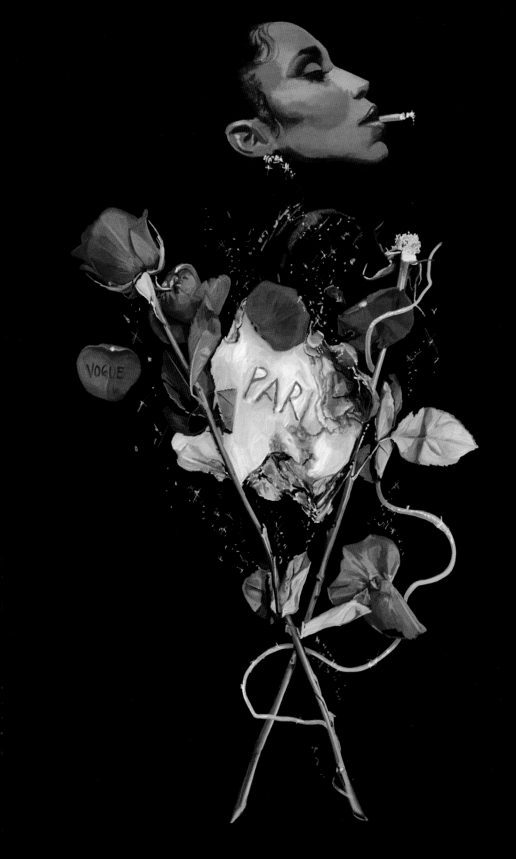

PARIS IS BURNING

by Munroe Bergdorf

I first watched *Paris Is Burning* when I was living in Brighton. I had just made my first Trans friend and she was like a mother to me. She was stunning, absolutely stunning. But also completely, through lack of a better word, normal. There was nothing out of the ordinary really about her. She was just an incredible person. But she was also Trans. Up until that point I hadn't knowingly been close friends with a Trans person. I got to know her, hear her story and where she'd come from, what she'd been through. She was the first person who actually told me, "I think you're Trans." Up until that point I knew it but I was in denial. Doing her "Mother Trans" bit, trying to get me to understand myself, she recommended films that I should watch. She showed me *Paris Is Burning*. The 1990 documentary film chronicles the underground New York City ballroom culture and the legendary Houses that competed in it. But it's about so much more. The real-life Black, Italian, Latinx, gay, and Transgender cast offer a window into a world on the fringes of society. The film is such a central part of queer culture, you'll know much of its lingo without even realizing where it's from. House Mothers, reading, realness,

---

Illustration by Fernando Monroy

shade, opulence—all phrases immortalized in *Paris Is Burning*. Our culture, so often erased or hidden to protect ourselves, recorded forever.

I'll never forget watching *Paris* for the first time. I can see it so clearly, even now. I remember my friend was cooking while I was watching it and I was just crying throughout the whole thing. So much of what they were saying was how I'd felt my entire life and I didn't know how to put it into words. Words have power. Their words spoke me into being. Take away the fact that it's in New York, take away the fact that it's about the ballroom scene, take away the fact that it's the 1980s. I felt the same way as so many of those characters. To see my feelings put into words and pictures was so overwhelming for me. *Paris Is Burning* was really the first time I managed to see that and feel that. It was an awakening and an education. Up until that point I think it's safe to say I was fairly uneducated when it comes to queer history. The queer history that I did know was extremely white. I knew about Quentin Crisp. I knew about Oscar Wilde . . . and in the eighties I'd heard Frankie Goes to Hollywood and the glam-electro bands like Erasure. But it was all white. I knew about Madonna's "Vogue" before I knew where Madonna's "Vogue" came from. They were echoes. *Paris Is Burning* was the first time I visited the source of all this culture. I came face to face with the originators, and they looked just like me.

I saw queer history through a white lens, because that's what I had been immediately exposed to. To be able to identify the root and to figure out that I had a direct link to the provenance of so much queer history was extremely empowering for me. It involved me and it allowed me to access a power that took my difference and made it positive, turning it into something that I could always get power from. That's what happens when you realize you connect to those who went before you; they become an immense source of ancestral power that you can draw from whenever you need to. You are not the first to walk this path. Our stories echo each other. Black and Brown Trans women have trod this ground, clearing a path for you. They are there when you need to call on them, stretching back thousands of years. This is the power of connecting to your true family. Stand in that power.

In *Paris Is Burning*, Mother of the House of LaBeija, Pepper LaBeija, reminisces about her own mother finding her mink coat and burning it: "She don't want me in girl's clothes, she can't take it." When I first told my own mother that I was Trans, she did not take it well whatsoever. It was very much, "Well, don't we have a say in this?" I think she felt that she was going to lose her child. She thought that I was going to turn up one day on her doorstep and I wouldn't be the same person. Of course that's not what happens. That situation just goes to show that people fear what they don't know. What a lot of parents of Trans kids or their children who are Trans don't realize is that you're not losing a child, you're gaining a happier child. You're gaining someone who understands and loves themselves enough to make a very difficult decision, which is beginning a transition. Being Trans is not a choice. But making the choice to love yourself and be who you are authentically is. And that's a choice that should be celebrated. As soon as my mum saw me being who I am and being successful in what I want to achieve for myself, our relationship got so much better, because actually she realized she'd got everything to gain by being there for her child and understanding and educating herself to better herself as a person. Not just as a mother, but as a person, so that she could be there. I had to do the same as well. I had to understand how difficult it was for my parent; she hadn't had the exposure to Trans culture that I had; she grew up in a transphobic country. All countries are transphobic. We live in a transphobic society, so the likelihood is that you probably are, too. We weren't having the conversations that we are having now. My mother and I had a real journey, but now my mum is so supportive of me and she sends me articles that I'm in before I even see them and tells me when I've got a good write-up and tells me what she thinks about certain looks that I'll post or whatnot. I would never have thought ever that we'd be on this page. . . . It's never really about clothes, it's never really about makeup; it's about not understanding and also being afraid of what society is going to think about your child.

I just wanted my mother to understand that this is who I am. When I first told her about being Trans, unfortunately, I didn't go about it the best way. At the time, I didn't see the humanity in my parents. When you're younger you see your parents almost as gods and you don't understand that they're just people too and they get things wrong. In your late twenties and thirties you realize your parents are just human beings that get things wrong, just as you do. Up until that point I hadn't really realized that, and I wish that I had. But I think at the same time, I had the weight of the world on my shoulders. It's so scary coming out, no matter how you're coming out, because it's almost like you're confronted with having to know all of the answers and knowing nothing. So when you come out as gay it's almost as if you need to explain everything to people. It's like, wait a minute, I've just come out as gay, I know as much as you do. I hadn't had sex when I was fourteen but people were asking me all the time whether or not I'd had sex. They were just assuming I'd had sex because I was gay. When you come out as Trans, you're bombarded with a thousand different questions about what it means and you don't know, because you've literally just come out! It's like hatching from a shell and then being bombarded with an interview. Culture tells us who we are.

To see my feelings put into words and pictures was so overwhelming for me. *Paris Is Burning* was really the first time I managed to see that and feel that. It was an awakening and an education.

Paris Is Burning ignited a spark in me. It encouraged me to look further into Black queer history. It was the beginning of my awakening of self and community. Then I realized it was a Black Trans woman that started the whole fucking thing! They fought for the rights that so many of the modern queer community enjoy today. I learned about Marsha P. Johnson, who threw the first brick at the Stonewall riots, and what she stood for. I learned about sex work and how so much of our community are ostracized from society, and sex work is resistance, sex work is survival, and sex work is work for a lot of us. Going through my life I have known so many sex workers and seen the humanity in what they do and understood why it's important to make sure that all feminism is accessible and inclusive. I learned about Miss Major, who was also at the Stonewall riots. I learned about Sylvester from the New York disco era. I fell in love with Venus and Octavia through *Paris Is Burning*. Stunning aspiring model Octavia became somewhat of an idol to me. I could just see myself in her in a lot of ways. I could see Venus in me, maybe younger me. The power of seeing your authentic self reflected back for the first time. Their zest for life, even in the face of adversity, was something that deeply resonated with me. Their unwillingness to live as anything else other than themselves.

It is imperative for young Black queer people to see other people like us centered in our history and culture. If you don't see people that are like you, you start measuring yourself up to unrealistic and unattainable standards. It places the power in the embodiment of everything that you aren't, so then in a wider sense it contributes to things like white supremacy or the patriarchy. If we're only seeing power when it's depicted as male, if we're only seeing success when it's depicted as white, then that means that only men and only white people can be successful, because that's drilled into the consciousness of society. As a result it subjugates people. It limits dreams. It narrows thoughts. It's important to see possibility, to create an image of something we can aspire to. When I was younger the same tropes came up again and again when it came to Trans people, and coded language when it came to young Black people. Language and ideas meant to limit and control and keep down. You end up feeling like you're a guest in this country, you end up feeling like you need to pretend about who you are. You don't feel like you can be yourself and be successful. So you try to make yourself whiter, you try to make yourself cis, you try to make yourself straight, which is a losing battle. You can't make yourself any of those things, you either are or you aren't. I tried to be the representation that I didn't have as a kid, because I know how isolating it can make you feel to not see yourself in aspirational roles. I don't take lightly the fact that with a lot of the modeling jobs I do or a lot of the rooms I'm even in, I'm the first Trans person to be in those rooms, and the first Black Trans person to be in those rooms, and the first Black Trans woman to work with those brands, and the first Black Trans woman to be on those magazine covers. It sets a really important standard, that I'm not gonna be the last. I may be the first, but I hopefully won't be the last. I do it knowing that I am fulfilling the dreams of Octavia. I do it with her and for her.

You are not the first to walk this path. Our stories echo each other. Black and Brown Trans women have trod this ground, clearing a path for you.

Some days I can't believe that I have these opportunities, and the number of Black Trans women that have come before me and chipped away at this glass ceiling so I could break through. I don't take that lightly by any stretch of the imagination. It's overwhelming, honestly. I have these realizations daily. I just sometimes sit there by myself thinking, this is absolutely mad. I'm thoroughly aware of how many Black Trans women have come before me and I want to honor them and make sure our history is celebrated, because that's our history. That's our legacy as a community. I'm chipping away at the ceiling that's above me, so that people that come after me can get further than I'm gonna get in my career. I look forward to Trans world leaders and Nobel Peace Prize winners, everything that I don't get to squeeze into my life. I want to see a Trans Beyoncé. I want to see Trans MPs. I want to see Trans world leaders. I want to see more Trans CEOs than there are now. I want to see us achieving in every single facet of society in every single way. I have hope that in the future we will live in a much more understanding and respectful world than we do now.

Paris Is Burning **ignited a spark in me. It encouraged me to look further into Black queer history. It was the beginning of my awakening of self and community.**

Jennie Livingston, the director of *Paris Is Burning*, was an out lesbian and campaigner with AIDS activist group ACT UP. An active member of our queer community. She is also white. One thing you can't escape when watching the film, and something the cast have spoken about since, is that Black and Brown people provided all the content and then other people made money off it. Black and Brown bodies literally created Voguing, and white people profited from it. Just like today, Black queer culture is co-opted by white capitalism. Unfortunately, white society has never been able or willing to understand the Black experience as a whole. Even through what we saw as a response to the murder of George Floyd, Blackness is always consumed as trends. Black people aren't consumed or understood as a whole person, or our humanity is not honored in the same way that whiteness is. There's an apathy with white society to Black lives. We see Black people killed all the time by police, the people that are meant to be there to protect us. But there's just not the same shock as if, say, a white woman was killed or a white man was killed in the same way that Black men are, with the same frequency that Black people are. Instantaneously Black men are assumed to be criminals before the whole situation is understood. So where does that come from? Black culture is literally pulled apart and consumed insofar as Black music is seen as a trend, Black hair is seen as a trend, Black style is seen as a trend, Black skin is seen as a trend. Black bodies are seen as a trend. Black slang is seen as a trend. But when we take the whole Black person, the humanity, it's not seen in a consistent way. It's consumed in parts as trends and as we saw with George Floyd, we had two weeks of white people being engaged in being anti-racist and being vocal against racism, but again it's fallen off the radar because the consumption of Blackness is frivolous. We must own what we create.

Self-knowledge, empowerment, and acceptance come with age. They come with experience. They come with being assertive as a human being and being dedicated to educating yourself about the world around you. But there's no way I was gonna be able to answer all the questions that even adults would have for me about being Trans. It's unfair to assume that young Trans people have all of the answers about being Trans because so many of them are just finding themselves. This is why it's really important to look to Trans history and to educate ourselves, because the words are there. We can't just be resting on people that are trying to find their own way.

> I'm thoroughly aware of how many Black Trans women have come before me and I want to honor them and make sure our history is celebrated, because that's our history. That's our legacy as a community.

Being Trans within monotheistic societies—cultures with religions that worship one god, like Christianity and Islam—is subversive and threatening to the status quo. In these religions the basis of humanity is man and woman, and that impacts on all of society. So when you're going against that, you're going against the kind of fabric of society. You're also peeling back and revealing that this binary approach is just imposed on society, this is just one version of reality. Look at ancient Polynesia or South Asia. The Mahu exist in some Polynesian cultures. In the Indian subcontinent there's the Hijra. In Native American culture there's Two-Spirit. Ancient societies recognized more than two genders. Two-gender societies are attached to religion, and if you're not religious, then you don't need to believe in the idea that there's just two genders. There are some religious people that don't believe that either. Religion changes as it grows and society changes and grows. Even social institutions such as marriage change. It's very important that people recognize that Trans people aren't anything new. That, if anything, we are older than a lot of the newer religions. We're older than Christianity, we're older than Islam. We just are, we've always been here. There is power in this knowledge. Tap into that power.

Near the end of the documentary *Paris Is Burning* we learn that one of the main characters, Venus Xtravaganza, a beautiful and a young Black Trans woman who is also a sex worker, is found under a bed. She's been murdered by a client. Unfortunately this narrative repeats, especially within American society and South American society, where Black Trans women are routinely killed. Here in the UK, Naomi Hersi was a Black Transgender woman who was murdered by somebody whom she met for sex. There is a worldwide narrative when it comes to Black Transgender women, an apathy toward Black lives. Thought experiment: ask yourself, if this was a white woman or a white rich woman that was killed, would there be more outrage than when a poor Black Trans woman is killed? Unfortunately, many of the issues raised by the film still ring true. I'm happy that I have fulfilled the dreams of Octavia. I'm really happy about that. But I would also love to see the dreams of other Black Trans women being fulfilled. Having to see Black Trans women's names hashtagged over and over and over again is an outrage. Over Pride 2020 I believe seven Black Trans women were murdered, all in different ways. We're impacted so much more when it comes to the violence of men because we're pushed to the fringes of society where a lot of us need to rely on sex work for survival, which puts us at a greater physical risk. All feminism is not inclusive. It prioritizes who should have access to liberation, and unless feminism is intersectional then it can't exist as a non-oppressive tool. So I also want to see the dreams of Venus Xtravaganza come true. I want to see the dreams of all Black Trans women come true and I want to see us supported within society, not neglected and forced into situations that put us in immediate danger and ultimately result in us being murdered.

In honor of those who have walked before us, let's take action, to create a world where Trans women can live safely, free to fulfill their own dreams.

Words have power. Let's speak their names—say them out loud with me now. Tap into their power. Honor their lives.

Dorian Corey

Pepper LaBeija

Junior LaBeija

Willi Ninja

Freddie Pendavis

Kim Pendavis

Paris Dupree

Octavia St. Laurent

Angie Xtravaganza

Danny Xtravaganza and

Venus Xtravaganza

Munroe Bergdorf

When *Teen Vogue* wrote of Munroe Bergdorf, "She's a powerful and unstoppable force and the world should take notice," in April 2018, they were right. In the past two years the model, activist, and Doctor of Letters has become recognized globally for her activism. In August 2020, not only did *British Vogue* name her in the Top 25 Most Influential Women in the UK (alongside Rihanna and the Queen) but *Teen Vogue* featured her on the cover of their coveted September issue. Munroe has most recently been announced as the winner of *Attitude*'s Hero Award 2020, presented by Edward Enninful.

In 2018, Munroe's debut authored television documentary, *What Makes a Woman* premiered on major UK network Channel 4. An hour-long documentary that bravely explores the changing perceptions of gender and identity in today's society, it solidified Munroe as an important progressive voice in UK culture.

Further cementing the significance of activism, in 2020 she was appointed as a UN Women UK Changemaker. Munroe regularly consults for global FTSE 100 businesses for their inclusivity and diversity schemes, including the world's largest beauty brand, L'Oréal Paris, where she sits on their UK Diversity and Inclusion Advisory Board to influence and inform the brand and be a voice for the Black, Trans, and queer community.

She has fronted campaigns for beauty, fashion, and lifestyle brands Illamasqua, Uniqlo, and Calvin Klein. And in 2021, Munroe will be releasing her debut literary offering, *Transitional*, published by Bloomsbury.

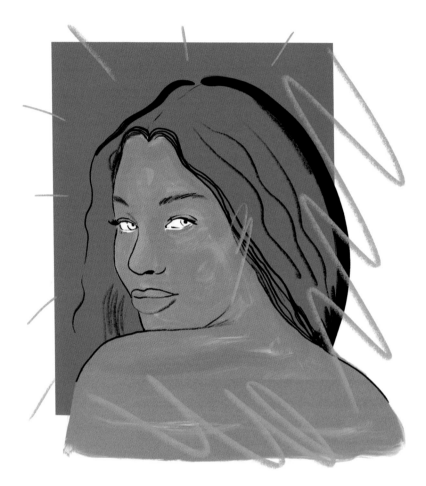

Illustration by Sam Russell Walker

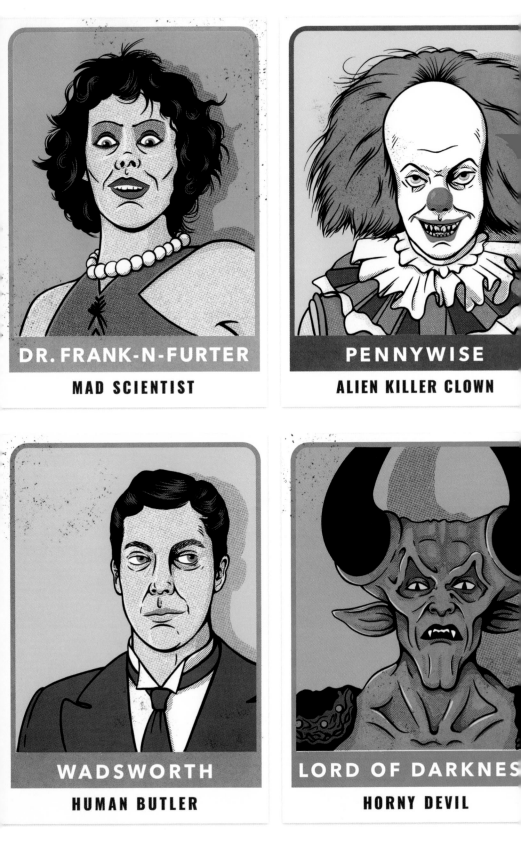

DR. FRANK-N-FURTER

MAD SCIENTIST

PENNYWISE

ALIEN KILLER CLOWN

WADSWORTH

HUMAN BUTLER

LORD OF DARKNES

HORNY DEVIL

TIM CURRY

by Mae Martin

I was first introduced to Tim Curry through the film *The Rocky Horror Picture Show*. The rock musical began life as a stage show in 1973 and was quickly adapted into a film, which was released in 1975. The story is bonkers; a mad scientist from outer space creates a Frankenstein-like creature to have sex with, and chaos ensues. *Rocky Horror* is a cult classic. Sell-out sing-a-long *Rocky Horror* showings still play around the world.

I was five when my dad showed me that film. There was a family connection to the musical; my grandmother was an agent in London and she represented Richard O'Brien, who wrote *Rocky Horror*. So when my dad was a teenager, aged about 14 or 15, the original stage musical of *Rocky Horror* was on at the Royal Court Theatre in London, and his dad, my grandfather, played the narrator in it. So my dad used to go to the Royal Court and sit and watch Tim Curry and his dad in this wild gay show. My dad was just passionate about it. He, and many others, found the whole atmosphere electrifying. My dad says there was a specific seat in the audience at the Royal Court where, if you sat in it, Tim Curry would usually come and put a feather boa around the audience

Illustration by Aimee David

member that was sitting there and sing to them his final ballad, "I'm Going Home." So my dad would always try to sit in that seat.

Dad was a superfan, a huge Bowie fan, too, and he'd describe this time of being young in London as all so cool; Mick Jagger being in the audience of *Rocky Horror* at one show where the cast was on acid . . . I think my dad was also in love with Patricia Quinn, who played Magenta. I never met my grandfather, but imagining him in fishnet stockings hanging out with those guys makes me feel certain we would have been best friends.

So when I was five, like really little—five is tiny—my dad sat me down and we watched the whole thing, all of the sex scenes and everything, and I think it completely blew my mind. Well, it must have completely blown my mind, because I WAS FIVE. I remember it vividly. Then I would demand to watch it all the time. When my dad and I drove to school in the mornings, we would do all the lines and we would sing all the songs and I'd be at school singing "Sweet Transvestite." The teachers were very freaked out.

As a child I definitely had an obsessive streak and my fandom was intense. There was a Holy Trinity of Bette Midler, Mae West, and Tim Curry. For me, I loved anything with Bette Midler. I was deeply devoted to her and to the movie *Hocus Pocus*. She's so confident, she's so in her body, she's so proud of herself, so sexy and unashamed. Mae West and Tim Curry have that same quality, too—Curry has a piratic twinkle in his eye that says "Come on, let's break the rules!" They're all so sex-positive, which I love. I remember watching videos of Bette Midler performing in bathhouses and stuff, like gay bathhouses—she's just outrageous. Frank-N-Furter and Bette Midler are actually not too far apart. But then I was named after Mae West, and that's a similar vibe that I find very attractive. I feel so weedy and wormy and awkward in my body and slightly on the more masculine side of that spectrum. Growing up, I felt like a scarecrow. A pile of sticks, struggling with feelings of being non-binary and trying to suppress my own femininity. So I'm just totally in awe of people who can confidently embody that sort of feminine glamour; I mean, Tim Curry's hips moving as he walks . . . I just love it.

Watching *Rocky Horror* so young had such a massive impact on me, expanding what I thought was possible for myself in terms of gender and sexuality. My dad spoke about Tim Curry with god-like reverence.

He deified him, would light up talking about watching him perform. I think he was totally besotted with him, like everyone was. To see this character who was so powerful, who totally defied any kind of labeling, was explosive; he's having sex with Brad, then in the next scene having sex with Janet, and nobody questions it. Nobody asks, "What are you?" Attraction conflates so many things, we want to possess and become and worship. I was wildly attracted to him. I was also desperate to be him. What an amazing message my parents were sending me by being so into *Rocky Horror*—that we're cool with everything and not only do we tolerate queerness but we think it's awesome.

Mae West and Tim Curry have that same quality, too—Curry has a piratic twinkle in his eye that says "Come on, let's break the rules!" They're all so sex-positive, which I love.

As I've got older I've been amazed at how it sometimes feels like we've slipped backward. I just can't believe how long ago that stage show was on, and people were loving it. Was there less focus on labels in the seventies? I feel like people weren't that obsessed with Bowie's sexuality. Bowie was Bowie. These days, if you're wearing eyeliner and high heels as a guy, people are desperate to hear you put a label on what you're doing and why you're doing it. It seems like it was a slightly more fluid time. Labels have huge value, of course; they allow us to use language to fight for our rights. And in terms of legal rights, things are infinitely better but, culturally, have we moved backward? I don't know, maybe I'm idealizing the past.

There's a sense that gender fluidity is a new and crazy thing. But really, in the timeline of human civilization, sexual and gender fluidity is not a new thing at all. As long as there have been humans there have been gender variances and different cultures that recognize multiple genders. It definitely sometimes gets painted as this kind of millennial, newfangled madness, where nobody has a gender anymore. It's so not true. The strict gender binary—that's quite a recent phenomenon, really. That's like a blip in human history and we're just trying to get back to fluidity.

Tim Curry, the man behind the Frank-N-Furter, was born in post-war England in 1946. In his childhood they were still rationing sweets! It would have taken real bravery to play that part and to field what I'm sure must've been some ignorant interviewers like that at the time. He was just so classy. Then later in childhood I saw *Muppet Treasure Island* and I was obsessed. I felt like Tim Curry's characters were always this siren call to adventure. Long John Silver in *Treasure Island*, all his characters, they have a sense of fun. He's always sexy because he's got this glint in his eye, even as the terrifying Pennywise in *It* or Darkness in *Legend*. My brother was really into that film. He just totally idolized Tim Curry in it.

> **There's a sense that gender fluidity is a new and crazy thing. But really, in the timeline of human civilization, sexual and gender fluidity is not a new thing at all. As long as there have been humans there have been gender variances and different cultures that recognize multiple genders.**

Curry wooed all of us—everyone in my family—and I think that sent a strong message to me, in terms of who I could be. I saw this interview where this woman was interviewing him and she was just kind of an awkward woman from Nebraska. She was like, "I can't believe I'm interviewing you, I feel like a transvestite." Such a weird thing to say! He replied, "I'm here to tell you, you look like a transvestite." So good. So celebratory. He's just really quick. I don't think he gets enough shout-outs in modern queer culture. I think we give a lot of shout-outs to RuPaul and people . . . not that they're not great, but how come people aren't worshipping at the altar of Tim Curry more often? I guess it's partly because he's refused to label himself; he hasn't been an outspoken activist, but that shouldn't diminish the contribution that he's made to queer culture.

It's hard to find footage of Tim Curry talking about his sexuality, so choosing Curry as my queer hero is maybe a bit subversive . . . but that's what he was all about. And it was irresistible. How else would a five-year-old start a lifelong obsession with a gender-queer, punk, sexual revolutionary? Curry's silence could be mistaken for conservatism or internalized homophobia. I don't think that's the case with him. I read recently that he said how amazing it was how many people had discovered different aspects of their sexuality through watching *Rocky Horror*.

The queer community has fought for its right to be seen, recognized, and protected. Perhaps the next step is the freedom not to be labeled. For your sexuality and gender to be yours. You share it with who you want, when you want. You don't owe it to anyone to explain who you are—you are just you. We're not there yet. It's important that we are visible and fight for the rights of others, and you don't get much more visible than playing Frank-N-Furter in the 1970s. I've definitely felt that frustration in my own career, with people just being strangely obsessed with wanting to put a label on my sexuality. If I say "I'm just me," then I feel like I'm almost being homophobic or ashamed of who I am. It's not that I'm saying I'm straight or being coy about my sexuality in any way, I just really don't have a label that I particularly ascribe to. I guess I'd say I'm bi, I date all genders, but I'm just a person. A strong queer community and being visible are hugely important, but I also want people to feel—I personally want to feel—like my sexuality is a dynamic human thing that is as nuanced and weird as I want it to be. I think everyone's is—not just in the LGBT+ community. It just seems strange, the way we categorize people.

> The queer community has fought for its right to be seen, recognized, and protected. Perhaps the next step is the freedom not to be labeled. For your sexuality and gender to be yours. You share it with who you want, when you want. You don't owe it to anyone to explain who you are—you are just you.

When you "come out"—basically label yourself—you step out of one prison of behavioral expectation and into a slightly different box that is not maybe as damaging as the previous one, but it is still restrictive in some ways. It can sometimes bulldoze over the nuances of sexual attraction or romantic attraction. Sexuality is so complex and, often, an evolving, changeable creature. When I first started a long-term relationship with a woman, for ease of communication I would say I was a lesbian. But I always felt weird about it because I've been in love with men, I've had relationships with men. Then I said I was bi and I received a lot of biphobia within the community. To experience such prejudice from a community that is so often the victim of discrimination, a community that is supposed to be a refuge, was really tough. I want to date who I want and be friends with who I want.

In his *Rocky Horror* role, Tim Curry embodied that freedom. The freedom to be. That type of self-acceptance, that celebration of life that is so irresistible and infectious. It's the definition of attractiveness. Curry's virility in the role smashes the binary. At the same time as being sexually dominant he's also a very vulnerable character; he has a feminine side that is also totally powerful. Language itself is so gendered; any time I start using language like "masculine" and "feminine," you then have to unpick all these things that we're taught. So often femininity in men is seen as a weakness and often those characters are victimized in some way. So to see this super character, so in charge, "powerful" is the only word I can think of. Like a lot of amazing drag queens as well, he's just so magnetic and in control.

> In his *Rocky Horror* role, Tim Curry embodied that freedom. The freedom to be. That type of self-acceptance, that celebration of life that is so irresistible and infectious.

That phrase—"Don't dream, be it"—when he's floating around in the pool at the end and they're all having a massive orgy? That is what I want from my life. My sexual orientation? It's being in that pool, getting off with tons of fit people of all genders. That's my orientation. That's kind of what I personally am into. Also, gender-wise, I definitely felt somewhere in the middle of the spectrum as a child and still do. I remember watching *Rocky Horror* and asking my parents, "Is he a man or a woman?" They said, "He's kind of both?" I was like, "cool." I asked, "Is he gay or straight?" They replied, "He's both." It just seemed like, oh great, the world's my oyster. That song at the end of *Rocky Horror* where he's got blue eyeshadow streaming down his face, singing "I'm Going Home" and he's kind of channeling this Judy Garland performance, like, later Judy Garland? Just iconic. Who needs labels? That tells you everything you'd ever need to know.

"Is he gay or straight?" They replied, "He's both." It just seemed like, oh great, the world's my oyster.

Mae Martin

Mae Martin is an award-winning Canadian comedian and writer whose drama *Feel Good*, which they created, co-wrote with Joe Hampson, and co-stars in the lead role alongside Charlotte Ritchie, Lisa Kudrow, and Sophie Thompson, is available on Channel 4 and Netflix and won the Edinburgh TV Award 2020 for Best Comedy Series. The second season of *Feel Good* is in production and will air exclusively on Netflix worldwide in 2021. Their most recent stand-up show, *Dope*, focused on addiction and was nominated for Best Comedy Show at the prestigious Edinburgh Comedy Awards while earning four- and five-star national reviews. The show has since been turned into a stand-up special for Netflix as part of their first global stand-up series, *Comedians of the World*. Mae's first non-fiction book, *Can Everyone Please Calm Down? A Guide to 21st Century Sexuality*, was published in 2019.

Since moving to the UK in 2011, Mae has also been awarded Best International Performer at the Brighton Fringe Festival and has been a finalist in the Hackney New Act of the Year Awards, the Musical Comedy Awards, and the Amused Moose Laughter Awards. On UK television, Mae has performed on shows such as Sky One's *The Russell Howard Hour*, *Comedy Central at the Comedy Store*, BBC Three's *Live at the BBC*, and *Uncle*. It was Mae's debut British TV appearance as the stand-up guest on BBC Three's *Russell Howard's Good News* that first catapulted them into the consciousness of the UK's online teen community. The clip gathered thousands of views on YouTube and Mae has emerged as a bright new role model for nervous teens everywhere, gaining a vast and engaged following.

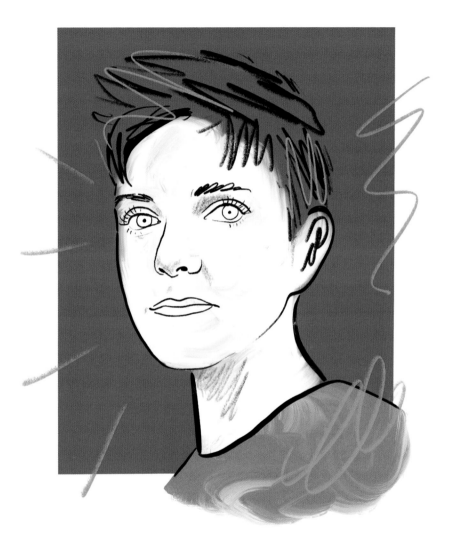

Illustration by Sam Russell Walker

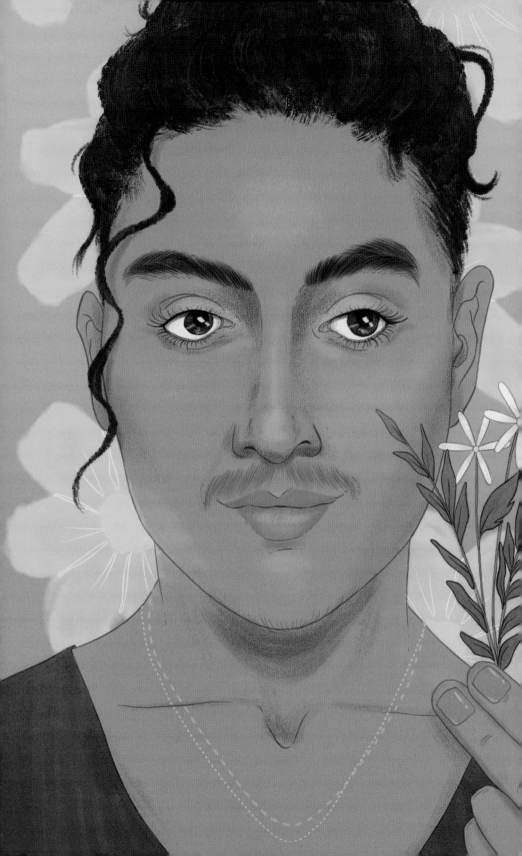

PIDGEON PAGONIS

by Hanne Gaby Odiele

My story is too common. Babies being given unnecessary operations. Parents lied to. Young people having to find out medical information for themselves. I hope my story educates society in general, and specifically, I want to reach out to other intersex people, to connect as a community, protect intersex people under law, to stop needless surgeries, and to accept and celebrate who we are in our awesome, beautiful uniqueness.

I underwent surgeries as a child and they were never really explained to me. I knew I couldn't have children from a young age and I couldn't have a period and I had been told that "something" was removed from me because it would give me cancer. In fact, the chances that I would get cancer on my undescended testes was statistically less than the chance of a woman getting breast cancer (we don't go around forcing healthy little girls to get breast amputations). That was what I was told, what my parents were told. But my parents were not told anything else more than that.

I found out that I was intersex at 17, I learned what it meant, what intersex is. That was around the same time I started modeling. I got discovered a couple of weeks after I knew

---

Illustration by Aorists/Anshika Khullar

the truth. I came across a teenage magazine, like a gossip idol teen magazine called *Fancy* in Holland. They had an article about an intersex woman who had surgeries, and they explained exactly what they were. Then for the first time I read the word "intersex." I learned that "intersex" is an umbrella term used to describe people born with sex characteristics that don't fit the typical binary notions of male and female bodies. It's much more common than people think. There are about as many intersex people as there are with red hair. In the article I found a phone number I could contact for a self-help group in Holland, which I did afterward.

I read the article and I was like, "Oh my god, surgeries—yes, no period—yes, no babies—yes." So I took the article and I took it to my doctor . . . and that's how I found out I was intersex. I started modeling shortly after that. Modeling for me was just kind of like, boosting my femininity. I was trying so badly to be a woman for so many years and it kind of boosted my ego. Like, "Oh yeah, I'm a full woman now, blah blah blah." I didn't tell anyone and I didn't have to tell anyone either. I just went with the flow and my career took off.

I used my career a little bit as an escape from that, until a couple of years ago, in 2015, when I started to see more possibilities for Trans models and in the media there was more representation of Trans folks and gender in general was more spoken about. This realization hit me, "Oh my god, I need to reach out to my community again." So I started looking at forums and seeing that young kids were still undergoing these surgeries. People who had surgery at thirteen years old are now having osteoporosis and no one is talking about this. I thought, "OK, I have to do something with this." That's why I contacted interACT and slowly but surely liberated myself as well. Since speaking out, I no longer really feel the need to be seen as a woman. My gender identity changed a little bit for myself. I would say I'm non-binary now, but for me that also doesn't mean anything has changed. For years I was trying so hard to be "this," now I'm just the same but I don't have to put a stamp on it anymore. It's very liberating.

I first became aware of Pidgeon Pagonis in a BuzzFeed video prior to meeting them. Pidgeon's visibility and activism inspired me to contact interACT in early 2016. We started conversations about getting me ready to speak up. The first person I met was Kimberly Zieselman, who at the time was president of interACT. We had a nice lunch and then she said,

"Oh, tonight there's a movie screening of Pidgeon," who was also part of interACT at the time. So we went to this queer LGBT+ center in Bushwick somewhere and I had a bunch of my friends join me. I told my friends, "Hey, so I'm gonna talk in a few months about this. I want you to come." I think my husband was there and a few of my other close friends. They heard me talk about intersex before but it used to come out at a moment when I was vulnerable and they were like, "Oh, it must be something really intense." But they never really understood the reality of it all. For them also seeing the video was like, "Oh my god, this is all so real and crazy."

Since speaking out, I no longer really feel the need to be seen as a woman. My gender identity changed a little bit for myself.

That was my first public outing as an intersex person. I remember putting on a hoodie. I kind of wanted to be invisible as much as possible in the audience. There were not that many people, but for me it was such a big deal, being there with other intersex people. Then I saw Pidgeon's movie for the first time; *The Son They Never Had*, it's called. Everyone in the audience was crying. I cried too. There were so many similarities between our stories. Afterward me and Pidgeon started talking, we hit it off immediately. Then from there we've been doing lots of talks together, we've done a video for *Teen Vogue*. We've been to multiple conferences, UN talks, and we also did some protests together. Pidgeon is my mentor. They are also a great friend to have. We don't have to just talk about intersex. We have fun, too. It's not all trauma, we can talk about movies!

Pidgeon's story changed my life. Suddenly my friends encouraged me to speak up, that I definitely should be talking about this, I needed to speak out publicly. They saw just how awful these surgeries are. Before it was an abstract concept to them. Pidgeon's film made it real. That's why stories are so important. Being visible and speaking your truth has such power. They also saw that it was about more than just a surgery—seeing the whole movie and the other intersex folks talk about it was, for them, put into a human context they could understand.

On my journey I've explored and challenged society's rigid definitions of sex and gender. Gender identity, easily said, is the way that you feel, how you see yourself, your identity. Then sex is sex characteristics, chromosomes . . . it's more biological but far more nuanced than even that. I see it more as all being on a spectrum. There are studies exploring how for many Trans people, their gender identity is also biological. As I've experienced in my own body, concepts and identities don't need to be cleanly binary, there can be nuance. There is real beauty and power in the non-binary. Pidgeon's activism has been such a source of inspiration to me. We have a lot of work to do as a community. We need to change a lot of things. Most importantly, we are trying to end interventions that are happening to young intersex kids, which is intersex surgery. It's a long history; doctors have systematically tried to erase intersex out of society. We need deeper acceptance, too, of intersex folks in general, being able to have intersex folk come out in public, and intersex people being safe to do so. There's so much shame and secrecy around it that we need to break through that as well. I love being part of the LGBTQIA community. It's wonderful.

> Pidgeon is my mentor. They are also a great friend to have. We don't have to just talk about intersex. We have fun, too. It's not all trauma.

I feel like we all have our own struggles and we are fighting together to get acceptance and to be equal; that's what we should all strive for. Our rights, our narratives, our battles intersect. Our community is strongest when it is inclusive.

Pidgeon's activism is so powerful because it's rooted in storytelling, in sharing their journey. That's how we can connect, to have empathy, to see how we are all connected as humans but also celebrate our differences and uniqueness. Pidgeon has done a couple of movies about their life and their experience as an intersex person, and also Pidgeon is the founder, together with Sean Saifa Wall, of the Intersex Justice Project, a person of color–led intersex advocacy group. Recently their main focus was on Lurie Children's Hospital in Chicago, where intersex surgeries were being performed on children.

Overall, intersex folks are still subjected to unnecessary surgeries in that hospital. The Intersex Justice Project has staged protests in front of the hospital, they've done social media campaigns, all to raise the public's awareness of this issue. Then finally, just recently, through many, many protests and also through some great online work, we had a breakthrough.

Members of the Trans community started retweeting information and then the whole hospital got bombarded with demands for doctors to apologize—and that actually happened! I can't overstate what a victory this was. This is the first time ever that a hospital has apologized and come forward to say, "Yes, we need to do better." They said they will stop any surgeries until further notice—a great first step for sure.

> Pidgeon's activism has been such a
> source of inspiration to me. We have
> a lot of work to do as a community.
> We need to change a lot of things.

Apologies are important, they're a step toward healing for a community that has been brutalized and erased and lied to. Action is even better. I want young intersex people to know that they can be whoever they are—don't listen to any of the bullshit, don't try to conform to any societal norm. We are free to explore who we are and accept and love our bodies. Also, being intersex doesn't have to completely dictate your whole life or identity. It's just a small part of you, like your eye color or your hair, something like that.

The intersex movement has a long way to go. One apology is great but we need to keep going because all LGBTQIA people across the world are in so much danger right now with politically crazy people in charge. It's very important that we keep going. We need to be protected by laws, so that young babies don't have to be operated on. It's really wrong.

I am very hopeful for the future. When I'm hanging out with younger intersex youth, it's so much easier now to talk about gender identity and differences. I feel like they are way more open than previous generations. I think slowly but surely there is a big shift happening. Non-binary identity is way more accepted now than ever before, in Western civilization at least. So yeah, I'm hopeful that the youth will change it all. We have to stay active and alert, we have to keep planning for a rise in oppressive laws.

In this day and age it might seem like everything is OK, but laws can change abruptly and push everything back a couple of decades very easily. Activists like Pidgeon Pagonis are telling our stories, educating society, and offering leadership in the intersex community. We are fighting to establish a protective legal framework so that this hopeful, amazing next generation of young people can flourish.

Hanne Gaby Odiele

At 17, Hanne Gaby Odiele was discovered by a modeling scout while attending a music festival in Belgium. They signed with a modeling agency in New York and shortly after made their debut on the runway. Odiele has walked for Alexander McQueen, Anna Sui, Balmain, Calvin Klein, Chanel, Dior, DKNY, Dries Van Noten, Etro, Fenty X Puma, Giambattista Valli, Givenchy, Lanvin, Michael Kors, Miu Miu, Philipp Plein, Prada, Saint Laurent, Tommy Hilfiger, Versace, and Zimmermann.

Odiele has been the face of some of the biggest designers in the world, including Alexander Wang, Balenciaga, Hugo Boss, Elisabetta Franchi, Jason Wu, Kenneth Cole, Maison Margiela, Marc Jacobs, Max Mara, Missoni, Moncler, Moschino, Mulberry, and Vera Wang.

Odiele has been featured in *Allure*, *Buro 24/7*, *Dazed*, *ELLE*, *Glamour*, *Harper's Bazaar*, *i-D*, *Interview*, *Love*, *Marie Claire*, the *New York Times*, *Numéro*, *Paper*, *Teen Vogue*, *Spur*, *V*, and *Vogue* magazines.

In 2017, Odiele revealed they were born intersex. Odiele is an advocate for intersex human rights and works closely with interACT Advocates for Intersex Youth, helping to raise awareness about the importance of human rights protection for intersex people worldwide. Odiele works tirelessly to empower and give a voice to others in the intersex community to help end the human rights violations that thousands of intersex people endure.

Hanne lives in New York with their husband.

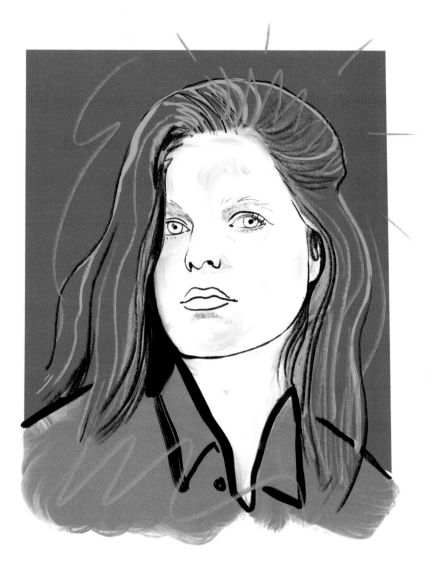

Illustration by Sam Russell Walker

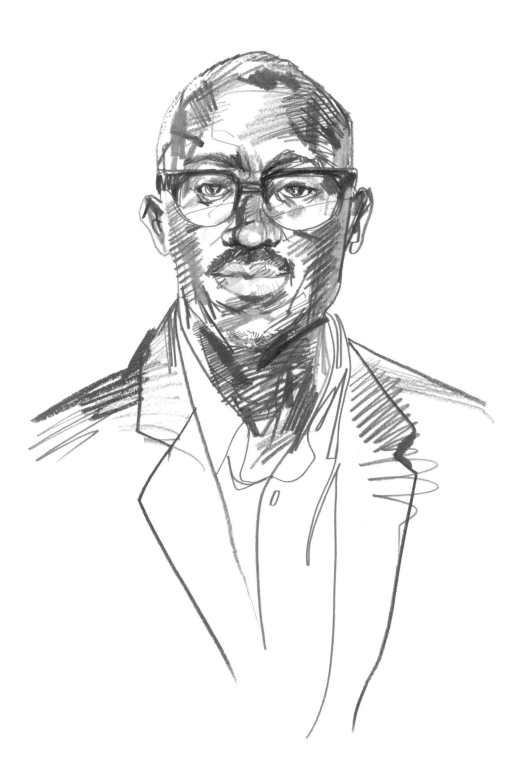

EDWARD ENNINFUL

by Paris Lees

Edward Enninful was born in Ghana in 1972; his mother was a seamstress, his father a major in the Ghanaian army. I can't be sure, but I have a feeling that if you had told this young Black couple at the time that four decades later their newborn son would go on to become one of the most influential figures in fashion, they'd have laughed you out of the room. If you'd told them he'd be regarded as one of the most recognizable people of color in Britain, that he would count royalty and A-list stars among his friends, that he would grace the cover of *Time* magazine, well, I suspect they'd have thought you were completely mad. Because Edward's story *is* mad.

I'm going to be honest, though, I didn't know much about Edward when he was named as the new editor-in-chief of *British Vogue* in 2017. I'd always loved fashion as in *clothes*, but hated fashion as in *the industry*, or at least the version of the industry I had in my head. Like every other queer kid in the noughties, I grew up addicted to *Sex and the City*, *Absolutely Fabulous*, and *The Devil Wears Prada*. I took the latter's message literally: fashion people look good but are, essentially, evil. "Fashion people" were the airheads

---

Illustration by Alex Mein

that Sacha Baron Cohen interviews in *Brüno*. I dismissed fashion as superficial, somewhere I would never be welcomed, and I was therefore happy to reject before it could reject me. But deep down, I craved a life of color, creativity, and glamour.

Nothing better illustrates this longing than the story of The Day I Snapped. It's 1 a.m. on a Monday and I'm standing outside the petrol station on Upper Parliament Street in Nottingham with my best friend, Steffi. It's the mid-noughties—or maybe 2004, maybe later. In any case, skinny jeans have just come in, because we're the only people not wearing them. I'm wearing a wig, an outrageously short skirt, and a bad attitude that I've not been able to shake since. I'm around 16, give or take a year, but no stranger to midnight adventures, having been climbing out of windows (or up through the coal grate) to go clubbing since I was 14. I'm tall and precocious, and doormen don't ask too many questions.

Steffi is a Trans woman of color, a few years older than me—my responsible adult, we love to joke. The Day I Snapped certainly isn't the first time people have been rude to us in public. The truth is, Steffi and I rarely leave the house without someone insulting us. The transphobia is bad enough, but I've seen Steffi face hostility due to the color of her skin, too. We usually let it go, reasoning that we can't spend all our time arguing with people. And anyway, aren't we asking for it? Going out of the house "dressed up"? What do we expect? We tell ourselves it's just the price we pay for expressing ourselves the way we do, the way we have to but don't yet fully understand why. And if we don't understand it, you can bet your bottom dollar no one else does.

1 a.m. We want cigarettes so we queue to be served at the 24-hour counter. Steffi can't decide what chocolate bar she wants. Two girls are behind us. One of them says, "For fuck's sake, hurry up, man." I can help feeling that that word "man" is loaded, intentional, but perhaps I'm just being paranoid. Steffi says, "Alright, darlin', no need to be rude." And then the other girl looks us up and down, her lips curled at the corner in disgust, and shouts, "That's a man. Look at 'em!" And they both laugh at us. One Black girl, one white girl. Like us, but the real thing.

That's when I snapped. There was no fight. No theatrics. Just a simple "Fuck off!" from me to them, to society, to the universe. So what if we "dress up" as girls? No one deserves to be treated like that. And I know I'm not going to put up with it anymore. Neither is Steffi. We've officially

Had Enough. By the time we spark up a cigarette something far more urgent has been ignited in us—rebellion.

I remember the conversation Steffi and I had as we walked home like it was yesterday. Walking through Nottingham's leafy avenues, we talked about our dreams. About a world that didn't exist. A world where people like us were celebrated, not stigmatized. She asked me something that has stayed with me since. "Do you think we'll ever do anything good?" I asked her what she meant. "You know, we could be the first transsexual to be on the cover of *Vogue* or something?" It's the sort of thing people would have laughed at you for saying back then, but we knew gay people had been on that journey. Black people. Steffi was obsessed with trailblazing Black women and would tell me I was the Kate Moss to her Naomi Campbell. We knew change was possible.

As the years went by, that night stayed stored in my memories, a foolish conversation about things that would never happen. As I went out into the world and came face to face with the harsh realities of life as a Trans woman, it became increasingly difficult to get out of bed in the morning, let alone break boundaries. There were bright spots of light in the darkness. I remember seeing Lea T model for Givenchy in 2010. She looked stunning. I can't overstate how revolutionary this was for me. I'd come to the conclusion that it might be possible to remove some of the stigma attached to Trans people, but I didn't dare to believe that we could be . . . aspirational.

But then Andreja Pejić arrived on the scene and it looked as though fashion was prepared to accept Girls Like Us for the first time. But *Vogue*? Like owning houses or having children, *Vogue* was something Other People did. Real people. In fact, I was so sure that *British Vogue* wasn't for the likes of me that I described the people who worked there as "privileged twats" in one of my columns for *Vice* as a young journalist. My *Vice* columns were intended to shock, but even so, as a writer, you watch what you say about publications in case you ever want to write for them. That didn't seem to apply in this case, though, because of course there was absolutely definitely no way I was ever going to be asked to write for *British Vogue*, never.

And so, in April 2017, when Edward was announced as *British Vogue*'s editor-in-chief, I didn't connect it with my story at all. I thought it was interesting that the powers that be had chosen a man, and a Black man too, a gay Black man. Perhaps those in the know in the world of fashion saw it coming, but for me it registered as a simple "Well, good for him."

Edward was talent-scouted on a train aged just 16—for millennials like me who hit puberty pre-Instagram, this sort of story was the stuff of legends. Stylist Simon Foxton approached Edward on the London Underground and asked him if he would like to model for *i-D*. Edward was shy and sheltered, having only been in London for four years. As he told *Time* magazine when he appeared on the cover last year: "I knew I couldn't just walk away from this, that something special was going to come out of it." Edward's mother had passed on to him a passion for clothing and bright colors, but she was understandably wary for her son. Edward begged. He saw a door into another world and was desperate to walk through it. It was a door I would one day follow him through.

Walking through Nottingham's leafy avenues, we talked about our dreams. About a world that didn't exist. A world where people like us were celebrated, not stigmatized. She asked me something that has stayed with me since. "Do you think we'll ever do anything good?"

He soon found that modeling wasn't his bag, though, and instead turned his attention (and eye) to creating beautiful images. His approach to creating images through concepts and storytelling soon got him a different kind of attention and so, at just 18, he was made fashion director of *i-D*. He was the youngest to fill the role. It wouldn't be the last time he would break boundaries.

When I got a call from *British Vogue* in 2017 asking me if I would like to write something for them, I was slightly taken aback. It was a month before Edward was announced as editor, and I had no idea the whirlwind he was about to bring not only to this British institution, but Britain itself. I didn't write for them again for another six months. When Giles Hattersley approached me and asked me if I would like to write something for the website, to mark Transgender Day of Remembrance, it looked very much like there was an open door for me at *British Vogue*. Was I dreaming?

But right while I was wondering if there was indeed a door or not, it swung wide open. I received an email asking me if I would like to be part of a feature on Britain's "New Suffragettes," along with six other women. Edward wanted to celebrate the achievements of the suffragettes by profiling women pushing for equality in 2018, and he wanted it to reflect modern, diverse Britain. There would be a lovely write-up in the magazine, Edward's second edition. There would be a photoshoot. It took a while for me to process this at first. That meant *Vogue* stylists, right? *Vogue* lighting? *Vogue* Photoshop? It was a no-brainer. Of course it was yes.

It couldn't have been better timing. I'd just had a bad breakup and was feeling utterly depressed at the increasing transphobia of the British press. Anti-Trans headlines proliferated in newspapers; *The Times* said children were being "sacrificed to appease the Trans lobby" and mocked Trans women as men in wigs and fishnet tights. I've written for pretty much every paper in Britain except the *Daily Mail*, but after years of asking journalists to approach the subject with fairness and accuracy, I was feeling utterly drained. Like that night outside the petrol station ten years earlier, I'd had enough. When Edward threw me a lifeline of hope, I grabbed it.

But just as Edward Enninful's *British Vogue* came calling, a very different offer came in—*Celebrity Big Brother*. It was billed as "the year of the woman" and the producers promised a concept that harked back to *Big Brother*'s early years as an interesting social experiment. They offered me a lot of money. It may surprise you, but journalism isn't exactly a get-rich-quick scheme, and activism less so. It was a life-changing amount, six figures. Enough to buy a house. Not in London, perhaps, but a house somewhere.

In a weird twist of fate, the *Vogue* photoshoot was scheduled for the same day I was due to film my intro tape for *Big Brother*. I could have asked if we could have filmed on another day, but deep down I knew I couldn't do both. Two very different doors had opened up for me. Was I going to go down the reality TV route? Or follow in Carrie Bradshaw's Manolo Blahnik footsteps? There's no shame in doing reality TV, but I knew it would undermine my position as a serious writer. Saying no to the *Big Brother* money was the most difficult decision I've ever made. It was also the easiest. I knew I'd rather die poor knowing I'd been in the glossy folds of *British Vogue*, if only once.

During the past three years, under his editorship, *British Vogue* is enjoying a renaissance. The Forces for Change issue, guest-edited by the Duchess of Sussex, Meghan Markle, is the best-selling edition of *British Vogue* ever. It featured a range of inspiring activists on the cover, including Laverne Cox—the first Trans woman of color to grace the cover—climate-change campaigner Greta Thunberg, and mental health advocate Matt Haig. Who would have predicted that? Digital traffic is up 51 percent and people are subscribing en masse. Put simply, *British Vogue* has never been this successful—it's also never been this diverse. *British Vogue* is now full of people, both in the mag and behind the scenes, who never thought they'd get a seat at the table. Now it's our table.

Edward's celebration of diversity isn't a bid to be "woke," though. He's not a campaigner in the formal sense, although anyone who wishes to celebrate difference is by default an "activist" in a society hell-bent on preserving white, male, heterosexual power structures. And he's not famous for being gay or Black. He's the editor because he's talented and has an eye for telling stories through fashion. He celebrates diversity because there is diverse talent out there to celebrate.

Last year I was invited by Edward's partner and *British Vogue*'s Creative Digital Director Alec Maxwell to take part in a film celebrating the Trans community. I was amazed when I saw the final cut. I discovered so many amazing people I'd never heard of before. Me, who thought she knew every Trans person on the planet. And it really felt like we'd finally gone past simply removing stigma against Trans people to somewhere I'm not sure I ever really believed we'd reach: a world where Trans people were not only not-reviled but, dare I say it, cool. Being Trans had become aspirational. It felt millions of miles away from The Day I Snapped.

> *British Vogue* is now full of people, both in the mag and behind the scenes, who never thought they'd get a seat at the table. Now it's our table.

Over the past few years I've been lucky enough to get to know Alec and Edward as friends—and they're as unlike the stereotypes about "fashion people" as could be. Edward wants the world to be a more beautiful place, in every sense. But it's an aspiration he believes should be open to everyone, no matter the color of your skin, who you love, or what happens to be between your legs. And no, I'm not just being nice about my "boss." If you don't believe me, here's Oprah on Edward, who he put on the cover in 2018: "I have never experienced in all my dealings with people in that world anyone who was more kind and generous of spirit. I mean, it just doesn't happen."

Edward's world may be beautifully scented, but it's not all roses. As he wrote during the Black Lives Matter protests in 2020: "I am lucky to have enormous privilege in my world, but as a man of colour, and as a gay man, I could not escape the sense that it doesn't matter what you've achieved, or what you've contributed to society, your life can still feel worthless. When I step out of my door in the morning, to take a walk or to wander alone, I am always aware of increased personal danger because of the colour of my skin . . . My mother told me to watch myself whenever I left the house. I still feel that same sense of anxiety today when I step out of my front door."

I can never know what it feels like to walk the Earth as a person of color, but I empathize. I recently reconnected with an old school friend, a white gay man, who told me he still remembers the stares he would get walking between classes. The constant fear of being attacked. Being spat at. That noise still lives in his head, over a decade later. Mine too. I don't wish to present myself as a victim, but the pain experienced in childhood can affect you for the rest of your life. And it's not just in our heads. Hate crimes against Trans people and people of color have ballooned in recent years, as Britain starts to feel like an increasingly hostile place for anyone who doesn't fit the "norm." Edward made headlines recently after revealing he was prevented from entering Vogue House by a security guard who tried to direct him to the delivery entrance. The editor-in-chief. It wasn't the first time.

Edward has changed my life. Would brands like Pantene have wanted to work with me if it weren't for my connection to *British Vogue*? Maybe. But there's no denying my life has become exponentially better since he became part of it. He's an undeniable force for good in the British media, whether it's making Dame Judi Dench the oldest star to grace the cover of *British Vogue*, or putting NHS nurses and other key workers front of shop during the coronavirus lockdown. To quote Oprah again: "Edward understands that images are political, that they say who and

He's an undeniable force for good in the British media.

what matters." He knows that we *all* matter and that the light of human dignity burns in all of us.

I didn't speak to my father for fifteen years. Edward didn't speak to his for twenty. The choices we made as teenagers didn't make sense to them, but time has made our case for us. Edward's father is incredibly proud of his son, particularly his OBE from the Queen, just as my own father is brimming with pride at the woman I've become. As I find myself saying about so much of our world these days, it's all so unlikely, yet here we are. Edward, like me, wasn't supposed to have all this. And yes, like me, he had amazing opportunities come his way, but only someone with talent and fire in their belly can translate that into becoming one of the most influential men in our culture. Edward Enninful hasn't just changed my life, he's changing this country and offering a vision of the Britain we could be, and a world worth fighting for.

Tomorrow I'm interviewing Oscar-winner Sam Smith at The Savoy for *British Vogue*. The last time I sat down in The Savoy's sumptuous suites was to interview Emma Watson. After that, I'm off to Paris. I've never been before. I couldn't afford to, either financially or emotionally—travel has always sent my anxiety through the roof and stirred up all those old feelings of fear, shame, and low self-esteem. But thanks to Edward, I'm going as a Contributing Editor of *British Vogue,* and I'll be holding my head high. As Morgan M. Page wrote about Aiyyana Maracle in a profile for *The Queer Bible*: "There are certain people who make things possible that were not before." Edward Enninful is one of them.

Paris Lees

Paris Lees was born in Hucknall, Nottinghamshire. Described as "the voice of a generation" by *i-D* magazine, and "the fearless, vital voice we need" by *Dazed*, Lees is a multi-award-winning writer and campaigner, widely known for igniting a much-needed discussion about Trans rights in Britain. A contributing editor at *British Vogue*, she has written everywhere from *The Guardian* to the *Telegraph*, the *Sun* to *Attitude* magazine. She was the first Trans woman to present on BBC Radio 1 and Channel 4—and also the first to appear on the BBC's flagship political discussion program *Question Time*, where she drew praise from across the political spectrum.

She is the co-founder of All About Trans, an initiative to improve media representation. Through her work there she has met with hundreds of media professionals, leading to £1.5 million worth of television being commissioned, including the BBC's first sitcom to feature a Trans character as a lead role, *Boy Meets Girl*.

In 2016, she was made an honorary Doctor of Letters for her work to educate the public about gender diversity by the University of Brighton, an institution at which she graduated with a degree in English Literature just a few years earlier. In 2019, she was named as one of Pantene's three new brand ambassadors, going on to become the first openly Trans woman to feature in a mainstream television campaign in the UK. Her debut book, *What It Feels Like for a Girl*, publishes in 2021.

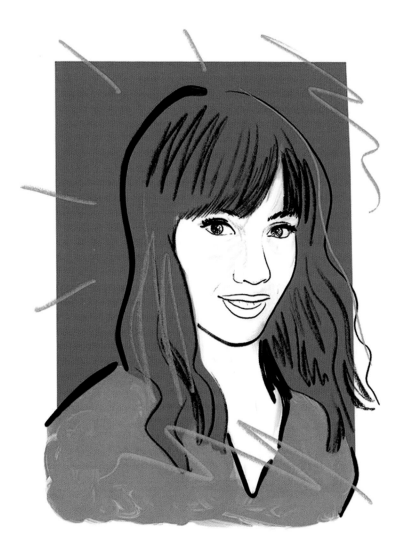

Illustration by Sam Russell Walker

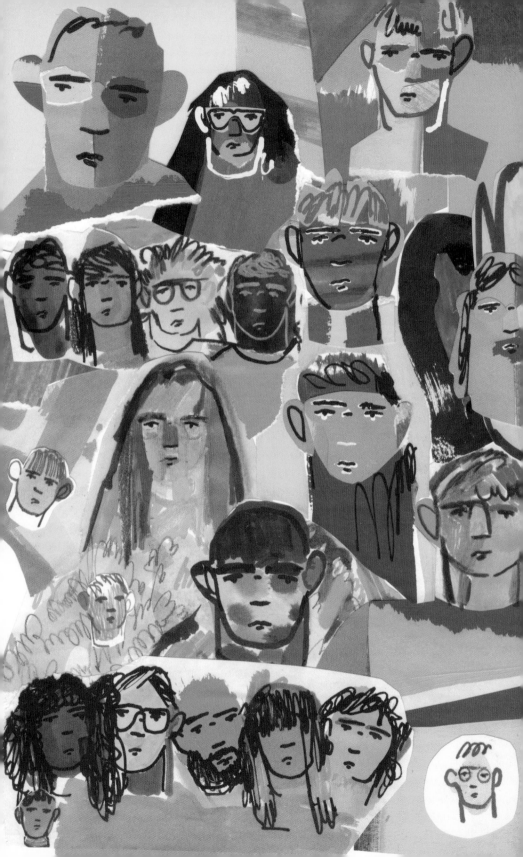

QUEER EYE

by Tan France

In 2003, I was living in Manchester, in the trendy suburb of Chorlton. There was a little hub in the middle of the neighborhood, with a bank on every corner and a Morrisons supermarket if you turned up the road toward town. My address was Wilbraham Road, right beside it. The local supermarket shouldn't be a particular point of interest, but it was the first place I'd ever seen LGBT people doing something as mundane as their weekly shop, normalizing an experience I had been nurtured—incorrectly—to feel was anything but. I was working a couple of jobs back then. The first was at British Gas, where I was a data inputter in the evening; in the daytime I worked as a visual merchandiser—the posh name for window dressers for the high-street fashion store Bershka.

It wasn't me who drove the plan forward to move to Manchester. It was my boyfriend. He wanted to live in a place where we could live more openly. We'd met in our hometown, a small Yorkshire town called Doncaster. We wanted to live without judgment and Manchester was the closest place to do it. We didn't do it exactly together, but we

Illustration by John Booth

moved at roughly the same time. I packed my bags for liberation just shy of my eighteenth birthday.

Oh my gosh, Manchester. It was absolutely eye-opening. I'd been going there for years anyway, because we have family close by, without ever discovering the city center. I only really knew the suburbs. South Manchester, and Chorlton in particular, was full of students and ex-students, which automatically meant that it was the most liberal place I'd ever lived in. We'd go out to the Gay Village around Canal Street and socialize among people who were not only openly gay but openly comfortable with their gayness. It was something I'd just never seen in my hometown, where being gay was still the subject of ridicule, gossip, and scorn. So, the majority of my experiences as a gay man I learned in Manchester.

I took a job at a bar called Gaia, which no longer exists. I'd pop into the bar next door, TriBeCa, before or after each shift, often both. If you left Gaia and crossed the main bridge on Canal Street and onto the other side of the road to the left, all the way down you got to Manto. Next door to that was a place I went to a lot. They were all different shades of gay, but because of the temperament and humor of Mancunians, specifically, Northerners generally, they represented a new kind of inclusivity, something I had never quite been able to imagine in my mind's eye. These were pretty much the places I lived in.

For me, these were the places where I learned not to hide any of my femininity, at all. On the most basic level, it was about not needing to hide those things that were natural to me that I had felt the need to keep covert before. If I had a limp wrist, I had a limp wrist. A high voice? That's fine, too. If I wanted to talk about Britney Spears, I could. It made me feel like I was safe to be the person I wanted to be and to no longer have to suppress the things inside of me that had previously been locked away. Because nobody, quite frankly, gave a fuck. I love Manchester for that.

The TV climate of the time was funny. Weird, not haha. It was the start of the millennium. Change felt imminent but not yet fully realized. Makeover shows were already in fashion, mainly hooked to a British star by the name of Laurence Llewelyn-Bowen, a dandy character who always felt like he might be a little on the downlow. You never quite knew—or we were never quite told—who this guy would bang on the weekend. Why would we? He was just choosing the shade of wallpaper for suburban living rooms. But he carried an air of cultivated fabulosity familiar to British TV audiences, a persona people might assume to be gay. I'm not suggesting he was. If he wasn't, so be it. But I assumed he was because of how effeminate he was, and as a kid I didn't understand the nuances of sexuality enough to know that it might be more complicated than that. Of course, that doesn't necessarily mean that someone is gay. But I assumed it did.

> These were the places where I learned not to hide any of my femininity, at all. On the most basic level, it was about not needing to hide those things that were natural to me that I had felt the need to keep covert before.

The first gay people I saw on TV were the cast of *Will & Grace*. I'd known there were gay characters in the seventies and eighties, but not many, and I didn't watch those shows anyway. But I would watch and be fascinated by the world of *Will & Grace*. What I found so fascinating was how clear it was to me that these people were not a version of me. They were either hyper-stereotyped versions of gayness, like the Jack character, or someone who was obviously played by a straight guy, like Will. Will would try to camp it up slightly but never quite enough to make a gay audience feel absolutely seen. These two extremes seemed to be on TV to make straight people feel comfortable about the idea of watching gay characters. And that was great, truly. They represented the possibilities of what a gay person might look like to that audience. But to a gay man watching the show it wasn't entirely clear that they took in the multitudes of gayness. What about the men who didn't have to try to camp it up?

Like I say, that was OK. *Will & Grace* was a scripted show with a clear intention. But then *Queer Eye* happened, and my mind was blown. It was the first show I'd watched gripped, where it was very clear that these people were gay, or queer—however they wanted to identify—24/7, around the clock, off camera as well as on. It was an important distinction for me. They talked in their own voices and said what they wanted to say, as identifiably real-life gay men. This was a first for me. The first time I felt like, what? We're allowed to be ourselves on TV? That is insane.

I should add here that there were other significant TV moments. There was the Brian Dowling win on *Big Brother*. But I came from a very religious household and we weren't allowed to watch *Big Brother*. I still don't watch a lot of reality TV because I find it too negative and I like to surround myself with as much positivity as possible. But I did watch *Queer as Folk*, the drama set five miles from my Chorlton home and in the Gay Village I worked and hung out in. Again, it was about actors acting being gay. There was such a difference in my mind between an actor playing being gay and a real person wanting to talk about their husband or boyfriend or the casual shag they might have had last night. Timothée Chalamet playing a gay role is quite wonderful, but it is a fantasy of what gay life looks like. It isn't real.

There were, however, many things to love about *Queer as Folk*. It was the first time we'd been privy to proper gay sex on TV and it even felt a little shocking to me. I was probably 15 or 16 when *Queer as Folk* aired and just shy of 18 when I moved to the city. So I went out into the village thinking, this is a little like what I saw on that show but not exactly, because on *Queer as Folk* they were straight men play-acting gayness. Reality is really quite different to that fantasy.

The scripted world never quite rings true to me. Even though *Queer Eye* was—and still is—a makeover show, the presenters said what they wanted to say in their honest voices. They were true queer men. They reimagined what the word "queer" meant to me. Back in the day, when I was growing up, the word was only associated with shame. There was a long time when hearing the word at school sent a shudder through me. I wouldn't hear it directed at myself because I was stupid enough or clever enough to pretend not to be queer. I can be angry for allowing myself to live that pretense at the time, but I forgive myself now because there was no option to behave any differently and remain unscathed. This is one of the reasons why I get it when people act from a place of shame and deny their true selves. Why did I have to convince these idiots that I was straight? Because the world is not set up for queer people. It's built around a "straight" model, whatever that is. So sometimes living an imaginary or modified life is a question of survival in small towns. It certainly was then.

For me, being gay wasn't a problem, but for other kids it was. "He's a queer," "he's a poof." That was a language I grew up with as routine. I heard it a lot, even if it wasn't directed at me, and the whole idea of being gay was equated, in those little moments of casual cruelty, with feeling ashamed of something at your core. It wasn't until I was in my thirties that I understood the word to mean something positive. *Queer Eye* must have triggered that. We're not something straight; we are something different from that and that's OK, that's beautiful. We are queer, and for me, that started to mean different or unique. The word started to shed some of its negativity. *Queer Eye* had a lot to do with that. Now it fills me with pride to think that I am one of those *Queer Eye* boys. I'm not dancing to the same beat as everybody else, and that is fine. That makes me feel strong. It's a source of great power, not having to conform to what people expect of you. I hate the word "normal" anyway, a word that now sounds like more of an insult than queer used to. Who, in all honesty, wants to be that bore?

I'll be honest. When I got the *Queer Eye* job I only watched half an episode of the first American series, because I didn't want to be inspired by the US original Fab Five and become a cheap knock-off of Carson. I didn't want to subconsciously channel him in any way. But the British version had changed something in me back then in Chorlton when it ended up popping on my TV one night. It chimed with my new life.

I can remember it coming on the TV as if it was yesterday. I was sitting with my boyfriend and was immediately struck by how fab these guys really were, in the best and worst possible way for the early 2000s. It was so weird that they referenced their life outside of the show, something actors on scripted drama or comedy could never do. They were naturally funny and charismatic and, most importantly, naturally queer. That felt so different to a script. It was so nice to imagine what their life might look like outside of the show—these men who didn't take off the costume of a gay man and disappear back to the arms of their girlfriends.

Even though *Queer Eye* was—and still is— a makeover show, the presenters said what they wanted to say in their honest voices. They were true queer men. They reimagined what the word "queer" meant to me.

Its appeal wasn't that it was a makeover show and that I couldn't wait to see the next episode. That it was nice, it was entertaining. What was truly revolutionary for me was that I was able to talk about it with my boyfriend and my friends, knowing that they were going back to their boyfriends or partners or however they articulated their queerness in a real way. That impacted me in the most positive way. It was something I simply hadn't seen before. Somebody on TV allowed to talk about what their life was like outside the show was something I had never experienced before. It brought a 360-degree gay experience right into the home. Not something that someone turned off and on for the camera. These men were working together—who knows what their relationships were like off screen, but on screen they were helping somebody improve their lives by bringing their own, rounded, fully gay experience to bear on the most important aspects of their lives. Gay men were useful, at last! Gay men weren't the butt of the joke anymore or wheeled on as a joke for comedic relief. Their opinions and expertise were respected, and their "gayness," that point of difference, was central. That they were introducing their experiences to other people in an affirmative, positive way made the show somehow holistic. "Queer" suddenly felt like the opposite of shame.

As gay men, our friends are to a large extent more important to us than our family. They are the ones who mold who we are at a time when our identity might feel under attack. We become a product of our friendship circle, especially when we first come out, especially if we are lucky enough to find friends who we love and who care properly for us. In our formative years, we start to take on little characteristics of our friends. It's part of our freedom and liberation, something we often have to learn. I know I did. Sometimes those relationships are much more important than those with our biological families.

My first ever gay friends came into my life at the same time as moving to Chorlton. The luxury of working in retail, especially visual merchandising, is that most of your co-workers are either female or gay. I didn't know that before I entered the industry; it was only ever about getting as close to the fashion world as I could. But the plethora of supportive women and gay male allies turned out to be a lovely perk of the job. I made friends with a guy five years older than me who had already been out for years. At 18 that was a big age gap. He felt so much more worldly wise than me. At almost exactly the same time I met a man in my office job; up until that moment, I had never even considered the possibility of being an open, out, gay man in the corporate world. It upended another incorrect preconception about how you might live a gay life. You can't be what you can't see. He was respected, people loved him, he was funny, and I had the most massive crush on him. Which was exactly not what I was expecting when I walked into the forbidding four walls of the British Gas offices!

> As gay men, our friends are to a large extent more important to us than our family. They are the ones who mold who we are at a time when our identity might feel under attack. We become a product of our friendship circle.

Believe me, it was the hugest crush. He was the exact image of everything I wanted to see as an emerging gay man coming out into the world. He looked like George Michael in his "Club Tropicana" days. So pretty, with a ridiculous suntan, Irish, with almost black hair and piercing blue eyes. He was slender, tall, and blew my mind. It wasn't so much that he knew I had a crush on him. He knew that everyone had a crush on him. He was just that type. Every woman, every man. He was such a sexy person. It wasn't just that he was a nice guy, either. He did something with that niceness—spotting that I was new to this gay world and taking me under his wing. I'd accompany him to the Gay Village and that was the first time I'd been out and about without my boyfriend. It was so nice not to have to rely on my partner to be my wingman.

Between these two men, I was allowed to be who I was and understand early on the value of gay friendship. I took on some of their characteristics, which still carry on in how I present myself as a gay man now. I was lucky. They were kind and supportive men. They weren't catty and there wasn't any competition between us. I wanted us to have fun together, cook together, sit and watch soap operas with one another. And that's exactly what we did. Those domestic friendships can in many ways be more formative than our love affairs. They are the relationships that shape you. Not the ones that break you.

I don't feel anger toward actors who play gay roles on TV or toward movies that cast straight actors in those roles. But it doesn't help the stigma, because there is still a disconnect. Ultimately, Heath Ledger and Jake Gyllenhaal would take their costumes off at the end of filming and return to a very different sort of life. Gay is not something that most people try on. *Queer Eye* was the first time I had seen our usefulness and purpose told fully. It was the first time, inevitably, that I felt seen.

**

I met the creator of the original *Queer Eye for the Straight Guy*, David Collins, early into my casting for the show. He was also the executive producer of the new iteration. David explained to me why the show was called what it was called, explaining the original reason for finding *Queer Eye for the Straight Guy* was that it was designed to show that we are supportive of our straight brothers and, therefore, there is no reason for a division to exist between us. There is no reason for us to hate them and for them to hate us, even if we have traditionally seen straight men as our oppressors.

Straight men are not just the people in the playgrounds making fun of us, telling us to walk and talk in a certain way, one that felt acceptable and unthreatening to them. No. They were our brothers, our uncles, our dads, and our cousins. They were not just the men who were oppressing or stifling us, they were the men who were teaching us. We needed to tell them, yes, we are here for you. Now be here for us. Even if you are going to try to tell us to live a life that is different to our true selves, we are still going to help you, because that is how evolved we are. I loved that he chose that title. We are still willing to help out the guys who wanted to fuck us over. That is the best answer to being a man. Also, I love that it's a wink to the fact that the men you are most scared of are the ones who might hold the secrets to your happiness. How brilliant is that?

David is the father of two wonderful twin daughters. He owns a company called Scout Productions with his ex-husband, Michael Williams. They created *Queer Eye* after attending a party, a gallery opening populated by a lot of gay men. A woman was parading her new husband up and down, saying how shitty he looked compared to all the gay men at the event. He walked over with a couple of friends and she began this rant again, to which they all started chipping in. No, all he needs to do is this and this or that or the other, then he's good to go. In that moment, David thought, OK, we could turn that into a show. It could be hilarious.

He decided to create a show to help straight men feel better about who they are. He's had several shows that have been a success since that one, and then, a few years ago, he had the very smart idea of trying to bring

Queer Eye back for the younger, newer digital audience and spearheaded our project. He's an incredibly impressive man, super kind and super sweet, always so lively. He's one of the most energetic men I've ever met, to the point where sometimes I will say to myself, OK, that is a lot of American! He's incredibly excitable on set.

> We needed to tell them, yes, we are here for you. Now be here for us. Even if you are going to try to tell us to live a life that is different to our true selves, we are still going to help you, because that is how evolved we are.

The reboot of the show happened so quickly. It wasn't just David who auditioned me; it was Michael Williams and Robert Eric, his partners in Scout Productions, and reps from Netflix and ITV, whose American studios produce our show. My audition process was hilarious. A friend of a friend who worked in Hollywood suggested me as a potential cast member. He said I'd retired already and would be perfect for it. I said, "No." I had no interest in being in entertainment. He gave my information to ITV anyway, they called, and again I told them, literally, I have no interest. I said, do not contact me again. There was a third try when I was asked if I would just give them twenty minutes on the phone. My husband said I should take the call. He said to me, "You talk about this all the time: Where are your people represented? In the straight or queer space? This is an opportunity to get to be a version of that. You might want to take this. It's unfiltered. It's real. It's not acting." I talked to a lovely man and those twenty minutes turned into two hours. At the end he said, "I've been looking for a version of you for six months. The auditions close tomorrow." I assumed he was saying it because he knew I didn't need the job. He said, "That couldn't be further from the truth. Hollywood people are the worst. Believe me, we'd tell you if you sucked."

He went to speak to Netflix and Scout and said he'd call in the next few days. Within twenty-four hours they'd called me back in. We did a Skype call and because there's a delay on Skype when you finish a call, I could see him jump up and scream, so I assumed they might've liked me. They invited me to go out to do chemistry tests with a bunch of forty or so other people. We were split out into groups of four and they'd watch who got along. Very early it became clear I was somebody they were trying to position other people with.

We went and did a live taping, unplanned, of what the first episode of the new *Queer Eye* would be, in somebody's house, looking through their stuff. We gave our comments and it was terrifying. I'd never been on camera before. A bunch of them get in your face; others are following you around. There isn't an angle or expression they missed. I wanted to cry, I struggled so much. I called my husband, said, "Don't worry, I did terribly, we can go back to our normal lives." Weirdly, a few days later they offered me the job. I had no idea why. I still don't know much about Carson on the original show. It was the UK original that I knew. But I have got to know Carson the person quite well since. We'll do appearances together, game shows in America. I adore Carson, he's so sweet with me and I know exactly the groundwork he did on my behalf. Without Carson, there would be no new version of the show. We have absolute respect for the originals, or the OG's as we call them, because they paved the way.

I was terrified doing *Queer Eye* all those years later, but they must've been fucking terrified back then, thinking of all the abuse you might get. It was a different time and place, on TV and out in the world. I can't imagine what being part of that absolutely groundbreaking team must have felt like. This was a time long before gay marriage, it even predates civil partnerships by several years in the UK. And yet their queerness was front and center in the show, absolutely unapologetically. There is no way you cannot see that as a risk as a TV presenter. Literally two years ago I was scared of it. They were super, super-brave men and I have mad respect for them. And they did it with grace, good humor, and absolute fearlessness. They led a conversation, majorly.

Cable was then as big as Netflix is now. Seeing gay men as real people, not just characters on TV, has a political impact. As wild as he can be, David Collins is not stupid. Far from it. He knew exactly what he was doing. He is well aware of the impact of both iterations of the show. He knew it would have a tangible part to play in social change. Stripping it all back, whether it's a gay, queer, or whatever person, however they choose to identify, I hope they feel inspired by our show to be whoever they are and to let the world see it.

Now I lean into my own gayness so hard. If you don't like it, so be it. We live in a very different world from the original cast members and get direct communication every minute of every day. We know the cultural impact the show's having, especially with the younger audience who I would like to believe are empowered to be who they truly are because they see others succeeding by being who they are. In any field, but in particular the creative field, you're expressing yourself and every facet of it. That was the one reason and only one reason why I wanted to join *Queer Eye*. I was in a very comfortable position. I didn't have to work again if I didn't want to. But I chose to and to put my whole life at risk because I wanted to change the conversations that I heard in my own communities.

There aren't many representatives of queer people of color on TV. Yes, there are Muslim people, for sure, but generally there isn't enough representation of any cultures that aren't white or Black. There aren't many Latinos, Far East Asians, Middle Eastern people, people who aren't white or Black. There are as many queer proponents in those communities as there are anywhere else. Yet you do not get to see us. I knew what a risk it was—I was hyper aware—and I wasn't surprised by the barrage of offensive shit I got as a result, but that was a risk I was willing to take. I was so sick of hearing the same conversations between people who were white or Black because we didn't have anybody to look to. There wasn't an inkling of queerness in our TV or movie references. I found it almost comical, but not really.

The assumption is that these communities are so backward that there is no one to draw on for representation. I want to scream and say, no, this is insane. The Western world has had representation for fifteen, twenty, thirty years now. That helps. Seeing someone on TV who is white and gay, you start to understand the nuances of that community. That helps, whether it's super obvious or subconscious. When a child, friend, or colleague tells someone that they're gay, they understand what it is because they've seen it on TV. When you live in a community that has never seen that before, it makes that conversation a lot more complicated. They do not know what you're talking about because it's strange and unique. Those people are not backward, they just have no references. They are so often denied the luxuries that the white Western community enjoys. That's why it's important there are more people like me, offering the full breadth of what our community represents.

We can't relate to the white guy's story. Our homes don't relate to that life. In our cultural life, it's important for us to have references and representatives of people who look like us and live a similar life to us. It won't be exactly the same, but there are community and religious similarities people can draw on when they finally say to themselves, "If he can come out, then so can I."

> I was so sick of hearing the same conversations between people who were white or Black because we didn't have anybody to look to.

All this is before we've even got to the racism that exists within queer communities, a subject that is never talked about enough. I joke about this and I have no idea why I joke about it because it really is not in the slightest bit funny. I'll say to my husband, he'd never have looked at me in England. He would've been totally out of my league. I struggle gauging so much in the UK. I had two boyfriends—one for four and a half years, one for two and a half—and that was it, they were the only two people I could persuade to sleep with me. Then I went to America, where they had a little bit of exposure to queer people of color, and I wasn't seen as a cultural leper.

I'm not trying to denigrate the UK. My friends and family are there. I love them and I love it. I am not saying that the UK is more racist than the US but what I can say, from personal experience, is that I suffered more racism in the UK than I did in the US. I'm more likely to get called something disgusting while walking down the street in the UK than I am here. So, I struggle to gauge it. And often people would want to sleep with an Asian or Pakistani person but they definitely wouldn't want to take them home. What are their parents going to say? That's a real issue I've had. On dating websites I used, the amount of times I would see "white only" or "no Asians" I found incredibly frustrating. I look at the stuff that's expected from hot guys on shows and I know that if I were to post a picture of myself and Antoni were to post a picture of himself— and he is one of my favorite people on the planet, he's beautiful, and I love him—I know the comments he's going to get versus the comments I'll get will be vastly different. He gets to be a sexual creature. I don't. I get to be the nice version of the Muslim guy that you see. There's nothing sexual at all about me. I'm not allowed to be, in any way. No matter how far I think we've moved along in this process, those comments run deep.

They don't know how far it runs. They expect to see sexy from a white person, possibly a Black person; they don't allow it from somebody else.

* *

When people talk about *Queer Eye* celebrating the shallow end of gay culture, I will hold my hands up and say, you know what? To a certain extent, it does. But some of us really do value feeling good by looking a certain way and there should be absolutely no shame in that. It doesn't mean that we don't contain further depths. What we do so much more is to establish, in a very short amount of time, an emotional connection with strangers and that, right from the first episode I ever saw of the show, was the beauty of it. It is our job, as it was of the Queer Eyes that went before us, to make sure that those people come to the end of the week loving themselves and caring for themselves in the best way possible. We use our diverse skills to facilitate those conversations. That's what the show is.

If by the end of the week the person doesn't have what I consider to be the best outfit in the world, I couldn't give a shit. I don't need to like it. It doesn't have to be something that I would wear. The point is that it has to make them feel good and that we have unlocked the thing within them that makes them feel good. That's all that matters. Yes, there is a touch of the superficial there. But everything we do is just to make sure they feel happier and can see a light at the end of the tunnel, where they could only see darkness before. We are dealing with people, mostly, who feel incredibly down on themselves. There is not a lot of hope, or at least they don't see a lot of hope. We are encouraging them to care for themselves, love themselves, to enjoy and take pride in who they are. What better way to show them than using physical tools to be able to facilitate that conversation?

My life itself hasn't changed so much since becoming part of the second wave of *Queer Eye*. I still live in the same house I lived in when the show started, go to the same gym, and shop at the same grocery store. My physical life hasn't changed. I still have the same husband—thank god!—and the same friends. The only thing that has changed is that I am more connected to people I would never once have been connected to. The major change is that I can feel, and am reminded regularly of this, what being an example to people means. It's so weird to get used to the idea of people always knowing your name on the street. It takes a lot of getting used to and I quite regularly say something nervous, stupid, or uncomfortable. But people reaching out and saying I am the first version of themselves they've seen on TV? That is what this was for. That's why I did it. That's why I finally took that call.

Breaking the representation barrier mattered. I don't suffer from false modesty, in any way, shape, or form, and shattering the glass ceiling of Asian gay men on TV mattered. I understand my position in the world now better than ever. Because I fucking fought for it. I had to put up with so much rubbish over the years. So, I can say with my head held high, that I am shedding light on something that hasn't been seen before, because I put myself in a personal position of great risk to do it. I feel like I've achieved something now. If I can say nothing else about my life, that I made people feel seen is more than enough. I owe all that to *Queer Eye*, to David, to the original Fab Five.

If I were on a show on Channel 4, I would hit a somewhat limited number of people. That's not the case with Netflix. This isn't about drinking their Kool Aid, either; it's about being lucky enough to be housed on a global platform. To have seen a person who looked and sounded like me on TV as a kid would've changed my life. I felt so alone back then, for the longest time, thinking nobody cares about our stories because you just don't see gay Asians anywhere. I felt low for a very long time. I wouldn't have felt so alone if I had seen someone else breaking out of their strict community. It means people in Pakistan see it. Anybody with access to a Netflix account can now see it. And they can be seen. They know I'm gay on TV, but I'm also gay at home, living a happy, open life with my husband . . . and they could, too.

Breaking the representation barrier mattered . . . I understand my position in the world now better than ever.

Tan France

Tan France has been a successful fashion designer behind the scenes for over fifteen years and has recently stepped into the spotlight as the star of Emmy-winning makeover hit, and Netflix re-boot, *Queer Eye*. Surrounded by an all-new cast, France is the witty wardrobe wiz leading the charge in the fashion department and is ready to make America fabulous again, one makeover at a time. This experience is so much more than just new clothes to the British-born fashion adviser, however, as it's also about real-life issues, changes, and acceptance on all sides.

Following the global success of *Queer Eye*, Tan recently released his *New York Times* best-selling memoir *Naturally Tan*, as well as the first season of his viral YouTube series *Dressing Funny*, which features him making over his celebrity friends, including Tina Fey, Amy Poehler, Nick Kroll, Miranda Sings, Pete Davidson, and John Mulaney. Tan also hosts a new global fashion design competition series for Netflix called *Next in Fashion*, which is sure to solidify him as one of the most influential tastemakers in the world.

Prior to his media career, Tan was the creative mind behind successful brands including the popular ladies' clothing lines Kingdom & State and Rachel Parcell, Inc. In his early years, he spent his summers working in his grandfather's denim factory while he secretly enrolled in fashion college in preparation to start a new chapter as a fabulous design star.

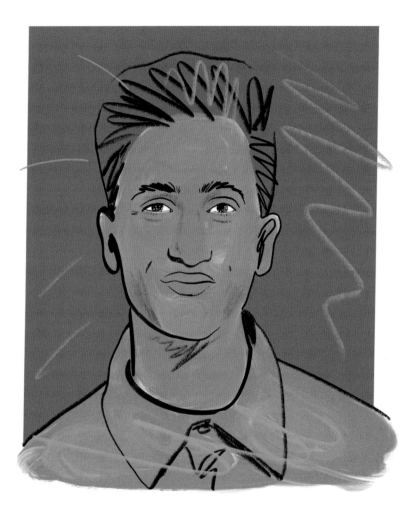

Illustration by Sam Russell Walker

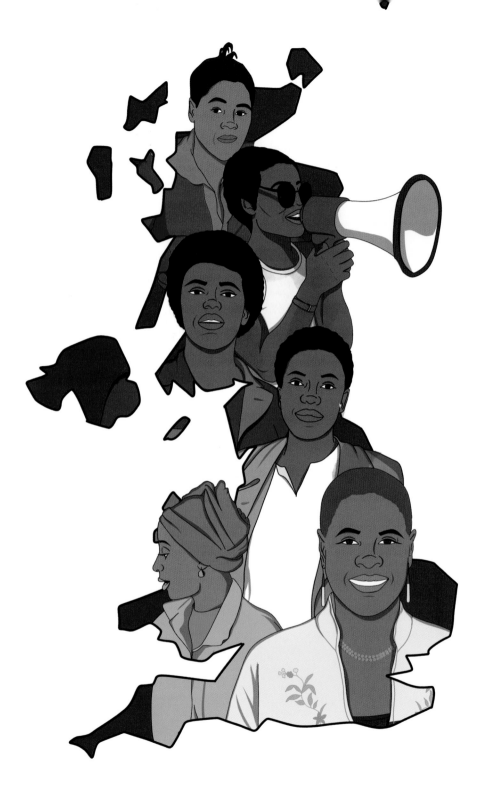

Parys Gardene

BLACK BRITISH LESBIANS

by Paula Akpan

Born and raised in London, and having lived in South London for the last three years, it feels almost shameful to share that I only began learning about the UK Black Women's Movement a few years ago. Having looked to African-American feminists as the default on theorizing Black women's liberation, I wasn't aware of the rich and complicated history of *Black Women Organising* in the UK that was, quite literally, on my doorstep.

As academics Akwugo Emejulu and Francesca Sobande note, "too often when we think about Black feminist theory and activism, we look to the particular Black American experience and seek to universalise and apply it to Europe," positioning racism and anti-Blackness as an import into European countries, like the UK, and erasing histories of anti-imperialist action from Black feminists in those nation states.[1]

1 Akwugo Emejulu and Francesca Sobande, *To Exist Is to Resist: Black Feminism in Europe* (London: Pluto Press, 2019), p.5.

Illustration by Parys Gardener

I quickly devoured as much as I could about Black women's activism in Britain in the seventies and eighties, which included protesting police harassment and brutality, advocating for fair pay and more childcare facilities for Black women workers, involvement in tenants' and squatters' campaigns, mobilizing against abuses within the education system, and organizing joint activities with Black women's liberation groups around the globe.[2] I read up on Black women's caucuses, mainly the Brixton Black Women's Group and the Organisation for Women of Asian and African Descent (OWAAD), and how they became critical spaces for campaigning across issues affecting Black women. These hubs were essential for women who had "become angry about male domination of groups like the British Black Panther Party and Black Liberation Front, and the suppression of gender issues within the Black movement," as well as those who "felt alienated by what they perceived as the reluctance of the women's liberation movement to address the realities of racism both within and outside of feminist groups."[3]

It felt like I was finding myself. Learning about the work that had been done before I was even born further bolstered my understanding of my positionality as a Black woman within Britain. I was able to draw parallels between my own experiences and those of the Black women who had rallied and protested for us to be seen and our needs to be met legally, economically, reproductively, emotionally, and more. Personally knowing what it means to feel deviant and like I was asking too much of Black men and white women to recognize how my Blackness and my womanhood are indivisible, the frustrations of Black women organizers resonated and reverberated around my body. But I had also found myself in other ways, primarily within my queerness. By the time I had begun researching the UK Black Women's Movement, I knew I was a lesbian and was trying to understand what it meant to be a Black lesbian; what it meant to desire and covet women and femmes within this Black woman's body under white heteronormativity.

2 Beverley Bryan, Stella Dadzie, and Suzanne Scafe, *The Heart of the Race: Black Women's Lives in Britain* (London: Verso, 2018), pp.150–154.

3 Brixton Black Women's Group, *Black Women Organising: The Brixton Black Women's Group and the Organisation for Women of African and Asian Descent* (London: Past Tense, 2017), p.i.

However, the more I researched, the more I understood that something critical and potent has also emerged during this period of mobilization of Black women: the demarcation of the Black lesbian within the activist space. Within a movement where issues specific to Black womanhood were seen as divisive within Black Power and white feminist spaces, in turn, issues of sexuality and lesbianism were pushed to the margins of the UK Black Women's Movement. And this was not an isolated issue. Speaking to a US context, lesbian feminist and scholar Barbara Smith writes, "I will never forget the period of Black nationalism, power, and pride, which, despite its benefits, had a stranglehold on our identities. A blueprint was made for being Black and lord help you if you deviated in the slightest way . . . How relieved we were to find, as our awareness increased and our own Black women's movement grew, that we were not crazy, that the brothers had in fact created a sex-biased definition of 'Blackness' that served only them. And yet, in finding each other, some of us have fallen into the same pattern—have decided that if a sister doesn't dress like me, talk like me, walk like me, and even sleep like me, then she's really not a sister."[4] In a space brimming with radical imaginations built around the needs of Black women, Black lesbians still found themselves navigating tricky and unstable terrain—both within and beyond Black women's liberation groups.

Britain in the eighties was aflutter with AIDS anxiety, rising homophobic attitudes, increasingly anti-Black immigration legislation, and Thatcherite assertions that the progressive policies from the "loony Left" around race, sexuality, and feminist issues had provided a breeding ground for militancy amongst these outsider groups.[5] Within a nation "struggling to recover its identity after the trauma of decolonisation,"[6] the Black lesbian was considered a dangerous threat to Britain's white Christian sensibilities; one who was simultaneously an "extremist Black" and a "diseased queer."[7]

4   Barbara Smith, *Home Girls: A Black Feminist Anthology* (New Brunswick: Rutgers University Press, 2000), p.xiii.

5   Anna Marie Smith, *New Right Discourse on Race and Sexuality: Britain 1968–1990* (Cambridge University Press, 1994), pp.42–43.

6   Ibid., p.25.

7   Ibid., p.35.

Considering the widely spread anti-lesbian and anti-gay discourse taking place, it's little wonder that Black British lesbians found themselves fearful of even entertaining the thought of joining Black women's groups. Reflecting on the Brixton Black Women's Group, which was founded in 1973, member Gail Lewis shares that she had questioned if she could even join as she had recently come out as a lesbian: "I thought about it for a long time and then thought no, I can't possibly go to a Black women's group because I'm a dyke, and then one day I just took the courage and went..."[8] Lewis goes on to highlight that "in the late seventies/early eighties, lesbianism was not seen as a political issue; it was seen as something you did privately and was, therefore, your own business."[9]

While some Black women within the Brixton Black Women's Group and OWAAD, the latter formed in 1978, felt that "sexual preference" was too unseemly to publicly discuss,[10] others prioritized confronting racism in Britain. One case study within *The Heart of the Race: Black Women's Lives in Britain* reads: "I think if you're a Black woman, you've got to begin with racism. It's not a choice, it's a necessity. There are a few Black women around now, who don't want to deal with that reality and prefer sitting around talking about their sexual preferences or concentrating on strictly women's issues like male violence. But the majority of Black women would see those kinds of things as 'luxury' issues ... If women want to sit around discussing who they go to bed with, that must be because it's the most important thing in their lives and that's all they want to deal with. In my mind, that's a privilege most of us don't have."[11] OWAAD members describe the question of sexuality being posed as "how could we 'waste time' discussing lesbianism, heterosexuality and bisexuality when there were so many more pressing issues."[12] In one fell swoop, the needs of Black lesbians are relegated as a non-issue in the grand scheme of Black women's liberation, undermined as if issues of sexuality are little more than schoolyard gossip or idle chatter.

Writing about the characterizations of lesbian and gay sexuality by those on the Left, Robin Podolsky asserts that "we were considered self-

8 Brixton Black Women's Group, *Black Women Organising*, p.5.

9 Ibid., p.8.

10 Ibid., p.33.

11 Bryan, Dadzie, and Scafe, *The Heart of the Race*, p.174.

12 Brixton Black Women's Group, *Black Women Organising*, pp.33–34.

indulgent distractions from struggle . . . [an example of] 'bourgeois decadence.'"[13] This is an all-too-familiar feeling for many of us; in the face of abject anti-Blackness and gender-based violence pertaining specifically to cis womanhood, Black queer folks dare to try to add inconsequential demands to the mix based on sexuality and gender presentation. We're told that once Black and/or woman-based equity is achieved, then we can focus on LGBTQ+ issues—but not before, because right now we're focusing on the real problems at hand. From this, a distrust can be fostered because it's clear that we're not "serious" about the struggle at hand, preferring to just fret about who we're sleeping with.

This distrust toward Black lesbians within the movement even resulted in a reluctance to share resources with them. When a Black lesbian group requested the use of the Brixton Black Women's Group's center for meetings in 1979/80, it created chaos among the members as "[they couldn't] possibly have lesbians meeting in our centre, what would the community say? They'll know."[14] It's abundantly clear that, to the minds of straight Black women organizers, Black lesbians didn't form part of the aforementioned community. Even at present, we're often erased from "the Black community" as a whole. I can't begin to count the number of times I've witnessed cis Black men and women tweet about how Black LGBTQ+ people put their "bedroom practices" ahead of their Blackness or a "Black Agenda," or even pit "the Black community" against the "LGBT community" when speaking on violence against Black people. We are invisibilized.

The myth of all feminists being nothing more than lesbians haunted Black women organizing groups. It "has acted as an accusation and a deterrent to keep non-Lesbian Black feminists from manifesting themselves, for fear it will be hurled against them," writes Barbara Smith.[15] With many Black men in the movement deeming Black feminism as divisive and splitting the movement, women within the UK Black Women's Movement were often labeled as "lesbians" by way of insult. With Black

13 Robin Podolsky, "Sacrificing Queers and Other 'Proletarian' Artifacts," *Radical America* 25.1 (1991), cited in Cathy J. Cohen, "Punks, Bulldaggers, and Welfare Queens: The Radical Potential of Queer Politics?" in *Black Queer Studies: A Critical Anthology*, ed. E. Patrick Johnson and Mae G. Henderson (Durham: Duke University Press, 2005), pp. 21–51 (p.27).

14 Brixton Black Women's Group, *Black Women Organising*, p.9.

15 Smith, *Home Girls: A Black Feminist Anthology*, p.xxxii.

lesbians deemed as "too ugly to get a man" or "man-haters," referring to Black feminists as such, lesbians or not, served as a way to undermine their work, while still centering men. Lewis remembers being asked,[16] "Do you think that Black feminism is becoming so strong now that all Black women are going to become lesbians?"[17] OWAAD members recall that the negative wielding of lesbianism was used with regularity: "It was...a weapon the brother could use against us, as supposedly illustrative of our lack of seriousness. Political men who had witnessed the disintegration of the Black movement and felt threatened by a vibrant Black women's movement could, and did, use it against us. Perhaps the favourite and most effective line of attack against Black women organising has been, and still is, that we were all 'frustrated lesbians.' And Black ones at that!"[18] Leveling such a charge was an effective tactic as it affirmed the belief that these issues were not relevant to Black women's overall political agenda.

We're told that once Black and/or woman-based equity is achieved, then we can focus on LGBTQ+ issues—but not before, because right now we're focusing on the real problems at hand.

In a climate where Black women organizers wanted to be taken just as seriously as their male counterparts, lesbianism and all its ills was an affront to their credibility as community organizers and political activists. "The attack was that we were all just a bunch of lesbians, implying that we had just got together to discuss our sexual preferences and weren't serious about taking anything else up which had relevance to the Black community. We were determined to prove them wrong on this because it was a label which really undermined what we had set out to do at the time," writes another *Heart of the Race* case study.[19]

Incorporating the lesbophobic violence and oppression that Black

16 Ann Allen Shockley, "The Black Lesbian in American Literature: An Overview," in Smith, *Home Girls: A Black Feminist Anthology*, pp. 83–93 (p.85).

17 Brixton Black Women's Group, *Black Women Organising*, p.17.

18 Brixton Black Women's Group, *Black Women Organising*, p.34.

19 Bryan, Dadzie, and Scafe, *The Heart of the Race*, p.150.

lesbians faced within their politic was not conducive for groups like OWAAD until they were able to find a way to make it acceptable to their cause. Founding members attempted to do this by stating that being lesbian was an inherently anti-imperialist position as "such self-definition . . . involved a challenge to both our traditional cultures and cultural imperialism."[20] An attempt to deflect criticism from OWAAD members who had noted an absence of discourse on sexuality, this reworked definition uprooted sexuality from the crude sphere of "sexual activity" and made it a more "politically respectable" topic.

The explosive issue of sexuality, alongside other structural problems like differing priorities with Asian members of the group, contributed to OWAAD's eventual demise in 1983. How lesbianism was dealt with within the Black Women's Movement demonstrated that, even within this deeply transformative period, many Black women organizers were not sufficiently equipped or simply prepared to hear the voices or concerns of Black lesbians. Having endured accusations of "splitting the movement" themselves, a similar structure was able to pervade these Black women organizing groups, this time with Black lesbians as the agents of divisiveness.

But unfortunately for many queer Black people, the reality is that we cannot, or don't want to, disengage from these spaces. Political scientist Cathy J. Cohen writes: "Any lesbian, gay, bisexual or trans-gendered person of color who has experienced exclusion from indigenous institutions, such as the exclusion many openly gay Black men have encountered from some Black churches responding to AIDS, recognises that even within marginal groups there are normative rules determining community membership and power. However, in spite of the unequal power relationships located in marginal communities, I am still not interested in disassociating politically from those communities, for queerness, as it is currently constructed, offers no viable political alternative . . ."[21] It's in a bleak political space that many of us find ourselves, with political agendas often demanding us to leave parts of ourselves at the door. In a conversation with my flatmate,

20 Brixton Black Women's Group, *Black Women Organising*, p.32.
21 Cohen, "Punks, Bulldaggers, and Welfare Queens" in Johnson and Henderson, *Black Queer Studies: A Critical Anthology*, pp. 21–51 (p.35).

writer and activist Rianna Walcott, we concluded that, when it comes to navigating Black communities as a Black queer person, divorcing ourselves completely from them is often not an option—there is an understanding that some of us have had to fortify ourselves to enter spaces with homophobic and transphobic elders and family members in lieu of robust Black queer spaces where we can feel whole. It feels like a sacrificing of self at times: political and familial communities in exchange for comfort. And, of course, there are others of us who have had to put our safety and well-being ahead of community ties, leaving us politically and, in some cases, physically homeless.

Learning about the plight of Black British lesbians during this era is one of the main reasons why I decided to go back to university to study a master's in Black British History. Through my research, I want to contribute toward the mapping out of Black lesbian lives in the UK: If the Black Women's Movement was a hostile space for Black lesbians, what were the alternatives? How and where did they organize and commune? And how did they process the violence that they were subjected to from all sides? Right now, I've got a whole host of questions that I hope to find some answers to over the years.

> When it comes to navigating Black communities as a Black queer person, divorcing ourselves completely from them is often not an option— there is an understanding that some of us have had to fortify ourselves to enter spaces with homophobic and transphobic elders and family members in lieu of robust Black queer spaces where we can feel whole.

I'm under no illusions as to what a difficult undertaking this will be, considering the way the figure of the Black lesbian has been historically maligned and demonized. The impositions of living under anti-Black heteronormative patriarchy have meant that many Black lesbians and queer women have often had to live their lives in the shadows—often prioritizing safety, family, and community above all. As a result, it feels like we have so few Black British lesbians and queer women, particularly within the activism sphere, whose stories we can locate and position within history. We deserve more than what we currently have; we are owed a much richer and robust understanding of our histories, our contributions, and our communities.

Considering how deeply personal and painful these experiences are, it has never been more urgent to do the work of documenting them before our queer elders pass on, with their stories departing with them. The labor and intellectual contributions of Black lesbians in the UK have long been obscured, erased, and deemed irrelevant by historians, but as novelist Alice Walker poignantly writes, people do not discard their "geniuses" and "if they are thrown away, it is our duty as artists, scholars, and witnesses for the future to collect them again for the sake of our children . . . if necessary, bone by bone."[22]

22 Alice Walker, *In Search of Our Mothers' Gardens* (New York: Harcourt Brace Jovanovich, 1983), cited in Patricia Hill Collins, *Black Feminist Thought* (New York: Routledge Classics, 2009).

Paula Akpan

Paula Akpan is a journalist, historian, and public speaker. A sociology graduate from the University of Nottingham, her work mainly focuses on Blackness, queerness, and social politics. She regularly writes for a variety of publications, including *Vogue*, *Teen Vogue*, *Independent*, *Stylist*, *VICE*, *i-D*, *Bustle*, *TimeOut London*, and more. She's also a published essayist, writing on Black women and community in Slay In Your Lane's anthology *Loud Black Girls*.

Paula is currently a fully funded master's student at Goldsmiths, studying Black British History with an interest in mapping out the lives and activism of Black British lesbians and queer women during the seventies and eighties. Alongside her writing and academic endeavors, she is also the director of a charitable incorporated company called The Black Queer Travel Guide, a digital resource prioritizing Black queer travelers and their safety as they navigate the world, through offering experiences, advice, and information on destinations around the globe.

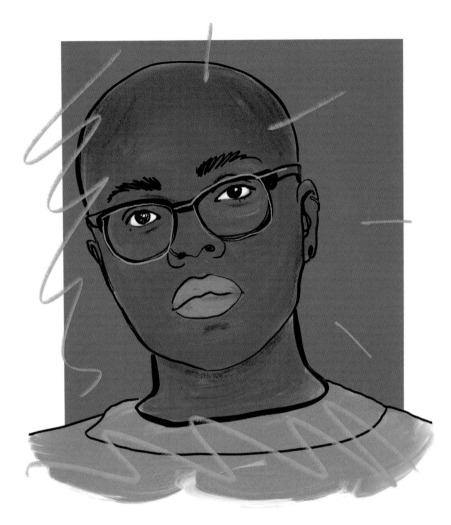

Illustration by Sam Russell Walker

Willi Ninja, Mother of the House of Ninja, was one of many legendary Mothers and Fathers of the Houses of the Ball Scen which from the 1970s to today has offered home, family, creativity and joy to Black and Latino queer and trans yout Ballroom culture draws on Harlem Renaissance dance culture and high fashion to create beauty and poise on a shoestrin

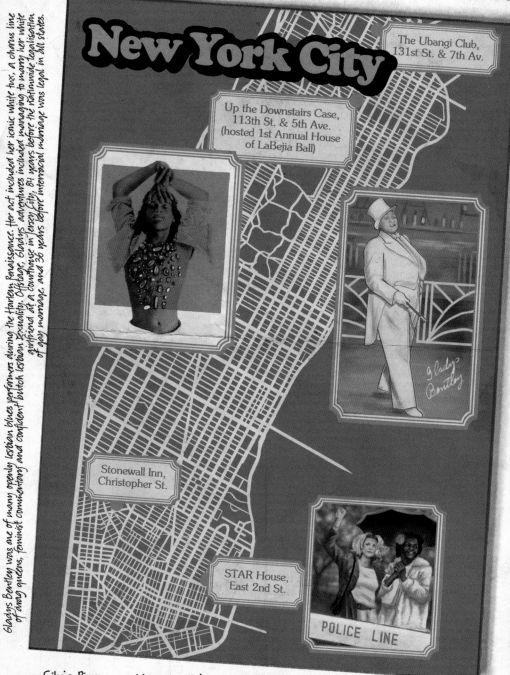

New York City

The Ubangi Club, 131st St. & 7th Av.

Up the Downstairs Case, 113th St. & 5th Ave. (hosted 1st Annual House of LaBejia Ball)

Stonewall Inn, Christopher St.

STAR House, East 2nd St.

POLICE LINE

9 Lady Bentley

Gladys Bentley was one of many openly lesbian blues performers during the Harlem Renaissance. Her act included her iconic white tux, a chorus line of drag queens, feminist commentary and confident butch lesbian sexuality. Offstage, Gladys adventures included managing to many her white girlfriend at a courthouse in Jersey City. 84 years before the nationwide legalisation of gay marriage, and 36 years before interracial marriage was legal in all states.

Silvia Rivera and Marsha P Johnson's STAR (Street Transvestite Action Revolutionaries) were prominent in the post-Stonewall explosion of queer political action. STAR House was an apartment offering refuge to homeless trans youth. Marsha and Silvia worked tirelessly for trans struggles to be included in the growing gay rights movement.

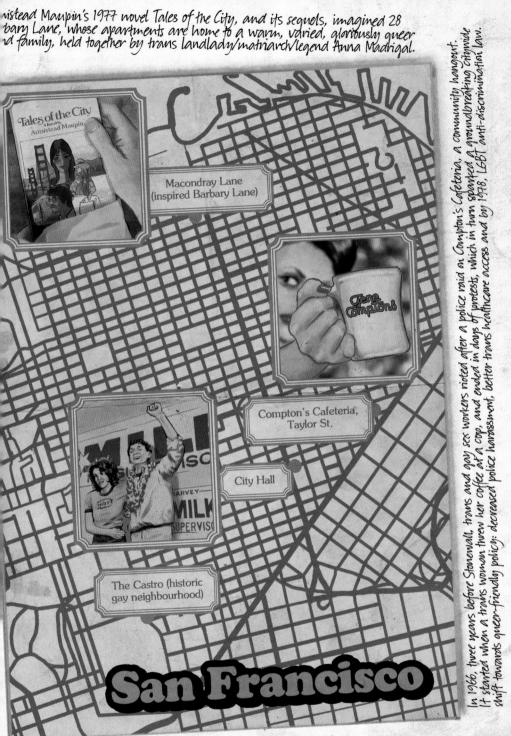

istead Maupin's 1977 novel Tales of the City, and its sequels, imagined 28 bary Lane, whose apartments are home to a warm, varied, gloriously queer d family, held together by trans landlady/matriarch/legend Anna Madrigal.

Macondray Lane
(inspired Barbary Lane)

Compton's Cafeteria,
Taylor St,

City Hall

The Castro (historic
gay neighbourhood)

San Francisco

In 1966, three years before Stonewall, trans and gay sex workers rioted after a police raid on Compton's Cafeteria, a community hangout. It started when a trans woman threw her coffee at a cop, and ended in days of protest, which in turn sparked a groundbreaking citywide policy: decreased police harassment, better trans healthcare access and by 1978, LGBT anti-discrimination law. shift towards queer-friendly policy:

One of the first openly gay public officials in the USA, Harvey Milk was elected to the city board of supervisors in 1977. Milk was murdered after only eleven months in office, but his political legacy shines on into the 21st century.

Words of Wisdom

04

Centering on the arts, these are words to feed your mind. The writers' intellectual rigor and passion for their subjects will inspire a deep dive into the worlds of art, literature, philosophy, and film. The beautiful thing about this book is recognizing that LGBTQ+ people have always been a part of society, but, tragically, these queer narratives have been forcibly erased or hidden. Words of Wisdom celebrates the lives and works of culture's most brilliant original minds. The entries are beautifully written works of art in their own right—Cassara's piece even mirrors the very form of an Almodóvar film—and they're wildly exciting. Enjoy!

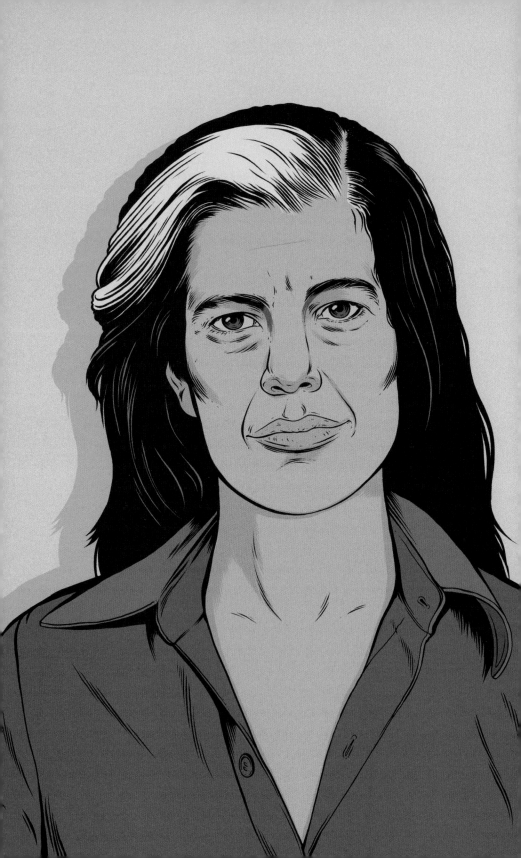

SUSAN SONTAG

by Amelia Abraham

I have a memory. I think I was about thirteen years old—probably wearing dungarees, or at least, that's how I like to imagine my proto-lesbian self. I was kneeling in my parents' living room and slotting a VHS into the recorder. The film was called *The Adventures of Priscilla, Queen of the Desert*, a nineties cult classic about two drag queens and a Transgender woman who go on a road trip across the Australian outback. It was the first time I had watched the film and I remember the opening scene distinctly: a drag queen in a big blonde wig pads onto the stage in a dingy club and starts doing a number, a lip sync to a dramatic seventies ballad. "What the hell is this?" I thought—I had never seen drag before, but I was instantly hooked. The film's strapline, which was printed across the VHS box, seemed appropriate: "Drag is the drug," it read.

Looking back now, there's one moment that really stands out in my mind from *Priscilla*, and that's when Guy Pearce's character, Felicia, sits atop the giant silver stiletto that's fixed to the roof of the tour bus the queens are traveling in, and performs a stellar lip sync to a song from the opera *Madame Butterfly*. First, we're given a close-up of the beauty

Illustration by Louise Pomeroy

look—high, arched eyebrows painted rudely onto Pearce's face—before the camera slowly pans outward to the reveal: the outfit, a glistening silver-sequined catsuit, then that ridiculous giant shoe, then the vast expanse of the Australian desert. The final touch, although I wouldn't quite clock it until I rewatched the film years later, is the graffiti that was sprayed onto the side of the bus in a previous scene: "AIDS fuckers go home." Horribly homophobic, yes, but Pearce's performance steals the shot, as if to say: "Whatever insult you throw at me, I'll always be fabulous."

I didn't know it yet, but watching this film was a pivotal moment in a long-standing love affair for me. A love affair with all things camp.

I've been consuming camp for as long as I can remember, before I learned that there was a word for it. Bands I loved, like the Spice Girls and Steps, were camp; so were the aunts in *Sabrina the Teenage Witch*, and my favorite childhood film, *Hocus Pocus*—mostly because it had Bette Midler in it, and anything Bette Midler does is camp. The first cassette single I bought was Cher's *Believe* (guilty), which was iconically camp—whether or not it flew under my seven-year-old radar. I loved to watch the high-drama performances on the Eurovision Song Contest, too. And remember that *Simpsons* episode "Homer's Phobia," where the godfather of camp and trash, the filmmaker John Waters, plays Marge's new gay best friend, the owner of a kitsch bric-a-brac store? Definitely my favorite *Simpsons* episode, and one of my earliest memories of camp.

A lot of us have camp tastes when we're children—some of us grow out of them, others grow up to be homosexual. It turned out that I am in the latter group, which meant that, at nineteen, now more familiar with the word "camp" and newly familiar with my own queerness, I wanted to know more about it. I understood that "camp" was often used as a way to describe someone or something effeminate, usually gay men. It was also a term used to describe a lot of the kind of films, TV shows, and pop music I liked. But what made them camp exactly, I wasn't sure. In all honesty, I was a little confused by the word. Was it a way of being? Or a way of seeing things? In fact, until I found the writer Susan Sontag's famous 1964 essay, "Notes on 'Camp,'" I don't think I could have put it into words.

Sontag's essay explains that camp is a sensibility, a "mode of aestheticism," "a private code," "a badge of identity, even." The hallmark of camp, she says, is the spirit of extravagance. It can be broad (as disparate as Bette Midler and John Waters are, their camp qualities unite them), but

Watching this film was a pivotal moment in a long-standing love affair for me. A love affair with all things camp.

certainly not everything can be camp; in fact, it's really quite particular. "Indeed the essence of camp is its love of the unnatural: of artifice and exaggeration," Sontag writes, adding that "camp sees everything in quotation marks." It is something that ties together theatricality, irony, and, sometimes, a certain self-awareness. While the aforementioned director John Waters's films know themselves to be camp (think a drag queen playing the matriarch of a suburban family), some 1930s musicals, for instance, are camp without meaning to be. Sontag divides it up into two neat categories for us: there is an accidental kind of camp, or "naive camp," she says, and a more "deliberate camp," that is aware of itself.

> "Camp" was often used as a way to describe someone or something effeminate, usually gay men. It was also a term used to describe a lot of the kind of films, TV shows, and pop music I liked. But what made them camp exactly, I wasn't sure.

As for the link between camp and homosexuality, "it has to be explained," muses Sontag (actually, she was going to call the essay "Notes on Homosexuality," but later changed her mind). The dandy writer Oscar Wilde was an early forerunner of camp, she notes—hence why "Notes on 'Camp,'" is dedicated to him—but of course there are many more examples. The word "camp" was used explicitly for one of the first times in the gay writer Christopher Isherwood's 1954 novel *The World in the Evening*. It could be read into the affected performances of Joan Crawford or Bette Davis, both gay icons in their own right. It surfaced in the gauche outfits worn by a closeted Liberace, the tongue-in-cheek appeal of the Village People, and as aforementioned, the questionable outfit taste exhibited by Cher. It has defined the gay Spanish filmmaker Pedro Almodóvar's colorful films and, of course, it is the main quality of a movie like *Priscilla*. "While it's not true that camp taste is homosexual taste," writes Sontag, "there is no doubt a particular affinity and overlap."

How do we explain this affinity and overlap? Well, camp, in all of its theatricality and fun, has been used by the gay community as a "solvent of morality," Sontag argues. In other words, it has been harnessed as a kind of self-defense mechanism or a clever mode of deflection, in a world that hasn't always been accepting toward LGBTQ+ people. Just as Guy Pearce's lip sync to *Madame Butterfly* on a giant silver stiletto detracts from the homophobic slur on the side of the bus, in Sontag's words, "camp neutralises moral indignation," and instead, she claims, it "sponsors playfulness."

Reading Sontag's essay as a nineteen-year-old, and one who was grappling with my sexuality, something seemed to slip into place. "Notes on 'Camp'" not only helped me to grasp the meaning of camp or to explain a lot of my weird cultural tastes, but it gave me something extra. Just months after confronting all of the difficult feelings that came with sleeping with a girl for the first time, in camp, I felt like I had inherited a special gift, a secret language, a very particular kind of humor. Camp felt like a weapon to use against the world when I might find myself up against homophobia—a source of joy in difficult times. But on top of that, I had gained something else. In Sontag, I had found a new queer hero.

**

Susan Sontag was born Susan Rosenblatt in New York City in 1933, to a Jewish family who were not particularly religious. Her father died of tuberculosis when she was five, and seven years later, her mother, Mildred, remarried a US Army captain called Nathan Sontag, from whom Sontag borrowed her name (according to some sources, because it sounded more American). Susan had a tense relationship with her mother, who was cold, distant, and apparently more interested in men and alcohol than her two daughters. They moved around a lot as Susan was growing up—first Long Island, then Tucson, Arizona, then to the San Fernando Valley in California, which, with its bungalows and palm trees, would have resembled the archetypal dream of American middle-class suburbia.

It was the young girl living here and attending North Hollywood High School, who—according to Sontag's biographer Benjamin Moser, at least—started to resemble the woman that Susan would become. In his mammoth 2019 biography, *Sontag*, he paints a picture of the extremely precocious teenager who would grow up to be one of the greatest minds of her generation, a writer, a critic, a philosopher, a fiction writer, a filmmaker, and a political activist. When she was just fourteen, Sontag's school principal told her parents that their daughter had read more books than her English teacher, and at fifteen, she was not only reading the highbrow literary magazine the *Partisan Review*, but had decided that she would write for it (of course, later she did). In her diaries, Sontag wrote about how she liked to pass an afternoon "immersing herself" in the collected works of André Gide.

> **In camp, I felt like I had inherited a special gift, a secret language, a very particular kind of humor. Camp felt like a weapon to use against the world when I might find myself up against homophobia—a source of joy in difficult times.**

Ever the overachiever, still at fifteen, Sontag started college at Berkeley, in California. If you choose to read her early diaries, which run from 1954 to 1963, and which were published posthumously by her son, David Rieff, Berkeley is where things get interesting from a queer perspective, as Sontag discovers herself and her sexuality. The girl in question's name was Harriet Sohmers Zwerling; she was five years older than Sontag and much more confident, while young Sontag was still awkward and insecure. "Harriet is quite tall, about 5'11," Sontag journaled right after they met. "Not pretty, but attractive all the same—she has a beautiful smile, and is, it was obvious to me, the minute I first talked to her— uniquely, wonderfully alive."

The two began a friendship that would quickly tip into a love affair, and Zwerling took Sontag to San Francisco to "teach her about the world of gay people." It was here that Sontag started making a list of gay slang that formed part of the basis for "Notes on 'Camp,'" ("drag," "swishy," "trade" are just a few examples). They went to a gay bar together, where the singer was a "very tall and beautiful blonde in a strapless gown," as Sontag remembers, as though describing one of the queens in *Priscilla*. "I wondered about her remarkably powerful voice. Harriet—smilingly—had to tell me she was a man." That night, Zwerling and Sontag slept together for the first time. "I know the truth now, I know how good and right it is to love," Sontag jotted down privately. "I have somehow been given permission to live."

Her words—written in a rush of joy—made me feel connected to something bigger than me; this night was not dissimilar to the first time I had been to a gay club and slept with a girl, fifty years later. But until I read these diaries, these were the kinds of experiences I had only read about in the context of gay men. Finally, here was someone with the same experience, albeit across decades and an ocean.

Sadly, Sontag's relationship with Harriet was stopped short when she won a place at college in Chicago. Partly grappling with her sexuality—and what her attraction to women might mean for how the rest of her life might play out—in Chicago, Sontag seemed to suddenly abandon her journey into exploring relationships with women, and met Philip Rieff, a lecturer with whom she found an instant intellectual connection and academic admiration. They got married almost immediately. She was still only seventeen. Two years later, at the staggeringly young age of nineteen—the same age at which I was just discovering my sexuality, gay bars, and Sontag's work—she gave birth to her first and only child, David.

According to Moser, Sontag didn't take all that well to family life, finding it confining, suffocating even, and so she applied for a teaching job to regain some autonomy. Eventually, when she was awarded a spot to study at Oxford University, she decided to leave her marriage and son behind in America—and on 5 September 1957, she set sail for Europe. She only lasted a few months at Oxford before tiring of its stuffiness and eloping to Paris, where she would rejoin Zwerling. They rekindled their romance and started living together in a hotel, with Sontag making money by doing walk-ons in New Wave films. This rekindling was, apparently, the motivation she needed to return to America and end her marriage, handing Rieff a letter that would lead to a divorce, and years of animosity and custody battles.

At this point, Sontag moved to New York with David and began the next chapter of her life. The year was 1958, and until now Sontag had only written one book, the book on Freud that she—according to Moser at least—had ghostwritten for her husband. She set her mind to writing her own work, and in 1963 she published *The Benefactor*, an experimental philosophical novel that won her praise from the likes of Hannah Arendt and Jacques Derrida. But it remained a niche book, confined to lofty literary circles. Really, it was "Notes on 'Camp,'" published one year later—and her first contribution to the aforementioned magazine

Partisan Review—that blew up in the media, with some outraged that this "language of homosexuals" could be deemed worthy of such study, others finding the essay to be brilliant. Either way, it earned Sontag instant fame, putting her on the map as the literary woman about town and cultural commentator whose voice would inspire and intimidate thousands of young writers like myself for generations to come.

**

After I first read "Notes on 'Camp,'" I went in search of Sontag's other books, and found that, similarly, they made other intangible ideas feel tangible. They took on nebulous topics I had spent a lot of time thinking about but had struggled to theorize. *Against Interpretation*, which contains "Notes on 'Camp'" and which was published in 1966, questions the ways that we are taught to respond to works of art, through thinking and feeling. *On Photography* (1977) looks at the complex relationship between photography and voyeurism, and *Illness as Metaphor* (1978) asks how and why we imbue certain illnesses with meaning. As I consumed her always considered, always eloquent writing, I noticed that Sontag seemed to give equal gravitas to what we might consider "high culture" and "low culture," always keen to analyze the things that the rest of us think of as ordinary. This seemed to me like a good way of looking at the world. As her son, David, famously said of her: "My mother was someone who was interested in everything."

But it wasn't just through her writing that I got to know Sontag; it was through photographs, too. Of which there are many that stand out to me. One is the shot of her taken in New York City by Jill Krementz, in 1974, in which she is smoking a long, thin cigarette nonchalantly, and staring directly into the camera, holding our glare. Another is the beautiful and very well-known 1975 Peter Hujar portrait of a youthful-looking Sontag lying on the bed in a ribbed sweater, gazing upward absentmindedly. And then, of course, there are the images of her taken later in life, with her (practically trademarked) thick gray streak of hair jumping out of the frame, many of which were captured by her long-term lover, the renowned photographer Annie Leibovitz. To this day, the only thing that makes me feel OK about my own rapidly graying hair.

After Harriet and Philip, Sontag had a string of relationships with both men and women, but her relationship with Leibovitz was arguably her most significant. They met in 1989, when Leibovitz was taking Sontag's headshot for the book *AIDS and Its Metaphors*, a follow-up to *Illness as Metaphor*, that examined the cultural connotations of the HIV virus, which was ravaging the New York City in which Sontag lived at the time. According to Moser's book, Sontag and Leibovitz instantly started a relationship, but when Sontag's assistant asked her about it, she initially denied it, and bristled at the use of the term "lesbian," saying that she didn't like labels, particularly that one. From talking to countless people who knew the couple, Moser describes how Sontag was cruel to Leibovitz, mocking, patronizing, sometimes tormenting her.

As I consumed her always considered, always eloquent writing, I noticed that Sontag seemed to give equal gravitas to what we might consider "high culture" and "low culture," always keen to analyze the things that the rest of us think of as ordinary.

Their relationship was the longest of Sontag's life, lasting fifteen years, but both women were famously private about it, at least until after Sontag's death in 2004. Controversially, in the autobiographical book *A Photographer's Life 1990–2005*, Leibovitz published photographs of Sontag naked, as well as images of a vulnerable, brittle Sontag in her hospital bed, not long before cancer (leukemia) took her life in 2004. That Sontag never came out publicly is something that she has been criticized for. But as the incredible New York writer, and Sontag's friend, Fran Lebowitz says in the documentary *Regarding Susan Sontag*, "This is an unfair thing to say about anyone, but to me it's an age thing—for someone my age it is a private thing . . . for someone my age it has to be a secret thing." The gay American poet and cultural critic Wayne Koestenbaum, who is also in the documentary, takes another approach: "Does the author of 'Notes on "Camp"' have to come out?" he asks.

From Sontag's writing, it's clear that she struggled with her own sexuality, but that this struggle drove her passion, her work: "My desire to write is connected to my homosexuality," she wrote. "I need the identity as a weapon to match the weapon that society has against me. I am just becoming aware of how guilty I feel being queer." These words have made me question why I have forged a career writing mostly about my own sexual identity as well as LGBTQ+ issues, whether it's a kind of self-defence mechanism, or a way of owning my own narrative.

Choosing to only write about her sexuality privately suggests that Sontag was perhaps ashamed of this part of herself. Or perhaps she simply felt that her sexuality was no one else's business. Or perhaps it was more complicated than that; Susan had a son, she was a very public figure, and she was often condescendingly labeled a "woman writer"—she may have felt compromised, or like she was up against enough already. Plus, to put things into perspective, she met Leibovitz at the height of the AIDS epidemic (highly stigmatized and described by some as the "gay disease"), homosexuality itself was still illegal in parts of America until as late as 2003, and Sontag was living in a time when there were very few gay or bisexual women in the public eye. Many people did know about her love life, of course, but for her to discuss it more openly may have impacted her career, her family, her personal relationships.

In many ways, Sontag was a victim of the time in which she lived, a time when same-sex love affairs were often shrouded in secrecy, when a lot of people lived "in the closet." That David Rieff, Benjamin Moser, and Annie Leibovitz have exposed so much of Sontag's intimate life since her death brings up ethical questions about a person's right to privacy when they are no longer with us. But it has also given more of her queer history to the world, and in doing so has allowed people like me to discover her as a (complicated) role model, to think of her in the canon of great LGBTQ+ thinkers along with the likes of James Baldwin and Gertrude Stein. Sontag's diaries remain a rare and honest testament to what it means to be a young woman falling in love with another woman for the very first time. I both see my own experiences in them and feel grateful that I am living in what is, for the most part, a much more accepting era.

Today, when I revisit "Notes on 'Camp,'" I find a lot of it to still ring true. But in a time when gay culture isn't quite so hidden as it was in Sontag's day, and there hopefully isn't quite so much "moral indignation" around homosexuality in the West, you have to ask whether camp holds the same importance or meaning, whether we still need a "solvent of morality" or "a private code." When I had the chance to interview the "godfather of camp" John Waters a few years ago, I mentioned the word "camp" to him offhand and he sounded shocked. "Camp!" he exclaimed, "I don't know anyone that would ever say the word 'camp' out loud, it's like an 80-year-old gay man in a 1950s antique shop under a Tiffany lampshade." If even the connoisseur of camp is beginning to see it as irrelevant, I thought, has its elusive nature finally got the better of us?

Sontag's diaries remain a rare and honest testament to what it means to be a young woman falling in love with another woman for the very first time. I both see my own experiences in them and feel grateful that I am living in what is, for the most part, a much more accepting era.

It was certainly starting to feel that way, at least until 2019, when the Metropolitan Museum of Art in New York chose camp as the theme for their annual lead costume exhibition, and for the celeb-packed Met Gala that goes with it. Sontag's essay was the bible for the show, with curator Andrew Bolton building an entire exhibition around camp's influences on fashion. Articles entitled "What Is Camp?" sprang up across the internet. Harry Styles channeled camp on the Met Gala red carpet in an effeminate Gucci look. Lady Gaga appeared in a magenta dress so big that several assistants had to carry her train. Joan Collins dazzled in a high-camp, white and feathered Valentino dress. Suddenly, camp was back on the agenda.

Over the last few years, other interrogations of camp have appeared within queer circles. The avant-garde gay filmmaker Bruce LaBruce wrote a manifesto for "camp/anti-camp" that broadened camp's definition for the twenty-first century ("Conservative Camp: Sarah Palin" or "Bad Straight Camp: Arnold Schwarzenegger and Jeff Koons") and arguing that, since gay culture has become ripe for co-option, camp is now basically everywhere. Then there's ButchCamp, the Instagram account celebrating "camp" in dyke culture. A whole breed of camp of its own, dyke camp is described by one excellent article on *The Outline*: "Dyke camp is not camp as we know it, the aesthetic sensibility derived from the gay community that glorifies kitsch and irony; the camp of *Priscilla, Queen of the Desert* and Rita Hayworth, Bette Davis, and RuPaul," writes Mikaella Clements, the article's author. "Rather, it's a movement directed, for the first time, not by the tastes of gay men but gay women: a specific brand of humor, manners, and sensibilities guided by lesbian identity." Elsewhere, there's the work of Madison Moore, the academic whose book *Fabulous: The Rise of the Beautiful Eccentric* builds on camp, arguing that fabulousness—in both style and behavior—is a defiant response to the struggles of living while marginalized, particularly for queer people of color.

Look hard enough and it's obvious that camp still captures the cultural imagination, unfolds and evolves over time. While Sontag acknowledged the relationship between camp and homosexuality, she has been deeply criticized over the years for suggesting that camp is apolitical, a matter of "style over substance." I have to disagree; I have known camp to be deeply political, and I believe that—as someone observing it firsthand in gay bars, and struggling with her own experiences of moral indignation—Sontag would have understood it this way, too, even if she didn't fully demonstrate that, driven (probably) by gay shame in distancing herself from her subject matter.

As a gay woman, camp, for me, has encapsulated a thread that has run throughout my life that is so much more than simply aesthetic. Like the scene in *Priscilla*, where camp becomes a mode of resistance, camp is my queer friends dancing alone to Madonna in their bedrooms as teenagers because they didn't fit in at school, it is seeing gender-nonconforming people performing as drag kings and queens to upend gender stereotypes, it is proud effeminacy in the face of a "masc for masc" gay culture that is still deeply misogynistic. It is in the pop culture in-jokes of GIFs and the irony that makes a great meme so hilarious and subversive. It is a particular type of trash we consume, from *Real Housewives* to *RuPaul's Drag Race*, when we are feeling overwhelmed with everything going on in the world. It is truly great pop music, it is celebrity feuds, it is catty one-liners.

Maybe to you, camp is none of these things, but that doesn't matter. It might be that no two people will ever entirely agree on what is and isn't camp—and in that sense, camp is as difficult to encapsulate as it has always been. For this reason, I think of camp the same way I think about Sontag's life and body of work: a gift that keeps on giving, but one that you'll never fully get the measure of. Like camp itself, Sontag remains elusive, unconquerable, and constantly outsmarting us. But her words were there when I needed them, giving me kinship, comfort, relief.

It might be that no two people will ever entirely agree on what is and isn't camp.

Amelia Abraham

Amelia Abraham is a London-based journalist and author. She has worked as an editor at both *VICE* and *Dazed*, and writes for *The Guardian*, *Vogue*, and other titles. Her first book, *Queer Intentions: A (Personal) Journey Through LGBTQ+ Culture*, was published by Picador in 2019. A first-person exploration of the mainstreaming of queer culture, Amelia goes to Britain's first same-sex wedding, travels to RuPaul's DragCon in LA, parties at Pride parades across Europe, and investigates the violence experienced by Trans people in New York City. Munroe Bergdorf described it as "an intersectional and insightful journey through the nuances of the queer experience." Amelia's second book, *We Can Do Better Than This*, is an edited anthology, asking queer pop stars, performers, academics, and activists the question: "If you could change something to make life better for LGBTQ+ people, what would it be?" The result is a definitive and global guide to queer activism. Outside of writing and editing, Amelia curates and speaks at events usually revolving around LGBTQ+ rights or queer culture. In 2018, she gave a TEDx Talk called "Why Feminists Should Support Transgender Rights." She wants to write the greatest lesbian rom-com of all time, but hasn't got round to it yet.

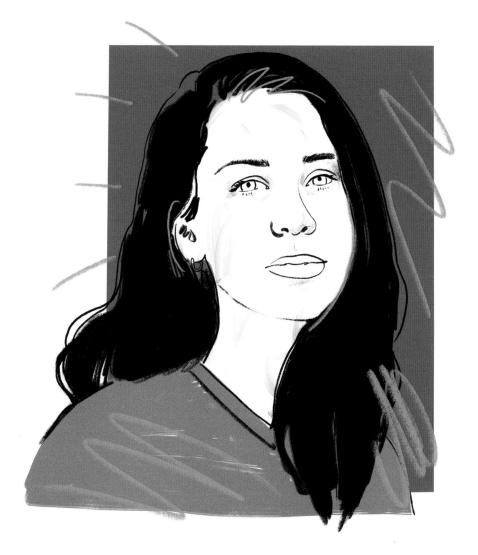

Illustration by Sam Russell Walker

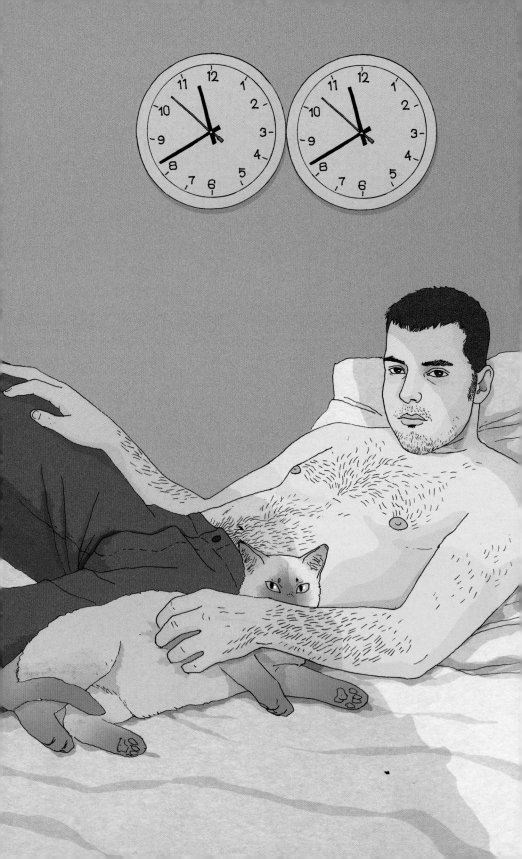

EVER FÉLIX GONZÁLEZ-TORRES!

by Hans Ulrich Obrist

"As a gay man . . . I am forced by culture and by language to always live a life of 'in-between.'"

—FÉLIX GONZÁLEZ-TORRES

The very first time I met Félix González-Torres was at the Noho Star, in New York. A few years prior, Dominique Gonzalez-Foerster had told me how inspirational they found him and his work, how he took art off the wall, and how for him art was no longer about occupying space, but about creating a genuine interaction between the work and the viewer. In González-Torres's eyes, art should create a resonant generosity and engagement. He would make works of art that slowly disappeared as people took

Illustration by José Angel Nazabal

them home, or works that were about the body, without ever showing one. Our first meeting was about exactly this: González-Torres led an intense conversation about the role of the body and its representation within forms of art that were prevalent at the time.

He described this trend as a "kitsch of the body," criticizing the ways in which artists would cast body parts in plaster or bronze in order to talk about bodies, and noting how the body and its representation are far more complex than any sculptural copy:

[. . .] the body at this time in our history, at this time in our culture, is defined not just by the flesh but is defined also by the law, by legislation, by language first of all. Therefore, when we feel pain in the body, when we feel decay in the body, when we feel pleasure in the body, all those issues are very much related to the law or the symbolic order, in that case to the phallocentric order.[1]

For his early show at Andrea Rosen Gallery in New York, in 1990, González-Torres pushed the ephemerality of art to its extreme by creating an exhibition that could potentially disappear altogether. Comprising individual stacks of paper and candy, these slowly diminishing edifices resonated with the presence of loss within the artist's life: "At that time I was losing Ross, so I wanted to lose everything in order to rehearse that fear and just confront that fear and perhaps learn something from it. So I wanted even to lose my work, this stuff that is very important in my life, I also wanted to learn to let go."[2] The stacks of paper and candy were a physical manifestation of the idea that piece by piece they could be taken away by the visitors. González-Torres did not consider the static forms to be works of art in themselves, but rather the inherent value and meaning of the piece lay precisely in its mutability and slow demise within the space of the gallery. As his long-term partner, Ross Laycock, was dying of AIDS-related illnesses, González-Torres positioned the stacks as symbolic representations of his body and its gradual diminishment. As each piece of paper and each piece of candy was removed, causing each stack to grow smaller, so the body was placed in a parallel state of steady decline. Representing his partner's body in this way engendered a cathartic

1 Félix González-Torres in conversation with the author, 1994.

2 Ibid.

process of letting go, a strategy of acknowledging and embracing the lack of control that he had over the passing of his loved one.

The subtlety with which González-Torres approached themes of death and desire surprised audiences at the time. In line with the body art trend from which he distanced himself, they were perhaps accustomed to and expected a certain explicitness within the depiction of homosexual desire. As he said to Robert Storr: "Every time they see a clock or a stack of paper or a curtain, I want them to think twice."[3] In rethinking how ideological institutions could be challenged, he insisted that the only way to actually change the power structures in place was to become part of them; they will always replicate themselves and, he said, "if we are attached to them like a virus we will replicate together with these institutions."[4]

What is striking about González-Torres's understanding of art's function is his radical approach to the distinction between a copy and an original; for him, there are no originals. By placing at the center of each piece a certain set of parameters and conditions for production, which more often than not relied upon the triggering of the work via the audience, González-Torres utilized instability and precarity as key factors within this practice. This instability was something that spoke to his personal experience of being a gay man: "I enjoy that danger, that instability, that in-between-ness. If you want to relate it to a personal level, I think as a gay man that has a lot to do with my ways of being in which I am forced by culture and by language to always live a life of 'in-between.' "[5] This created an awareness for the viewer of the different movements and the given parameters that allowed such movements for different bodies. The responsibility of the viewer, specifically the necessity for their active engagement and acknowledgment of an interaction between bodies, was what rendered the work complete.

The ways in which the lack of an original challenged the art market is rooted in González-Torres's activism. The lack of distinction between the private and the public was also a subject treated in the work he made as part of Group Material (1979–96). Established by Julie Ault, Mundy McLoughlin, and Tim Rollins, the artist collective adopted an activist

3 González-Torres in conversation with Robert Storr, 1995.

4 González-Torres in conversation with the author, 1994.

5 Ibid.

stance against the art world's dependency on the market, which was fueled by the prevalence of Neo-Expressionist painting at the time. Their projects were durational and collaborative, such as the *AIDS Timeline* project (1989), with which González-Torres was involved. According to Group Material, this timeline, which reconstructed the narrative of AIDS as a counter to what was being propagated by the federal government, "indicts the government's inaction and society's complicity in that inaction."[6] A collaboration between González-Torres and agnès b. also addressed the question of body ownership and the self, which extended across private and public spaces. Together, they produced a T-shirt that read "Nobody owns me" on its back.

> **He took on the role of infiltrator, a kind of spy, whereby as a gay man he could no longer be identified and isolated as the enemy, but rather could subtly subvert people's ideas and prejudices about homosexual desire through his work.**

González-Torres was an artist who inspired multiple generations, both those of artists who came after him, but also those who came before. A great example of this is Christian Boltanski, an artist thirteen years González-Torres's senior and for whom he shared a mutual admiration. Boltanski was inspired by the idea that one could actually take the artwork away, the dispersion of a work, and dissemination. I remember my first meeting with him, with Annette Messager. They told me that the exhibitions we remember are the ones that change the rules of the game. González-Torres's work did just that: by allowing people to actively engage with the work, to take part of it home, he bridged the gap between the work and the viewer. Moreover, the engagement wasn't merely allowed, it was essential to the work: "I need the viewer, I need a public for that work to exist. Without a viewer, without a public, this work has no meaning."[7] A duality was therefore created in which the

6   Richard Meyer, exhibition brochure, *AIDS Timeline*, University Art Museum, Berkeley, 1989.

7   González-Torres in conversation with the author, 1994.

viewer had a responsibility to render the work complete. This concept was hugely inspiring to me and prompted the idea for my touring exhibition, *Take Me (I'm Yours)* (1995–2017), in which visitors were permitted to take away the works on display, such that the exhibition itself would enter into a process of dispersal. González-Torres was involved in this project, and his works became an integral part of it.

The idea to change the rules of the game also became the trigger for *do it*, a project that Boltanski, Bertrand Lavier, and I initiated in 1993. For *do it*, we thought about the ways in which art could travel, about how we could create other structures of dissemination. The idea for the exhibition was to present "how-to" manuals, instructions for each work that would allow anyone in the entire world to reproduce and reperform the exhibition. At its center, *do it* began from an interest in the idea that art could travel not as object but as a kind of score, so that it could be performed over and over again, many years from now, and at different places simultaneously.

The conceptual approach of *do it* found multiple resonances with González-Torres's work. For his works using stacks of paper and candy that could be taken away, he had precise instructions about how they were to be produced and displayed. Despite the inevitable element of unpredictability and instability inherent to the process of interpreting a set of instructions that could never be fully controlled, they nevertheless resulted in the stacks having a clear form regardless of the context in which they were installed. It is for this reason that we invited González-Torres to participate in *do it*, and since the inauguration in 1995, his work has been one of the most frequently realized during the project's actualization in more than 160 countries worldwide. The candy stacks have been shown in different ways, but always under the guidance of his instruction; it is a case of repetition and difference—a repetition that grew from the difference in itself.

During my time working for museum in progress, in Vienna—a museum, which, much like *Take Me (I'm Yours)*, was in itself about dispersion—we invited González-Torres to be part of a billboard project for Austrian Airlines. Among other artists, he was asked to produce an advertisement campaign that would be shown on billboards all over the city; he decided to make a portrait of Austrian Airlines. González-Torres's portraits frequently create an intimate presence through bodily or physical absence. They often exist only as titles, referring to individual lives of significant meaning, but which remain unknown to the viewer. González-Torres related his understanding of portraits to the connotations that one can associate with a photograph, which he found to be the most interesting aspect of its interpretation: "In order for us to read a photograph we have to have a language transaction. The only way we can read a photograph is through language. So I decided to go the other way, to get rid of the image and just use the language."[8] It was in this vein that González-Torres made a corporate portrait of the airline: in silver letters on a green background, numerous destinations were shown, accompanied by the year Austrian Airlines flew there for the first time. Within this image, people's personal memories were connected with collective memory and the political changes that were occurring in these places.

The exhibitions we remember are the ones that change the rules of the game. González-Torres's work did just that: by allowing people to actively engage with the work, to take part of it home, he bridged the gap between the work and the viewer. Moreover, the engagement wasn't merely allowed, it was essential to the work.

In the same year that we completed this billboard project, I also invited González-Torres to partake in a project at the Musée d'Art Moderne de la Ville de Paris, where I was working as the migratory curator. Being the migratory curator meant that during this time I would invite artists to the museum, and they would realize an exhibition that, in whichever way they chose, would migrate from the building of the museum and appear in other, unexpected locations: the *migrateur* project. González-Torres had a very romantic relationship with Paris. Whenever he came, he would stay at the Little Palace Hotel—the same hotel that he and Laycock would go to—their favorite place in the city. After Laycock passed away, he would return to the same place in homage to the time spent there with him. By this time, we were well acquainted and would

8   Ibid.

send each other letters. He told me about the slow sunsets in Miami—a place he often returned to during his illness and where his life came to an end far too soon. While we were working on his exhibition at the Musée d'Art Moderne, we would start our day by going to Carette, a little patisserie in Trocadéro, where we had breakfast before we went to the museum. One day during breakfast, he had this wonderful idea that the exhibition would not only happen in the museum's public spaces but should also happen in the employees' offices. His idea was to have fresh flowers in the museum's offices in order to create a more human, positive, and gentle environment. This beautiful idea of subtly transforming the institution by placing these flowers in the office has stayed with me ever since.

Hans Ulrich Obrist

Hans Ulrich Obrist was born in Zurich but now lives in London, where he is artistic director of the Serpentine Galleries. Prior to this, he was the curator of the Musée d'Art Moderne de la Ville de Paris. Since his first show *World Soup (The Kitchen Show)* in 1991 he has curated more than 300 shows.

In 2011 Obrist received the CCS Bard Award for Curatorial Excellence, in 2015 he was awarded the International Folkwang Prize, and in 2018 he was presented with the Award for Excellence in the Arts by the Appraisers Association of America. Obrist has lectured internationally at academic and art institutions, and is contributing editor to several magazines and journals.

His recent publications include *Ways of Curating* (2015), *The Age of Earthquakes* (2015), *Lives of the Artists, Lives of Architects* (2015), *Mondialité* (2017), *Somewhere Totally Else* (2018), and *The Athens Dialogues* (2018).

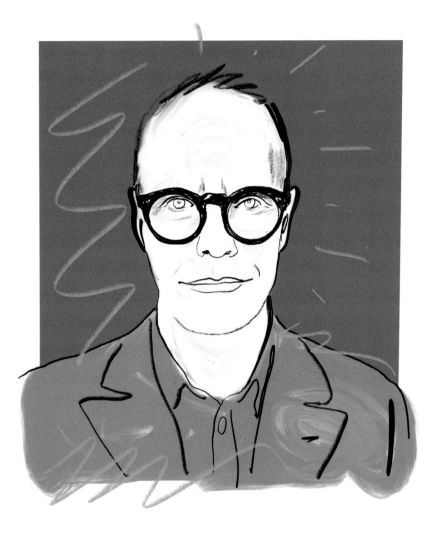

Illustration by Sam Russell Walker

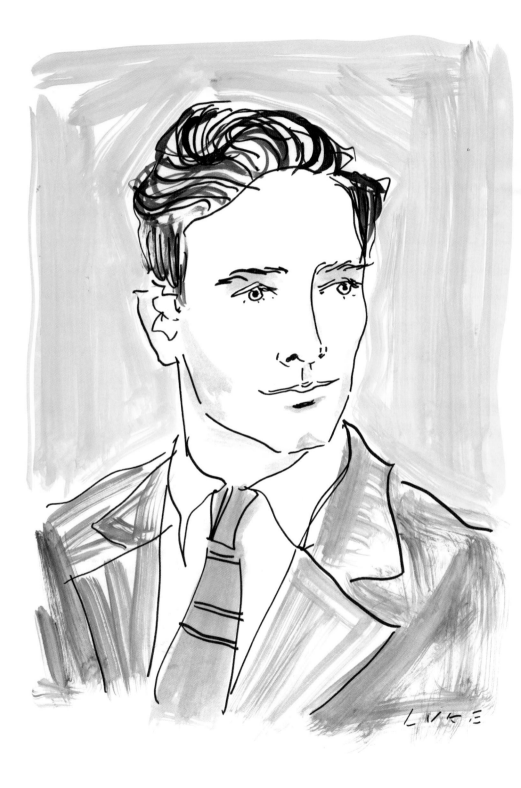

PIER PAOLO PASOLINI

by Juliet Jacques

Growing up, I didn't have many ideals of what a queer life might look like, and most of the ones available through television felt uninspiring to me. It wasn't so much that I was looking for people who were Trans like I was—although a few options *would* have been nice—nor that I was seeking anything so dreary as a *role model*, whose behavior had to always be perfect to avoid discrediting us in a society endlessly looking for reasons to hate us. What I wanted, as actor Laverne Cox would later call it, was a *possibility model*: someone who would show me that you could be lesbian, gay, bisexual, Trans, or queer *and* achieve something of worth, maybe in a field traditionally open only to heterosexual, cisgender people.

As a student, having spent my youth desperately trying to fit in with heterosexual, cisgender people, I decided I was going to look for possibility models in film. Cinema had only seldom interested me before: music had been my passion. Through their record sleeves, my favorite bands had introduced me to European and arthouse films, which I had never quite picked up in the BBC2 or Channel 4 listings. Joy Division

---

Illustration by Luke Edward Hall

made me aware of German director Werner Herzog, through a reference to his *Stroszek* (1977) etched into the grooves of their compilation LP *Still* (1981); The Brilliant Corners put Jean-Pierre Léaud, the star of François Truffaut's coming-of-age film *The 400 Blows* (1959) on the cover of one of their albums; The Smiths had Candy Darling, the Transgender superstar from Andy Warhol's *Women in Revolt* (1971), on the front of their 1987 single "Sheila Take a Bow." I sought them all out and loved them, and so I decided to give myself a crash course in film studies, wondering if the world of cinema might provide some better inspirations than that of television.

One biography that really stood out was that of Pier Paolo Pasolini. He made me feel like I could do almost anything, as he did almost everything that I wanted to: filmmaker, actor, playwright, poet, novelist, journalist, political activist, and even (like me) a football fan and player. In the United Kingdom, he was primarily known as a director, having made twelve films, including his debut *Accattone* (1961) and *Theorem* (1968) with Terence Stamp, as well as the brilliant *The Gospel According to St. Matthew* (1964) and an adaptation of the ancient Greek myth *Medea* (1969), starring Maria Callas. His violent death also seemed to be linked to his film work; he was murdered in 1975, aged 53, shortly after finishing *Salò,* based on the Marquis de Sade's novel *120 Days of Sodom,* which affronted a number of powerful people in Italy with its brutal depiction of sexual domination in the final years of Mussolini's fascist regime—and was swiftly banned from British cinemas. In Italy, he was best known for his literary output, not all translated into English. Asked in his final interview how he defined himself, Pasolini replied: "On my passport, I say *writer.*" These days, as an author and filmmaker, I do the same.

Pasolini was born in Bologna—one of Italy's most left-wing cities—on 5 March 1922, six months before Mussolini took power in a coup known as the March on Rome. Throughout his life, Pasolini could not help but get caught up in his country's extraordinarily turbulent politics: when he was four, his father, Carlo Alberto, a lieutenant in the Italian army, identified 15-year-old Anteo Zamboni as the person who had attempted to assassinate Mussolini in Bologna on 11 October 1926, leading to Zamboni being killed and Carlo Alberto converting to fascism. The family then left Bologna; Pasolini returned to study literature at the university in 1939, having been writing poetry since he was seven. There, he became more interested in cinema, and captained the Faculty of Letters football team. (Clearly, he was a better player than me; I never got beyond the Under-12s B team at my local club, Horley Town, in 1993.)

One biography that really stood out was that of Pier Paolo Pasolini. He made me feel like I could do almost anything, as he did almost everything that I wanted to: filmmaker, actor, playwright, poet, novelist, journalist, political activist, and even (like me) a football fan and player.

He published his first volume of poetry in the minority Friulan language in 1942, and edited a magazine called *Il Setaccio* (*The Sieve*) until he was fired by its fascist director. He managed to avoid conscription into the Wehrmacht after the Germans occupied northern Italy and set up the puppet Republic of Salò in September 1943; his 19-year-old brother Guido died in a partisan ambush in February 1945.

As Mussolini's regime collapsed, Pasolini shifted toward communism. The reaction against fascism meant that at the end of World War II, Italy had Europe's largest Communist Party—the PCI—outside the Soviet Union, but Pasolini was slow to join it. Despite being an atheist, he spoke out against Pope Pius XII's decision to excommunicate communists from the church—an act that made Italy's orthodox communists suspicious of him, and marked him out in Italy's chaotic and still deeply conservative post-war political landscape. In September 1949, *L'Unità*—the PCI's newspaper—denounced the "deleterious influences of certain ideological and philosophical trends of the various Gides and Sartres . . . who pose as progressives, but in reality welcome the most deleterious aspects of bourgeois degeneration" after Pasolini was accused of sexual misconduct with three 16-year-old boys, in a time and place where *any* homosexual activity, whatever the participants' ages, was outlawed. While he did not deny the allegations, Pasolini said the right-wing Christian Democrat party instigated the criminal proceedings and informed the local press in order to smear him. Although he was ultimately acquitted of the indecency charges, he was fired from his teaching job and expelled from the local Communist Party, and he moved to Rome with his mother in 1950.

His literary career took off in the mid-1950s when he published his first important collection of Friulan poems and a novel, *Ragazzi di vita* (*Hustlers*), which brought an obscenity lawsuit. Pasolini was exonerated, but increasingly treated with suspicion by the Italian government and the tabloid press. He further alienated the PCI in 1956 when he published *Polemics in Verse*, a volume attacking Marxist intellectuals, but he regained their favor when they welcomed his second novel *Una vita violenta* (*A Violent Life*)—a story about young male hustlers in Rome's poorest districts who convert to communism—and wrote a column on a wide range of topics for the PCI magazine *Vie Nuove* from 1960 to 1965.

He worked with the great Italian neorealist director Federico Fellini on the script for *Le notti di Cabiria* (*Nights of Cabiria*) in 1957, and directed his first feature film, *Accattone*, in 1961. This story of pimps, prostitutes, and thieves aroused controversy, and his short film *La Ricotta* (1963), in which Orson Welles plays a filmmaker (obviously a stand-in for Pasolini) making a work about the crucifixion, was censored, with Pasolini tried for "offense to the Italian state and religion." Nonetheless, his film career continued, with international acclaim for *The Gospel According to St. Matthew* in 1964 and *Theorem* in 1968. He made a trilogy of bawdy adaptations of classic literary works, starting with Boccaccio's *Decameron* (1971), before Chaucer's *Canterbury Tales* (1972) and *Arabian Nights* (1974). *Salò* had its premiere at the Paris Film Festival on 23 November 1975, three weeks after Pasolini's death. It was soon recognized as one of the most extreme films ever made, showing four powerful men—a duke, a bishop, a magistrate, and a president—imprisoning eighteen youths in a palace and subjecting them to prolonged sexual torture and humiliation. Having long been aware of it, and put off for years by its foreboding reputation, I only saw it for the first time in 2018. I was surprised to find that it was, in places, strangely beautiful, balancing the authorities' exaggerated evil with acts of solidarity and defiance among the captives, who knew that the regime was behaving in such a decadent manner because it was about to collapse. It was also a bold, brave indictment of the ways in which absolute power corrupts absolutely, one that I think will give me courage in my own writing and filmmaking in future, which is testament to its force as a work of art.

The bleak brutality of *Salò* may have been the logical conclusion to a career spent looking at how political and religious persecution worked to suppress the social and sexual potential of the working class, but its utter pessimism was at odds with much of Pasolini's earlier work, which had a strong humanistic streak. In one of his most gentle and emotionally generous films, *Love Meetings* (1965), Pasolini took a camera around Italy, asking people for their opinions on various topics regarding love, sex, and sexuality, including homosexuality, prostitution, sex education, and virginity. His interviewees were drawn from all social classes; Pasolini was just as likely to solicit the views of children in city slums as he was to ask those of feted Italian poet Giuseppe Ungaretti or novelist Alberto Moravia. My favorite scene is where he interrupts Bologna FC—who won the Italian championship in the year *Love Meetings* was shot—and questions their star players, Giacomo Bulgarelli and Ezio Pascutti, about how their Catholic upbringing has affected their attitudes to sex, and if abstinence is necessary for them to perform at their best on the pitch. (Pasolini later tried to persuade Bulgarelli to appear in his *Canterbury Tales*, but sadly, the footballer declined.) The resulting film, released just three years before the student uprisings of May 1968, gave rise to new feminist and LGBT movements in Italy, shows a country struggling to escape its social conservatism and its recent manifestation in Mussolini's fascism. It also captures how attitudes were slowly changing, and could be changed further if people were pushed in the right direction— something that should make it inspirational to queer advocates and activists in a time of global reaction against our advances. Sharing his fascination with politics, sexuality, and football as I did, *Love Meetings* showed me how I might reconcile apparently divergent interests in my work, making a virtue (and plenty of humor) out of combining them in such a playful fashion.

Pasolini's ability to provide comradely critique of those on his side, and to engage sensitively with those who weren't, came across in his poetry as much as his interviews. In *Gramsci's Ashes* (1957), Pasolini wrote about Marxist philosopher and PCI leader Antonio Gramsci, who had died in 1937, aged 46, after eleven years in prison, having been arrested under the emergency laws that Mussolini introduced after Zamboni's assassination attempt. At Gramsci's trial, the prosecutor had said: "For twenty years we must stop Gramsci's brain from functioning." Given his father's support for Gramsci's jailers and his own persecution by right-wing forces, Pasolini identified strongly with Gramsci, but also wrote about being "with you and against you; with you in my heart, in the light, against you in the dark of my gut." Writing by Gramsci's grave at Cimitero Acattolico in Testaccio, the non-Catholic cemetery in Rome where a number of well-known English Romantic poets were also buried, Pasolini wrote about how he saw common people as the inheritors of ancient culture and values, preferring a left-wing politics based on instinct, joy, and agricultural practices to Gramsci's theorizing about how to struggle on behalf of the urban, industrial proletariat. Above all, Pasolini expressed sympathy for Gramsci's commitment to improving Italian society, and the tortures he suffered for it.

Pasolini also displayed a desire to engage with his enemies, to understand them, and to find some good in their intellectual and spiritual traditions. This could be seen in his interview with the great American poet Ezra Pound, who moved to Italy in 1924 and was captured by the US Army in 1945, being imprisoned in a tiny cage in Pisa after being charged with treason. By 1967, when they met, Pound—then aged 82—had all but stopped talking, doing a silent photo-shoot with Italian photographer Lisetta Carmi the previous year, but Pasolini persuaded him to discuss experimental Italian literature on television. They did not talk about Pound's support for Mussolini—perhaps Pasolini suspected that if Pound had not recanted by now, he never would, and felt a conversation about writing would be as brilliant as one about Pound's politics would be appalling. With regard to both Gramsci and Pound, Pasolini taught me how to form a healthy, critical relationship with the people who inspired me to write, make films, and to get involved with political activism; he showed me how to engage critically with the positive parts of their work, and how and *when* it can be productive to reconsider their mistakes.

Pasolini's generosity was most visible, and most sustained, in what I consider to be his best film, *The Gospel According to St. Matthew* (1964). It was the second of his I saw; the first was *La Ricotta*, a furious satire of how, in Pasolini's view, the Roman Catholic church neglected its duty to help the poor in favor of building monuments to itself, ending with a homeless man accidentally dying on a cross on Welles's film set. After this, I was even more amazed that *The Gospel*, made by an openly gay, committed Marxist, turned out to be such a quietly beautiful retelling of the story of Christ. Its (sparse) dialogue was composed mostly of the scriptures, as Pasolini felt he could not possibly improve on their poetry, but he emphasized Christ's words about caring for the disadvantaged; its cast consisted mainly of non-professional actors, with 19-year-old Enrique Irazoqui as Jesus.

> **Pasolini taught me how to form a healthy, critical relationship with the people who inspired me to write, make films, and to get involved with political activism; he showed me how to engage critically with the positive parts of their work, and how and *when* it can be productive to reconsider their mistakes.**

Aged 20 and learning my way around European and arthouse cinema, I was mesmerized by the economy with which Pasolini told the story, with its unfussy black-and-white cinematography and long periods of silence. The result was so beautiful that in 2015, the Vatican City newspaper *L'Osservatore Romano*—surely not a supporter of Pasolini during his lifetime—named *The Gospel According to St. Matthew* as the best film ever made about Christ. To me, that seems completely fair. As a teenager undergoing a long (and, to be honest, continued) existential crisis, I flirted with religion, desperate to discover a higher meaning. I never managed to persuade myself into Christian belief, but nor could I share the scorn for faith expressed by the New Atheist writers (especially Richard Dawkins) who were prominent around the time I saw Pasolini's *Gospel*. The film taught me an invaluable lesson as I began to write short fiction for the first time: to be open to ideas, faiths, and traditions that were not my own, or to which I did not subscribe, as doing so would allow me to create characters and narratives with far more subtlety and sophistication.

Pasolini was extraordinarily prolific as a filmmaker, writer, and journalist, and as Italy's awkward post-war balance between its conservative Catholic and communist factions began to collapse, his voice became ever more influential—and, as such, dangerous. He continued to antagonize his own side with his criticisms of the student movement of the late 1960s, suggesting that their lack of class consciousness or tangible goals would fatally undermine their dream of revolution. (Jacques Lacan and Jean-Paul Sartre said similar things to the French students in May 1968, as they demonstrated across Paris.) In his poem "The PCI to Young People," composed after the Battle of Valle Giulia in Rome in March 1968, Pasolini wrote that he sympathized with the police, as they were "children of the poor," while the students were essentially middle-class. Again, Pasolini's determination to question orthodoxies wherever he saw them damaged his reputation on the left, many of whom did not take his provocation in context: a few lines later, Pasolini wrote that "obviously we are against the police as an institution." He managed to save his relationship with the PCI, calling them "the saving grace of Italy and its poor democratic institutions" in a famous article entitled "I Know" (1974), and from this point on, Pasolini's conflicts were not with the left or the center, but the right.

It is well known that Pasolini had just finished *Salò* when he died. It is less well known that he was also working on a novel, *Petrolio*, and that he planned to make just two more films after *Salò* before devoting himself to literature. Pasolini produced a documentary about the Piazza Fontana bombing that killed seventeen people outside a bank in Milan in December 1969, and in "I Know" he said he knew "the names of those responsible for the Milan massacre" as well as the bombings at an anti-fascist rally in Brescia in May 1974 and on a train in Bologna a few months later. He wrote: "I know because I'm an intellectual, a writer who tries to follow everything that happens, to imagine everything that is unknown or unspoken; who connects facts that may seem disparate, that puts together the disorganised and fragmentary pieces of an entire coherent political picture, who restores logic where arbitrariness, folly and mystery seem to rule." His next novel, he continued, would draw out the links between corrupt politicians and corporate interests; proclaiming this act of bravery most likely cost Pasolini his life.

On 2 November 1975, Pier Paolo Pasolini was murdered at the beach in Ostia, just outside Rome. He was beaten, burned, and repeatedly run over by his own car in a Mafia-style revenge killing, for which 17-year-old Pino Pelosi was convicted in 1976. Even before Pelosi retracted his confession in 2005, few believed that he was the killer, and certainly not that he acted alone. The motives remain unclear—further evidence uncovered in 2005 suggested that Pasolini may have gone to Ostia to meet thieves who had stolen reels cut from *Salò*, but the inquiry into the case was not continued, and his death remains unresolved.

In a recent article, the Wu Ming Foundation—a contemporary group of radical activists and authors—talked about how Pasolini had always been against the Italian state, in both its fascist and Christian-conservative iterations. Wu Ming quoted Italian politician Stefano Rodotà, who wrote in 1977 that Pasolini's life had been a "single trial" from 1960 onward, as he had often been dragged into courtrooms, endlessly attacked by the right-wing press, and even criticized by Sergio Leone, director of great "spaghetti westerns" such as *A Fistful of Dollars* (1964), for normalizing gay relationships. Another hero of mine who also died too young, the pioneering Italian LGBT rights activist and writer Mario Mieli (1952–83), suggested that "in beating and punishing Pasolini, Pelosi was unconsciously convinced that he was indirectly punishing and torturing his own homosexuality." In a homophobic society in which people were constantly killed for being queer, Mieli argued that *both* were victims—the best way to honor Pasolini would be to recognize the revolutionary potential of his critiques of sex, sexuality, and power.

In 2018, I visited Rome for the first time, having long been fascinated by the city—and having just watched several of Pasolini's films in a retrospective at my favorite cinema, the Close-Up Centre in London, for the first time. As well as meeting activists at Italy's largest LGBT organization, the Circolo di Cultura Omosessuale Mario Mieli, and Gramsci's grave, I went to Ostia to see the monument to Pasolini, designed by Mario Rosati and unveiled in 2005 in the park where he died. The gates appeared to be locked, to detract fascists from vandalizing it; more than forty years after his death, Pasolini retained the power to affront. We got in, and below the white, modernist sculpture were flowers and copies of Pasolini's poetry—clearly, he also retained the power to inspire. Reflecting on Pasolini's life, I thought about how he may not have been a perfect role model, but the possibilities he had opened for others seemed boundless.

Throughout my life, I have been a journalist, writer, filmmaker, and activist, and every time I have tried to move into a new field, I have found that Pier Paolo did it first, all the while keeping a consistent set of ethical principles running throughout his work. If I can achieve half as much with my life as he did with his, I will be quite content indeed.

Juliet Jacques

Juliet Jacques is a writer, filmmaker, academic, and broadcaster based in London. She has published two books, *Rayner Heppenstall: A Critical Study* and *Trans: A Memoir*, as well as a short story collection, *Variations*. Her short fiction, essays, journalism, and criticism have appeared in *The Guardian* (for whom she wrote a blog about her transition, called "A Transgender Journey," longlisted for the Orwell Prize in 2011), the *New York Times*, *Granta*, *London Review of Books*, *Frieze*, *Sight & Sound*, *TimeOut*, *Washington Post*, *Wire*, *Art Review*, and many other publications, while her short films have screened in galleries and festivals across the world.

Since 2017, Juliet has hosted Suite (212) on Resonance 104.4FM, which looks at the arts in their social, cultural, and political contexts. She was featured in the *Independent on Sunday Pink List* of influential LGBTQ+ people in 2011–2015, and was one of ten British LGBTQ+ writers chosen for an International Literature Showcase in 2019; *Trans: A Memoir* was runner-up in Polari's First LGBTQ Book of the Year award in 2016. She completed her PhD in Creative & Critical Writing at the University of Sussex in 2019, and now teaches at the Royal College of Art and elsewhere.

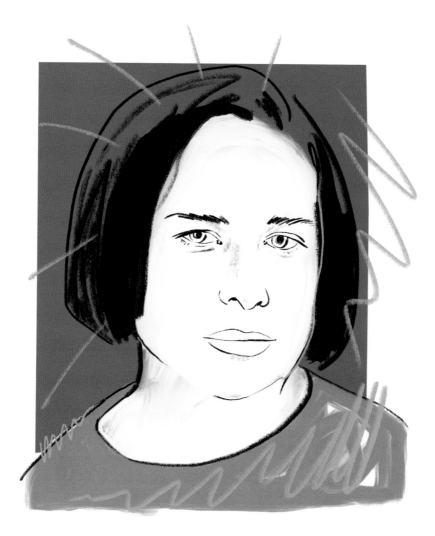

Illustration by Sam Russell Walker

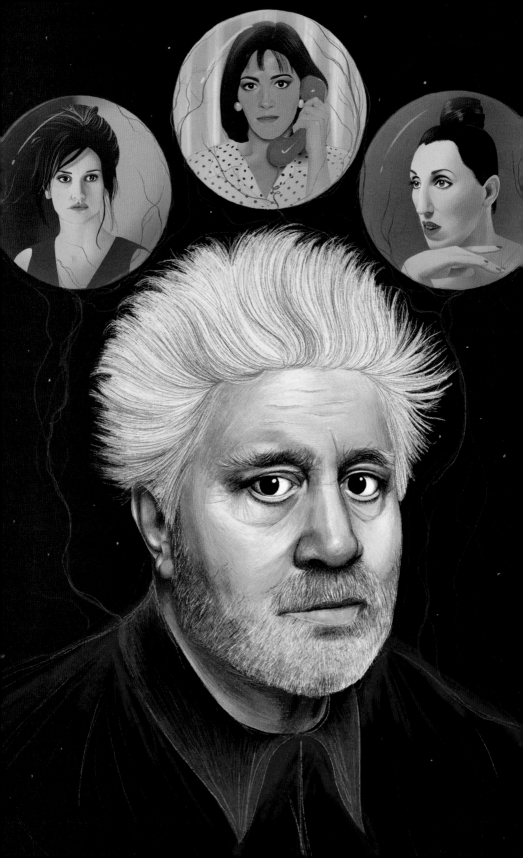

PEDRO ALMODÓVAR

by Joseph Cassara

One of my favorite scenes in cinematic history is from Pedro Almodóvar's 1982 screwball comedy *Labyrinth of Passion* (*Laberinto de pasiones*), a film about a sex-addict pop star named Sexilia who falls in love with Riza, the gay son of a Middle Eastern emperor. In the scene, Fabio McNamara—a gay punk who piques Riza's sexual interest—is posing for a photoshoot while Riza looks on. The concept is pure absurdity: Fabio lies on the floor, covered in blood, holding a rotary telephone receiver, wearing nothing but a faux-fur coat, and has gashes plastered on his exposed torso while one of the crew members holds a power drill near his blood-smeared face.

"Enjoy it, enjoy it more," the photographer instructs Fabio as he shrieks and squirms for the camera. "Look at it with lubricated eyes . . . Get closer to the drill. Desire that drill. Yes, yes, start to lick it. Yes, you like it. You love it. Yes, very good. Now cum a little. Yes, more . . . Fabio, now call a friend and ask permission to fuck the telephone . . . Now chat a little and invite them somewhere to eat a salad or something, maybe an empanada. Then you say: Listen, darling, I have to hang up because a crazy

Illustration by Stephanie Howe

murderer has come here to destroy my life. If I survive, I will call you and tell you all about it in great detail."

The critics did not like *Laberinto de pasiones*, but I did and still do. I loved it because it embodies so many elements that Almodóvar deploys so well in his early work: an over-the-top, dark, campy humor that to the wrong viewer would seem horrifying. It is, quite simply, too much—and that is the point. If humor is that which is unexpected, perhaps I've always loved Almodóvar's work because I never knew where each film, each scene, even each line would take me.

** **

I first encountered his work by accident, in October 2004, at the New York Film Festival. I was in my second year of high school, a wee little baby gay. I came out to some friends just a year earlier, though I would need to do this once or twice more to family. My friend M, a year older than me, had a father who worked at Alice Tully Hall in the Lincoln Center. I don't remember what M's father did, but he was some sort of stagehand, and as a result we were allowed free access to the hall, which I was told was world-renowned for its acoustics, though I was too young at the time to appreciate what that meant.

The first film we saw was Almodóvar's *Bad Education*, about two boys, Ignácio and Enrique, who are lovers in a Catholic boarding school in the 1960s. One of the boys is abused by a priest, and years later, when most of the movie is set, the men reunite. The movie is intense, with sprinkles of stylized humor, and was the first movie I had ever seen with an NC-17 rating. Think: church sex abuse, drug-addicted transsexuals, blowjobs, and murder. I remember sitting in one of the enclosed boxes at the back of the theater, with a square hole in the wall for us to see the screening in private. There is a moment where the camera lingers on Gael García Bernal's body as he does push-ups in bright-colored shorty-shorts, chest exposed. When he reached the top of the push-up, he would wiggle his butt, then release his upper body down toward the floor again. It was one of the film's many erotic moments, which is what I focused on at the time. Those moments gave me a hard on, and I was terrified that M would see. (I don't think she did.)

** **

I did not know, in 2004, when I stood backstage, that the Spanish director with the crazed white hair standing feet away from me, waiting for the Q&A to begin, would produce work that would alter the way I view the world and my own writing.

We did not know that Alice Tully Hall would close down for many years during a reconstruction project that was reconstructing—what?

M did not know that lodged in her father's brain was a tumor that would end his life within a year. Sometimes I wonder if he knew.

We don't think of time when we are that young—or maybe we do, but with a different set of terms. The future seems far off and distant, something that will eventually happen for us, not to us, but in the meantime, we projected our hopes and dreams onto our imagined future selves, into the realm of possibility.

The people who populate Almodóvar's early universe feel this way to me. McNamara, sniffing poppers across from punk rocker Alaska, at a café in Madrid, saying, "Pass me my lipstick, querida."

Now, the people who populate his films are constantly asked to confront the ways that pain stems from the passage of time.

What this shift signals to me is that either we are no longer the people we once thought we were or we remain the same but something irrevocable has changed in the world around us.

I've heard it said that if we love an artist's work, a good place to start is at the ends of things. If we begin with the most recent film, or painting, or book, we can go back and trace the ways that themes and preoccupations develop. Like a backward exploration of how style and aesthetics solidify in a person's work.

When I look at the past decade of Almodóvar's output—*Pain and Glory, Julieta, I'm So Excited, The Skin I Live In, Broken Embraces*—only one is a comedy. A sobering realization about a director whose early work was so deeply funny and raunchy.

In *Bad Education*, Ignácio goes in search of Enrique years after their boarding school days. In *High Heels*, a mother returns after a decade and a half to find her daughter is married to the mother's ex-boyfriend. In *Julieta*, a mother has a chance encounter with her daughter's childhood friend and is forced to reckon with the pain and guilt associated with her daughter's disappearance and estrangement. Even in *I'm So Excited*—the stand-alone comedy from the past decade—time is the ultimate constraint. The movie is about a group of three flamboyantly gay flight attendants who must calm a set of first-class passengers as the plane slowly descends into the ocean. The ultimate question is: Will the plane—like Spain's economy—crash, or will it not? And maybe more importantly, can we still laugh if a doomed fate seems inevitable?

**

I lived in Spain for a period of my life—the aimless years after college when I had no idea what I was doing and had no vocabulary to articulate my aimlessness. I bought a one-way ticket to Barcelona. My plan was to stay for six months, teach English, and that would be that.

I stayed for two years. Funny how that happens.

When I arrived, I met a Portuguese guy a couple of years my junior. L was beautiful and knew it, appreciated Almodóvar, and lived in a modernist building in L'Eixample with a flight-attendant roommate, also gay, who was never around. His apartment had tiled floors with a repeated block pattern. I would come to see these tiled floors as one of the signatures of the modernist movement and, to this day, they remind me of L. He had a huge cock, but preferred bottoming, which, in its unused potential, provided its own kind of heartbreak. But we had fun for a little while.

L introduced me to a short film called *The Cannibalistic Councillor*, about a politician in the conservative Partido Popular, played by Carmen Machi in a bright orange suit. The *cortomentraje* (short film) was written and directed by Almodóvar under the *nom de plume* Harry "Huracán" Caine and spans about eight minutes, as Machi sits at the kitchen table eating flan with one spoon, snorting a mound of coke with another, while telling a sleeping woman about her profound foot fetish and belief in polyamory. "Nothing is more democratic," she tells the sleeping woman, "than pleasure."

**

I've always been surprised that a director with such an unabashedly queer aesthetic and vulgar sense of humor could capture the attention and imagination of a Catholic country that had, hundreds of years ago,

I've heard it said that if we love an artist's work, a good place to start is at the ends of things.

devised the Inquisition—where gay men would be castrated and burned at the stake—and only 60 years ago abided by the rules of Franco's dictatorship. When I asked a Catalan friend why this was, he said, after laughing, "*Porque la gente esta loca*."

Yes, people are crazy. Also, fascinating. Or maybe just contradictory. The kernel of wisdom there is just as amusing to think about as it is horrifying. We all contain multitudes, sure, but I've always been wary of how fast norms and attitudes can shift. How they have the potential to regress gently, and then suddenly.

Almodóvar is very much a product of *La Movida Madrileña*: a period bookended by the death of Franco and the beginning of the AIDS epidemic; a time of intense social, artistic, and sexual exploration. Toward the end of the *La Movida*, in 1983, he released a film called *Dark Habits*, about a nunnery once filled with prostitutes, murderers, and drug addicts that falls into disrepair. I like to describe this movie in two words: naughty nuns. (*Very* Boccaccio.)

I received a DVD copy of *Dark Habits* from A, one of my students who had a mischievous laugh and a filthy sense of humor. A was a dentist in his early thirties who had just opened his own dental clinic, which specialized in traditional orthodontic treatment, and also, for whatever reason, Botox and fillers. He was very open about his own love for Botox. Sometimes when I used his lavatory after class, I would see, near the sink, the syringes he used to practice on his own face. I don't know how medical licensing works in Spain, and I asked no questions.

He had three quiet Basset Hounds, and we usually spent a good chunk of our time together walking the dogs around Poblenou. He'd tell me stories about himself and his porn-star friend gallivanting around circuit parties in Ibiza or play parties in El Gótico and I would correct his grammar and that was the class. Sometimes we had a coffee.

One of A's favorite actresses, Chus Lampreave, is in *Dark Habits*. She is also in *What Have I Done to Deserve This?*, a dark comedy about a working-class family living in an apartment complex in Madrid. Lampreave plays the deadpan grandmother who is addicted to bottled water and cupcakes, which she keeps under literal lock and key. When asked what she enjoys, her response is: "muffins, cemeteries, plastic bags, and money."

Toward the end of my first year there, I began to recognize the character archetypes from his films on the streets. The Chus Lampreave–

type *abuelas* (grandmothers) who walked around Les Corts in formal wear, or the hardened street walkers roaming the narrow alleys of El Raval, unafraid to touch a shoulder and promise you a good time. One Saturday night, a friend and I waited in line at the McDonald's on La Rambla at 3 a.m., like the faithful Americans we were, and watched a sex worker playing with a German tourist's hair. "What are you in the mood for tonight?" she asked him, in English.

"Oh," he said, avoiding eye contact by looking up at the menu. "I think I will take the double cheeseburger."

She rolled her eyes and walked away. But what a moment it was.

**

After a year of hopping around the city, renting rooms for stints of a couple of months at a time, I wanted to find a more permanent place to stay. I found an apartment in Les Corts that had a kitchen with very retro, olive-green tiles on the wall that immediately reminded me of the slow-pan shots that Almodóvar employs in the quiet moments before a scene begins, or when a scene is already in progress, but the characters are enveloped in silence: holding each other, or smoking a cigarette in the rain, or sucking someone off in a hotel room.

In my search for apartments and rooms for rent, the first place I looked at almost sent me into a depressive episode. There was almost no natural sunlight, dark-wood paneling everywhere, and each bedroom had beds that folded into the walls. And who the hell wants to do manual labor every morning and night just to get in or out of bed?

Each room had floor-to-ceiling wallpaper that depicted a snow-peaked mountain range. I'd describe these scenes as Mount Fuji adjacent, with the faded yellow veneer of age. It was atrocious, and I knew from the minute I stepped into the apartment that there was no amount of money someone could pay me to live there. To make things worse, it smelled like cat pee, which reminded me of the handsome man who had, just a month earlier, stood me up on a date. He sent me a text on WhatsApp to tell me that two of his cats had gotten sick, followed by a picture of five cats and a mess of indiscernible and various fluids. When I asked him how many cats he owned, he said seven, and look: I don't care how hot you are, that is beyond words.

In the second apartment, the landlady lived in the master bedroom but wanted to find a subletter while she went on a year-long yoga retreat in India. I didn't ask her about this, fearing she would give me a story that was reminiscent of *Eat, Pray, Love*. The apartment was a modernist wonderland with high ceilings and a stained-glass terrace in the back, which housed orchids that she encouraged her tenants to talk to. She was in the middle of reading her orchids *La sombra del viento*, one of those odd novels that is both a contemporary literary classic in Spain but also available at every supermarket next to the candy bars.

During the middle of our tour, one of the hottest Italian men I've ever landed eyes on walked from his bedroom to the bathroom. The curls in his hair could rival those of Shirley Temple and his gym muscles made me feel all kinds of yes. I wanted to move in immediately. But then the absurdity began, as it always seems to, when it is least expected.

She asked me what I did for work and I told her. She said, in a monologue that I neither asked for nor wanted, that she was lucky in this life to be able to combine both of her passions: she was an artist and a dog groomer. She showed me her canvases, which perhaps could best be described as "multimedia." She hot-glued dog fingernail clippings to canvases, and then smeared acrylic paint over everything. "You can touch it," she said, holding the canvas in front of me. It felt like some kind of test that I hadn't studied for.

"Oh, no," I said. "But thank you. I really like the—texture."

"No," she said. "You can touch it."

So I did. I touched it while fantasizing about all of the soap I would use to wash my hands later.

Despite the hot Italian, I no longer wanted to live there.

**

I eventually found an apartment that felt right, though in the coming months it would remind me of *The Skin I Live In*, Almodóvar's 2011 psychological horror movie that is about a plastic surgeon, played by Antonio Banderas, who keeps a woman imprisoned in his mansion.

At first, this apartment seemed amazing. The live-in landlord was a middle-aged Catalan painter whom I rarely saw. He had brutally chapped lips and never smiled, but who cares, I thought. He was always painting in his bedroom-studio. The place was within walking distance of the metro, the market, the language academy where I worked, and the gay nude beach, where every morning an exhibitionist with a cock the size of a baby's arm would jog up and down the beach for all the world to see. Everywhere around me, it seemed, the absurdity of life bubbled at the surface.

There were four bedrooms: one occupied by a handsome, but straight, German business student whose semester abroad ended a month after I moved in. When he left, a 50-something-year-old man from southern Spain moved in. He kept to himself and only stocked his shelf of the refrigerator with Estrella beer and probiotics. The last bedroom, I thought for months, was unoccupied.

Every inch of wall space in the flat was jammed with the landlord's paintings: highly stylized canvases done with acrylics. Every piece depicted the same woman. In one, she's playing volleyball. In another, she's lounging on a beach, drinking a piña colada. In yet another, she's wearing a fashionable hat and holding a shopping bag. Each is comprised of small dots that come together to form the shapes that become her body, in what I now know is called a stippling effect. Impressionistic would be a generous term—these were not Monets by any stretch of the imagination. I once described his work to a friend as being perfect for a beach house, but never for a library.

The one striking element that each painting had in common, which haunted me as I walked everywhere, was that she had no face. Her body had a head, with hair, but no facial features. Her arms had fingers; those fingers were nail polished—which made no sense to me because she couldn't see. Whenever I sat in the dining room, surrounded by eight or nine of the canvases on each wall, I had the feeling that this woman, whoever she was, was both staring at me but also not. Because she had no eyes.

**

Months later, I came home from an afternoon jog and there was a new person in the kitchen. It is a startling feeling to walk into your kitchen for a protein shake only to see a stranger there, preparing hard-boiled eggs. I assumed she was either a friend of the painter or a new tenant—which in a city like Barcelona, where people come and go frequently, is not odd. When I introduced myself, she told me that she had been living in the apartment for two years. I can only imagine what my reaction was like. Perhaps the look of doing mental math—the darting eyes, the look of gears clicking into place somewhere within—like the meme of the woman who, in four time-lapse boxes, slowly realizes some deep shit.

Then something did click. The unoccupied room.

In *The Skin I Live In*, the woman held captive in the mansion is kept in a bedroom on the second floor. She draws signs and symbols on the walls. She wears a mask and a body suit. The plastic-surgeon kidnapper and his complicit maid are constantly worried that she will injure herself. There are competing desires at play: keep her locked up, but make sure she doesn't bruise.

Whenever I sat in the dining room, surrounded by eight or nine of the canvases on each wall, I had the feeling that this woman, whoever she was, was both staring at me but also not. Because she had no eyes.

This roommate that I didn't realize I had was not being held captive. It turned out that she worked late nights and mornings as a care attendant at a geriatric center. I was home when she was at work, and vice versa.

But the more I saw her, the more I began to suspect that she was the woman in the paintings. The hairstyle was the same, as was the frame of her body. I couldn't help but see her as the painter's muse, whether or not this was true, and this made the faceless paintings feel even creepier.

I never learned much about her. I rarely saw her. She always took her meals to her bedroom. I never heard the sound of a television or a radio coming from her room. Nor did I ever see the painter and her interact.

But then one day, it was the beginning of summer—a beautiful Sunday when all of the families of Poblenou came outside to stroll down the Rambla. Boys were everywhere kicking footballs. I was going to meet a friend for a gin and tonic when I saw them in the park, holding hands. That is when I knew: she is the woman without a face. She is the woman behind the door.

* *

There were so many doors in that city. Of course, there still are doors, one would hope, but it's been years since my time there ran its course. What I love about city life, and maybe—I realize now as I write this—what I love about art is the feeling that behind every door there is a person with their own inner life, their own story and idiosyncrasies, and something, no matter how big or small, is *happening*.

To say that things happen in Almodóvar's films is an understatement. If Chekhov had a gun, then Almodóvar has dagger-dildos and a filthy safe word. Early on in his career, Spanish critics didn't quite know what to make of him. They called him melodramatic, which is not untrue, but the problem is when the word carries a sour taste in their mouth.

Was his work trivial or groundbreaking? they asked.

I ask, who were these critics, and why was the binary articulated in such a way, as if an artist must be one or the other?

If Chekhov had a gun, then Almodóvar has dagger-dildos and a filthy safe word.

On the plane ride that took me away from that period of my life, the flight attendants didn't sing The Pointer Sisters. The drunk man seated next to me did vomit in his mouth (twice!) and swallowed it both times. I tried to fall asleep, but couldn't. Our plane didn't descend into an ocean, though what a story that would've been. We landed at the Philadelphia airport, which is the beginning of another story altogether.

Years later, I still await Almodóvar's newest films with the same eagerness of a teenager, when anticipation meant something different to me than it does now. When we engage with art created by people who are still living, it feels like a friendship that has been sustained over years and miles. With each new book, or album, or film, or opera, they are saying to us: come in, it's been a moment, sit down, let me make you a cup of tea, I have so much to tell you, querida. A couple of hours pass. The visit has run its course, until the next time, whenever that is. We won't see each other again for a while, maybe a few years, but when we do, my god, will it be fabulous.

Knock, knock, Pedro. It's been a moment. Come in. We have so much to cover.

Joseph Cassara

Joseph Cassara is the author of the critically acclaimed novel *The House of Impossible Beauties*, which won the 2018 Edmund White Award for Debut Fiction, two International Latino Book Awards, the National Arts & Entertainment Journalism Award for Best Fiction Book, and was a finalist for the Lambda Literary Award for Gay Fiction. It was selected by Graham Norton as one of his Top Five Reads of 2018, as well as WH Smith's Fresh Talent program and Barnes and Noble's Discover Great New Writers list. Hailed as one of the most anticipated novels by dozens of newspapers and magazines, *The House of Impossible Beauties* was excerpted in the *Wall Street Journal* and *Buzzfeed*, and was listed as one of the best literary novels of the year by *Entertainment Weekly*, *Library Journal*, and the American Librarian Association's Over the Rainbow book list.

He is a graduate of Columbia University and the Iowa Writers' Workshop, and has received fellowships and grants from MacDowell, the Fine Arts Work Center in Provincetown, The Studios of Key West, and California Humanities. He currently serves as the George and Judy Marcus Endowed Chair of Creative Writing and assistant professor at San Francisco State University. He lives in California, where he is at work on a new novel and collection of essays.

The House of Impossible Beauties won Publishing Triangle's Edmund White Award for LGBT debut fiction in 2019, and was shortlisted for the Lambda Literary Award for Gay Fiction at the 31st Lambda Literary Awards.

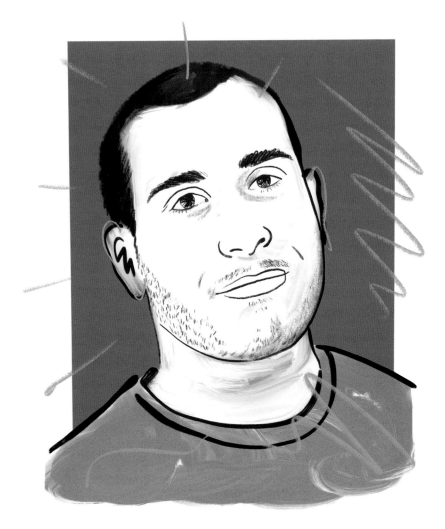

Illustration by Sam Russell Walker

I ASKED FOR ADONIS

NOT A DOUGHNUT

DAVID ROBILLIARD

by Russell Tovey

From a post-war, religious family home in the Channel Island of Guernsey, the poetic genius of artist David Robilliard was spawned. Leaving as soon as he could, Mr. Robilliard found his way to London, East London specifically, to find his people, his artistic voice, and to start on a journey of beautiful self-discovery.

I moved to London from Essex as fast as I could in the early 2000s. Not that I was born into any sort of Christian orthodoxy, or that my upbringing was stifled by conformity and pomp—I never suffered from any form of rejection, quite the opposite. It just felt like I couldn't ever be the person I was meant to be, if I didn't relocate to the capital. I have the impression that David's family remained in Guernsey, much like my own who have never strayed far from Essex. Though their most theatrical offspring had to flee the nest to truly realize who he was.

I discovered David's work during a retrospective at the ICA gallery in 2014. My personal journey of art discovery was still in its initial stages and David's work was

Illustration by Hollie Nudds

one of the first prominently queer British artists' voices that I had discovered. Prior to Robilliard, I only felt aware of overtly gay themes running through the work of British artists such as David Hockney and Patrick Proctor. Both game-changers, but it felt like they were from a different class or generation to myself and Robilliard. I connected to Robilliard because it felt like he could have been me, or at the very least it felt like we would have been friends.

It shocked at first. His work. So proud and raw. It astounded me how a young male artist in the late seventies/early eighties could be so obviously "out there" and gay. His colloquial street-level style and sharply dark humor, a combination of both images and text with vivid, proudly queer prosaic meanderings that were so accessible and universal in their themes of love, longing, and loneliness, all tingled with a contemporary optimism and courage. I looked to the works of Gilbert and George, their "Dirty Words" series, their earlier imagery of men in provocative, suggestive poses, their ability to project into their narrative an almost arrogant "up yours" to the establishment's disposition. This pride in identity, once again, led me to David. It didn't surprise me to discover that David and Gilbert and George had been firm friends and that they even considered him to be their most favorite writer and artist. They said he encapsulated the "Existers" spirit of the day . . . He was the "new master of the modern person. Looking, thinking, feeling, seeing, bitching."

David's work is full of honesty and romantic longing, and this "Existers" spirit of his was something that I longed to encapsulate. As a gay man myself, moving from Essex, first to North London and then East, I sensed in David's work the potential for an authentic life. An authentic gay life, full of excitement and lust, and relished with the possibility of love. Growing up under Section 28, the idea of open passion, mutual respect, and the potential for an honest and kind, happy gay relationship didn't really feel possible at first. Internalized homophobia pathed a rocky road in my mind: filled with pitfalls and secrecy. David's pride and honesty were an advocate for hope, advocating for an authentically lived gay experience. In his written word, it's all possible. It all feels so casual and in some of his verse . . . ordinary. Oh, to be gay and ordinary. To reach a moment in time where being "out and proud" is so uninteresting and average, so normalized and commonplace, that to exist in this sleepy sweet spot would feel kinda, well, meh. But for me, an average existence felt aspirational. Feeling like the "odd one-out," the "one-in-ten," the "shame-he's-never-going-to-have-kids" every time you entered a room, really did feel like a bore. Now it feels like I belong to a club of some of the luckiest few.

David's pride and honesty were
an advocate for hope.

David's partner, the artist Andrew Heard, was his muse. The inspiration for so many of his poems and drawings, all kept on scrappy note pads collecting frantically in his pockets, all carved out from a mania of emotions. Andrew twisted within him. Moving from poetry to painting, David leaped ahead, and although he only crafted around sixty painted canvases within his lifetime, each depicting a funny, poignant, emotionally unsettling, thought-provoking message. It feels inspiring to witness this out gay man, using his gay relationship and his gay life to create his artwork. As an actor, and now as a writer myself, partners, love, crushes, and relationships really have played huge roles in my acting capability: to access those deeper emotions, the ones that are truly needed to connect, to really flesh out and fully commit and sympathize with the character that you are inhabiting. You need to have had your heart crushed to act out anything with real gusto. David's relationship played out in his art, his jealousy and low self-esteem, paranoia and co-dependence, all there, bared in the open, stretched along a psychiatrist's couch for the world to analyze. They say actors can hide behind a role, but the best actors can hide inside a role. Roles allow us the space to express inner fears and desires through playing someone else. Writing is where I further channel my anxieties: copying and pasting my interior universe into an exterior world, telling stories of the everyman, the human experience, cherry picking from my own autobiography. Creativity really is therapy. David's work feels like his therapy. His anger and his love, his fears and his dreams—they spurt out in tightly held bundles of nuanced, sharply camp imagery and words.

His oeuvre allows us a chink into the past, a momentary time capsule for queer British life: a gay artist living in East London in the 1980s and thriving.

Humor is a fundamental tactic in tackling pain. The most magical gift you can offer a friend is the opportunity to laugh. The gift of something funny—that flourishes up some pithy wit, which facilitates a crack in their pain and lets some light into their dark—it's like nothing else on Earth. The gift of a momentary comedic release extended to someone struggling is almost spiritual. Primal screaming, broken by a belly laugh. That's magic. David chooses satire, sarcasm, irony, and wit for his tools of the trade. His quintessentially British voice speaks volumes to me. I know his tone. I feel his irony. It's a very unique thing, the British wit, something that as a society we seem to take for granted, our sarcastic raw underbelly only ever exposed when overseas visitors entrust our derision with verbatim. Only then do we realize the power we preside over our satirical cadence of choice. It takes a certain intellect to be able to subvert a language, mock it, spin it, twist it up, and then offer it back to us, served cold with cryptic audacity. Only then, in what seems like mere milliseconds, it is deciphered, analyzed, and presented straight back to us, ridiculed and flat. That's British humor. It's bloody smart. That's how David's voice connects universally. That's why his words speak directly to me.

They say actors can hide behind a role, but the best actors can hide inside a role.

Being from Essex, fundamentals of our culture include the ability to tell a good story. I remember as a kid, learning to sit back, watch, and listen to my parents when they chose to regale us with their tales of old, my mum of her rebellious teenage years, and my dad of his wild early twenties teaching water-skiing in Greece. I loved the feeling, sitting there, warm and relaxed in their presence, their confidence shimmering, basking in their performances, seeing them play out all the parts, all the voices and mannerisms, keeping a crowd entertained. I learned early on to watch them, study them, learn from them, be them. How those pratfalls and misguided jokes were spun into a magical moment of colloquial prose. The ability to not take yourself too seriously and only to be serious when it's truly essential. That's Essex. I may have inherited their gifts—I hope I have—my parents unaware they were even offering up such treasures for me to accept. My need to tell stories, to entertain, to captivate, and to hold an audience, keeping them hanging on for the punch line, even if they've heard it a hundred times—that's my parents' magic. You can't learn that, it's "something in the water," as my mum would say, it's inherent.

I can't speak for the Channel Islands, I can't speak for Guernsey, the island that David Robilliard rose up in and ran away from. I'm not sure of their people's ability to tell monolithic tales of great pathos and mirth or why and how David had to leave to be free, but whatever he felt, he has crafted work that has truly changed me.

David knew that he didn't have long to live when he was diagnosed with AIDS in 1988. His work took on a deeper satirical style, a coping mechanism, maybe for the stigmas and internal shame he felt for his own diagnosis. He even claimed it, allowing himself agency, and from then on introduced himself as David RobilliAIDS. I have always feared this disease, the product of an eighties child, the vivid red-topped headlines screamed of gay death and pain. It was an early death, an ignorant death, arrogant choices made for an easily avoidable death sentence ... silly you. Judged and vilified, it felt like the grim reaper sauntered into every room you entered, patiently clipping hawk-like nails along his well-sharpened scythe, fixating on you as you undressed beside your chosen mate for the evening.

David died within the same year of his diagnosis in 1988, aged just 36. This scares me. It scares me because he was so close to my age, just a small generation leap back. It scares me because it feels like it could have been me. We all imagine our own funerals, some may not admit it, but we do, it's the human condition. The tragic accident, the debilitating onset of disease. Rarely do we consider a time for when we are slowly being carried across a cemetery, our barren grave waiting patiently, after falling asleep peacefully in our own beds, happily, at the age of 99. No! It's the tragic stuff that takes over this fabricated location—the rows and rows of crying mourners, how could this happen, it's so sad, he's so young, so much left to do and say, what a loss. Ego is the casting director for our funeral's audience and script. I wonder how this really feels when a quick exit from this world becomes a reality.

I think of David in his bed at night in the last year of his life— how he must have tossed and turned, imagining and even planning his own funeral, knowing the inevitable was rapidly approaching with no control over when and how. The stories of friends, near and far, dropping like flies and how scared he must have been, reaching for his notebook and crumpled papers for comfort. This was the story of hundreds and thousands of gay men. I take comfort in the role of Prior in Tony Kushner's theater masterpiece, *Angels in America*. In my mind, David Robilliard dances alongside Prior Walter in the most fantastic way—ordinary men, that through art (Prior as a fantastical character in a play and David in the actual psychical creation of his art), can become heroes and voices for a lost generation. I imagine Prior would have loved Robilliard and Robilliard would have tolerated Prior as they read aloud Alan Bennett and Susan Sontag over coffee and pancakes.

How lucky it is to feel a semblance of safety now. To know that this disease is medically avoidable and manageable for so many of us, to the point of a full and healthy life with zero transmissions—how I wish our late brothers and sisters could see us now. I thought the world I was going into as a young gay man would be wrought with battles for survival and a determination to take up space, but so far as gay men and women, we live on an Earth, albeit a Western Earth, that protects us and our rights; nevertheless our battles have furrowed deeper. Protection, visibility, and amplification of the voices of the Trans and gender non-conforming community are now what we must strive to protect. I wonder how David would have considered this non-binary new world, what he would have written, and what he would have drawn. I think Robilliard would have liked playing with gender norms, considered his and others' pronoun options, challenged the art establishment with a fluidity in himself and his peers. Much like how his camp, street-level poetry style challenged the highbrow poetry establishment back then, he would have been quick to comment on the now and created work that would have certainly further exposed his own personal and unique awareness of humanity.

> **Protection, visibility, and amplification of the voices of the Trans and gender non-conforming community are now what we must strive to protect.**

I miss David and I didn't even know him. Many did. Gilbert and George still talk of him. Louisa Buck, art world critic and all-round wonderful person, laments on the majesties of his personality. There are still

Robilliard hand-holders in this world. He was special and his story has been neglected and his art overlooked. If a biopic of his life was made, I would love to play him and I'd like to know what he would have thought about that. I hope he would have thought it was a good idea . . . I'd promise him that I'd make him funny.

Missing someone you didn't know—because of the art that they leave behind, smacks to me like the hallmarks of a genius. There have been many great minds, the eminence of which you are well within your rights to invite to your theoretical dinner party, your fantastical banquet of kings, teeming with icons of history. But for me, the person I'd most like to have a quiet sit down and a nice cup of tea with . . . is David. We'd partake in a fat slice of cake and talk about boys. I'd empty out his pockets filled with crumpled notes and drawings, unfurl them, smooth them out on the table, and read them aloud, because that's what he wrote them for. To be read and listened to. I would feel unlimited pride to be reading them out for him. David Robilliard was, and is, a colossal talent. A cultural force kept on a simmering low light for far too many years, but any moment now, trust me, he's getting ready for a whole new world to discover him.

Russell Tovey

With an extensive background in film, television, and theater, award-winning actor Russell Tovey made his stage debut as part of the original company for Alan Bennett's 2004 play *The History Boys*, both at the National Theatre and on Broadway. He then reprised his role of Rudge in the much-loved 2006 film adaptation directed by Nicholas Hytner.

On stage, Russell was most recently seen as Joseph Pitt in the critically acclaimed *Angels in America* at the National Theatre alongside Nathan Lane and Andrew Garfield, and also appeared in *The Lover* and *The Collection* at the Harold Pinter Theatre, London. He last appeared on Broadway in the critically acclaimed Tony award–winning revival of *A View from the Bridge*, directed by Ivo van Hove.

On television, Russell's latest leading role is in the ITV/Hulu drama series *The Sister*, from *Luther* creator Neil Cross. He was recently nominated for a 2020 Critic's Choice Award for Best Supporting Actor for his role in the critically acclaimed BBC/HBO Drama series *Years and Years*, written by Russell T. Davies and starring Emma Thompson and Jessica Hynes. Other notable television credits include BBC's *Doctor Who*; critically acclaimed BBC TV mini-series *Little Dorrit*, *Sherlock*, HBO's *Looking*, *The Night Manager*, *What Remains*, *The Job Lot*, *Freedom Fighters: The Ray*, CW's *Legends of Tomorrow/The Flash*, and ABC's *Quantico*.

As well as acting, Russell has a successful podcast, *Talk Art*, with friend and gallerist Robert Diament, where they interview leading artists, curators, celebrities, and gallerists about their shared passion.

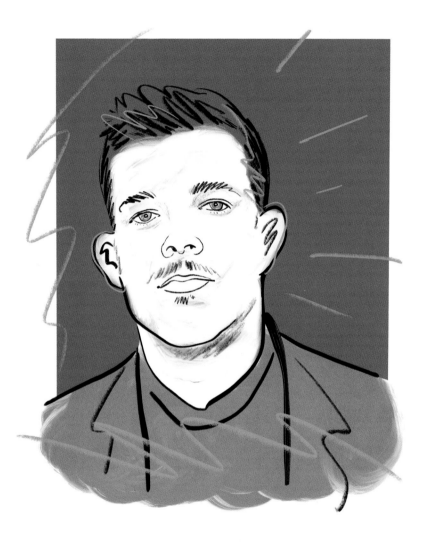

Illustration by Sam Russell Walker

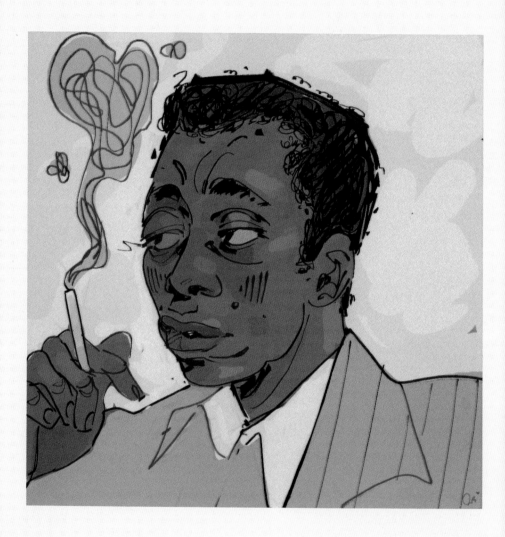

A LOVE LETTER TO JAMES BALDWIN

by Paul Mendez

I first became aware of James Baldwin when I was twenty. I was living in Tonbridge, Kent, and had just quit my degree in automotive engineering before the end of the first year. I lived with, and had been befriended by, a group of photography students, a relief after being bullied for nine months by the lads on my engineering course, three girlfriend-less Asian boys with customized cars and no self-respect. My new friends were white, middle-class, and thought of themselves as liberal and creative.

Illustration by Jannelly

I was working-class, Black, and had grown up around white people in the West Midlands. These Kentish types, to my eyes, were a superior kind of white people—people from whom I could learn the finer things in life. My diction changed, adopting theirs. I ate their unseasoned, more expensive food, smoked their mild weed, listened to their roots reggae vinyl, swayed to the music—toddler-like, against my body's natural rhythms—like they did, watched arthouse cinema with them, modeled for them. I had always thought of myself as being white, but now I thought of myself as being a privileged white, just like them.

Then, one of them—I can't remember who—pushed Baldwin's 1968 novel *Tell Me How Long the Train's Been Gone* into my hands. I cannot thank them enough, and they will probably never know what a life-saving thing they did for me, as I have lost touch with most of them. I only realize now, having recently reread it for the first time, that *Rainbow Milk*, my debut novel, could've been based directly on it, so deep did it penetrate. The original copy I read is long lost, and I do not remember whether I was told, on being handed the book, whether Baldwin was Black, or not; gay, or not. (In 2002, the Internet existed, but we did not yet go straight for it without thinking; we didn't even yet google much—we asked Jeeves; we still asked each other questions or phoned a friend; we still went to libraries, but perhaps I didn't bother—perhaps I just read the book and asked questions afterward; I don't remember, and I didn't start to keep a journal until two years later.) I, myself, was still in the closet, just about gripping it shut with the tips of my fingers from the inside, powerless to stop someone ripping it open from the outside, humiliating me, showing me up to be an incorrigible, rabid, AIDS-ridden pervert, as I was raised to believe homosexuals were, and worst of all, that I was unable to conceal it.

Tell Me How Long the Train's Been Gone was the first book I ever read that was written by a Black man. I thought I wanted to be an author until I was thirteen, when, I suppose subconsciously, I realized that books did not tend to be written by Black men, or at least I was not exposed to books written by Black men, so I altered my ambitions to suit what I did see Black men doing. There were Black men in my life who had nice cars, and my father drove a truck, so I thought I might become an automotive engineer and design chassis and engines—perhaps I might even work in Formula 1! (Failing all that, I'd become a chef, because my late grandmother, a Jamaican immigrant of the Windrush generation, was a wonderful cook.) I moved to study at West Kent, a partner college of Greenwich University, and found myself in agony, living against a truth I did not yet understand and was not yet able to accept. I stopped going to classes, quit, then read what Baldwin himself referred to as Train.

Leo Proudhammer is a thirty-nine-year-old bisexual actor who suffers a heart attack on stage. He manages to deliver his final lines while falling to his knees, drawing huge acclaim from the audience at the curtain, wowed by his authentic performance, assuming that the collapse was scripted. He is rushed to hospital and stabilized. Leo's trauma catalyzes the telling of his life story, from childhood, growing up in Harlem with a brother, Caleb, seven years older than him, whom he witnesses being beaten and arrested by police; the three girls their mother gave birth to between the brothers all having somehow perished. They were a loving family, but not free of the tensions typical of Black households in mid-century Harlem, that Baldwin has centered in all but one of his novels: a father, disempowered at work, working too hard for too little pay and under the relentless whip of systematic racism; a mother, disempowered in the home; a brother, the victim of police brutality; the protagonist, the great Black hope for both white and Black people; the Church, in which, perpetually, one or more members are seeking asylum, or escaping from its tyranny. Leo's childhood scenes are interspersed with depictions of life in his early twenties, training to be an actor with a downtown method school like the Actors Studio, a time of interracial heterosexual relationships, homoerotic experimentation, and subtly developing racial awareness.

> **I realized that books did not tend to be written by Black men, or at least I was not exposed to books written by Black men, so I altered my ambitions to suit what I did see Black men doing.**

It was only the second time I had ever read a book about a Black man, the first being *Othello*; I was not empowered to notice, much less challenge, as a teenager, the fact that the books on my English curriculum were all written by white men—from William Shakespeare to John Steinbeck, Thomas Hardy to F. Scott Fitzgerald, J. B. Priestley to Tennessee Williams; the poetry anthology I studied rattled through Geoffrey Chaucer to William Wordsworth, Samuel Taylor Coleridge to Ted Hughes, stopping, as far as I recall, at only one woman—Carol Ann Duffy—but never at a Black writer of either gender. The fifty books of that other volume I was raised with were written by men considered to be "white," even the ones named after women, like Ruth and Esther. Literature was white, and in that context, I was literate. It was not difficult, after that literary schooling, to take it upon myself, as an adult, to read the likes of Proust, Flaubert, Huxley, and Orwell, but it was a radical challenge for me to read fiction and non-fiction by Black people or, indeed, white women.

Train was a novel, by a Black man, so well written it could have come from the hand of a white man (so I would have thought, then) about the things Black people—who, in my view, could not or would not raise themselves up to be more like *normal* white people—suffered. For instance, I believed that when Stephen Lawrence was stabbed to death in 1993, his killers must have been acting in retaliation, however over-administered; I believed that the default condition of Black people was to suffer *because* of their Blackness. I grew up in Sandwell, an area of the West Midlands that, until the late 1990s, was a British National Party (BNP) stronghold. I had been called the N word all my life, and somehow thought I deserved to be called the N word; I thought it was *normal*. I didn't understand the weight of the word; I did not know its history. *Train* alone would not teach me, but it started me off on a journey, and the destination was a place where I no longer had to apologize for my intersectional—Black, male, gay, working-class, agnostic—identities.

The thing that strikes me most about Baldwin—now that I have access to every clip of his speeches and interviews, now that I've read all but one of his novels, now that I've been floored by my own reflection in his essays—is his courage, and his confidence in his own mind. He did not go to college. He knew he was brilliant and worth saving by something other than God; he left New York lest it killed him, and fled to Paris, then to Istanbul, then to the south of France, periodically returning to the US—even while being hounded by the FBI's COINTELPRO (Counterintelligence Program) project (run by J. Edgar Hoover, a closeted homosexual)—to tell it about itself in no uncertain terms, influencing the Black Power movement, marching side by side with Civil Rights campaigners, writing essays like "Letter from a Region in My Mind," that woke white America to the questions it needed to be asking itself about its role in the country's race problem, landing him the cover of *TIME* magazine, a first for a Black writer. He smoked like a chimney, drank like a fish; went to school with Richard Avedon; was taught English Literature by the man who wrote "Strange Fruit" and who adopted the Rosenberg children after their parents' execution; was besties with playwright Lorraine Hansberry, Harlem Renaissance painter Beauford Delaney, and Nina Simone; slept with Marlon Brando (if the Quincy Jones rumors are to be believed). But he was serious, and it is for this that I am in awe of him: what enabled a Black man from his background, barely older than I am now and pretty much openly gay, to rock up at the Cambridge University Union in February 1965—two whole years before the partial decriminalization of homosexuality in the UK and just seven days before the assassination of Malcolm X in Harlem—and in front of seven hundred elite students, and America's most-respected conservative intellectual, deliver a knockout argument about how the American Dream has been at the expense of the American Negro, to the ring of a minutes-long, each-to-a-man standing ovation and landslide debate victory? I don't think it's a coincidence that, less than a year after reading *Train*, I myself found the courage to come out, initially, as bisexual, as Leo Proudhammer and Baldwin himself preferred to self-identify.

For reasons I can only speculate on in hindsight, I left Baldwin—and Black writing—alone after this initial moment of revelation. I was not ready for it. I misremembered the most striking scene in *Train*: Caleb and Leo, as young men, have sex with each other, and I recalled this as a simple moment of Black same-gender love, a radical thing in itself in proper literature, but I must have chosen not to believe, until I reread the novel eighteen years later, that they were *brothers*, that the younger brother was loving the older brother in a way no one else could, and that, at least between them, it was a pure, beautiful, and shared moment of affirmation. It was just too much; these things were supposed to be outside the realm of Black experience. Like Leo, I would become an actor, via being a waiter, via getting a leg-up in society from sympathetic white creatives. Like Leo, his lover Black Christopher, and Rufus, the troubled, queer, jazz drummer in Baldwin's 1962 novel *Another Country*—the latter two both said to be avatars of the young James—I was forced to confront what my place is in this world as a Black man, but in my case, in the

I no longer had to apologize for my intersectional—Black, male, gay, working-class, agnostic—identities.

glare of Black Lives Matter, and after watching a string of Black male bodies lie unjustly dead.

I am lucky, so, so lucky, to have been able to consult James Baldwin, to know that others have been angry, before me; others have thought about white supremacy and how it affects all our lives, before me; thought about what it means to be gay in the Black community and in the Church, before me. He is the writer who has perhaps had the greatest impact on my life, and as I have not yet read every word he has written, it thrills me to think that there is more inspiration, more affirmation, still to come.

Paul Mendez

Paul Mendez is a British novelist, essayist, and screenwriter, born in the Black Country in 1982. Mendez disassociated himself from his family's Jehovah's Witness faith as a teenager, starting and quitting an engineering degree in Kent before moving to London to study drama, working variously as an escort, waiter, voice artist, and journalist. Influenced by Joy Division and Kanye West, the writings of James Baldwin, Marcel Proust, Joris-Karl Huysmans, and Alan Hollinghurst, and the Alejandro González Iñárritu film *Amores Perros*, Mendez began fictionalizing his own experiences, while the Andrea Levy novel *Small Island* awakened him to a deeper heritage as a descendant of the Windrush generation.

In 2020, Dialogue Books published his novel *Rainbow Milk*, a portrait of a Black British family between the Windrush era and the EU referendum, from the perspective of a queer young runaway. It featured on the *Observer*'s Top Ten Debut Novels list and was shortlisted for the Gordon Burn Prize, before being named on end-of-year lists by, among others, the *New Statesman*, *Attitude*, *The Guardian*, *Stylist*, *Mr Porter*, *i-D*, and the *White Review*. Mendez has contributed to *Esquire*, *The Face*, *Vogue*, the *Times Literary Supplement*, the *London Review of Books*, and the *Brixton Review of Books*, and is currently reading for an MA in Black British Literature at Goldsmiths, University of London.

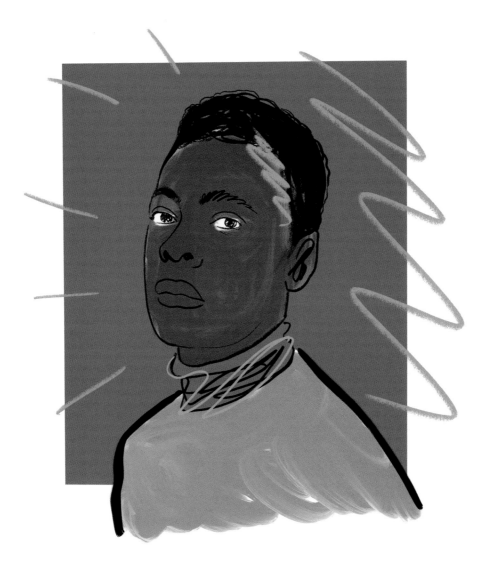

Illustration by Sam Russell Walker

Artists

The Queer Bible is a space that reflects the richness, beauty, and creativity of our diverse community. Our artists identify as LGBTQ+ or as allies drawn from around the world. Their contribution to the collection's visual identity has brought our subjects and writers alive in these pages. I'm proud to call them collaborators and friends.

ADAM JOHANNESSON

Adam Johannesson is an illustrator and graphic designer based in Scotland, who is a recent graduate of Gray's School of Art. Throughout his teen years he fell in love with the art of drag and began illustrating queens when he wanted to illustrate fashion on a more dramatic muse. He takes a great deal of inspiration from different eras and favors a more vintage feel in his work, and cites RuPaul as a muse for his art and identity.

AIMEE DAVID

Aimee David started her career working as a graphic designer for various design studios and start-ups before following her passion into illustration. She has been able to create custom illustrations in a variety of styles for emerging brands. When she's not working, she likes to screenprint, draw comics, read, and travel.

ALEX MEIN

Alex Mein is an artist and lecturer living and working in London. His work explores identity, portraiture, and observation. Casting individuals through his personal networks or social media, he draws people, often from the LGBTQIA+ community, in their personal, domestic spaces. Mein has also worked with brands such as Liberty London, Mulberry, and Nike, and currently lectures in Fashion Imaging and Illustration at London College of Fashion, UAL.

AMIR KHADAR

Amir Khadar is a Sierra Leonean–American multidisciplinary artist and educator from Minneapolis, Minnesota. Their main media are poetry, fibers, and digital art. Regardless of medium, their practice has always been grounded through Afro-futurism, black beauty, and ancestral practices. They have done extensive work with Parenting for Liberation, Wakanda Dream Lab, Forward Together, and the Astraea Lesbian Foundation for Justice. Amir is currently a student at Swarthmore College.

AORISTS/ANSHIKA KHULLAR

AORISTS is the pseudonym of Anshika Khullar, an illustrator based in Southampton, whose bold and vibrant work aims to showcase the ordinary as beautiful. Anshika is an Indian, non-binary Transgender creative with a BA in English Literature & Media from the University of Brighton. They have a focused interest in intersectional feminist narratives, a study which has invariably informed their art practice, with illustrations that are colorful, detail-oriented, and thoughtfully studded with hidden gems of metaphors made literal, often dealing in overarching socio-political themes.

AUSTIN STORIE

Austin Storie is a queer Latinx illustrator and student from the midwestern United States. Currently pursuing his BFA in Applied Drawing from Wichita State University, Austin enjoys creating works that merge his love of naturalistic, academic drawing with graphic design practices.

BROGAN BERTIE

Brogan Bertie is an illustrator from South London. They are currently smoking 40 a day because they are desperate to have Harvey Fierstein's gorgeous voice.

BUTCHER BILLY

Butcher Billy is a Brazilian illustrator who serves up a fresh slice of modern culture by splicing ideas, imagery, lyrics, and moods together forming his own unique form of contemporary nostalgia. Juxtaposing everything from *Wonder Woman* and *Watchmen* to Morrissey and *Breaking Bad*, his work is ironic, iconic, and very postmodern. Billy is also a creative director in a digital agency. He graduated in Graphic Design from the Pontifical Catholic University of Paraná, in Brazil.

CHEYNE

Cheyne (pronounced Shane) Gallarde is a multi-faceted artist born and raised in Hawaii. Prior to illustration, Cheyne was an award-winning fashion photographer. His illustration work reimagines drag queens as superheroes and villains. Cheyne's work is nostalgic, celebrating the sentimental look and grit of vintage comics while putting a modern twist on it. He won an Advertising Award for his comic art for MTV's 2019 Video Music Awards and was a contributing artist in the 2020 Pow!Wow! Festival. He won a National Advertising Award for his illustrations of LGBTQ icons for LOGOTV. In addition, he worked with Condé Nast to create the key visual and branding for their QUEEROES Awards show and with VH1 to create comic covers celebrating queer icon John Waters.

CLYM EVERNDEN

Clym Evernden is an award-winning artist and art director with a unique creative eye, named by the *Evening Standard* as one of "London's most influential people 2019." His signature ink-based style has evolved to encompass mixed media, animation and set design. A graduate of Central Saint Martins, Clym studied BA Fashion Design Womenswear prior to working solely as an artist. Clym has created artwork and animations and directed marketing campaigns for global brands such as Louis Vuitton, Hermès, Samsung, Audi, Christie's, and Moët Hennessy, and has been published on a variety of platforms, including television commercials and onsite installations.

EGO RODRIGUEZ

Ego Rodriguez is a queer artist based in London. His work hints to fashion, pulp, and nouveau. The message is a conversation of bright pop and human interactions, dynamic strokes and bold colors. He works a lot within the LGBTQ+ community, for some of the main publications, and also for Pride events worldwide.

FERNANDO MONROY

Fernando Monroy is a Mexican illustrator currently studying in Mexico City. His work references pop culture, reflecting the work of photographers, designers, and fashion. *Out* magazine named him one of twenty young queer artists to watch.

HOLLIE NUDDS

Hollie Nudds lives in East London working as an illustrator, mural artist, and sign writer. She has a BA in Fine Art. Hollie is a passionate explorer of queer history and themes in her practice.

JAMES DAVISON

James Davison is a London-based artist whose work explores color and geometric form in relation to the human body. His work is playful and celebrates his identity as a gay man. He has collaborated with brands such as Versace, Nike, and Adidas, and contributed to various fashion publications. Davison co-founded "SketchSesh"—a drawing project that works with creatives to produce live drawing sessions that explore identity, costume, and performance. He is an associate lecturer at Central Saint Martins and London College of Fashion.

JAMIE ELDER

Softly political and a quiet critique on modern society, Jamie's work looks at making conversations about social issues approachable and accessible without being intimidating and accusatory. He likes to turn the "normal" hyper-masculine representation of the male form and introduce his subjects as soft and delicate, challenging how the art world has historically seen queerness and masculinity. Jamie's work presents an idealized world of intimacy, humor, and vibrancy for life told through a warm and slow-moving narrative. There is a stillness in his work that is intriguing and comforting, while at the same time slightly unsettling and thought-provoking.

JANNELLY

Jannelly is a New Jersey–based artist who has been creating for many years. They have always drawn inspiration from television and film, especially when there's a great cast of characters. His/her art not only focuses on the design and personality of a character but also graphic illustrations, such as title cards or posters.

JOHN BOOTH

John Booth is a London-based illustrator, ceramicist, and textile designer renowned for his graphic aesthetic featuring multi-layered collages of textures and colors. His works are distinct and identifiable, bursting with color and texture. His diverse works seem to feature as often in the fashion world as they do on magazine covers and restaurant walls and in museum collections. He is currently focusing on his studio work—exploring ceramic objects and furniture as well as his textile print designs for luxury fashion and interior labels.

JOSÉ ANGEL NAZABAL

José Angel Nazabal is an architect, cartoonist, and visual artist. He graduated from the San Alejandro National Academy of Plastic Arts in the specialty of Painting and Drawing (2013), and later he graduated as an architect and urbanist from the Technological University of Havana "José Antonio Echeverría" (2019). His work has been exhibited and published in books and specialized art magazines, inside and outside Cuba.

LOUISE POMEROY

Louise is an illustrator and graphic artist based in London, originally from Brighton. Her work is a mix of hand-drawn line and digital color. Since graduating from Kingston University with a First Class Honours in illustration and a commendation in editorial, she has been awarded a D&AD Best Newblood for her book of illustrated shorts, *I Married a Toyboy Convict*. Selected clients include the *New York Times*, *Forbes*, *WIRED*, Google, and *The New Yorker*.

LUKE EDWARD HALL

Luke Edward Hall is a London-based artist and designer. He has worked on a broad range of commissions, from interior design and fashion projects to murals and illustration work for books, restaurants, and hotels. In October 2020, Luke's first large interior design and art direction project opened in Paris: a thirty-three-bedroom hotel and bistro. He has exhibited his drawings, paintings, and ceramics in London, Stockholm, and the United States. Luke has contributed to a wide range of magazines and in March 2019 he joined the *Financial Times* as a weekly columnist in *FT Weekend*, answering readers' questions on aesthetics, interior design, and stylish living.

PARYS GARDENER

Parys Gardener is a multi-award-winning contemporary digital illustrator from Bristol whose passion derives from creating artwork which represents women of color—particularly Black women—empowering them to feel seen and heard. She creates memorable work that can be described as pop art with a modern edge. Her work has been commissioned for a collaborative project with Banksy and her first solo exhibition was in Amsterdam in 2018/2019. She has been commissioned by brands such as Nike, Footlocker, Facebook, BBC, gal-dem, and more. She has been nominated for a Rise Award "Young Entrepreneur of the Year" 2019, and in the same year she became the recipient of the Precious Lifestyle Award for Visual Artist of the Year.

PATRICIO OLIVER

Patricio Oliver is an Argentinean graphic designer and illustrator, who graduated from the University of Buenos Aires, where he currently teaches Illustration and Typography. His work is mostly inspired by eighties pop culture, nature, cartoons, comic books, and queer culture—with a soft spot for the fascinating universe of drag performers.

SAM RUSSELL WALKER

Sam Russell Walker is a queer Scottish illustrator based in East London. Also working as an illustration agent, Sam regularly commissions and collaborates with talent across the creative industry. With a love of people, art, pop culture, and fashion—he enjoys creating bold and eye-catching portraits inspired by gestural line work and expressive mark making. Sam has created portraits for various arts, design, and culture outlets including *Wallpaper**, *Elephant* magazine, and The Queer Bible.

STEPHANIE HOWE

Stephanie Howe is an illustrator, printmaker, and animator who lives and works in the South East of England. Her illustrative practice is centered around telling stories throughout every piece of work, as narrative is the key to efficiently communicating each message, whether in a literal or in a metaphorical sense. Her works mainly revolve around the subjects of nature, TV and film, and day-to-day life. She works in digital and watercolor mediums to create each concept, and has an undying love for Risograph and screen printing.

A Note on the Endpapers and Maps

By Alex Farebrother-Naylor

The Endpapers

The intention with the endpapers is a cheeky response to the idea that LGBTQIA people are "unnatural." For many queer people, including the artist, the rich variety of sexual behavior and gender in animals and the natural world was a joyous and liberating discovery that affirmed their difference as a valuable and beautiful contribution to our world rather than a detrimental aberration.

HYENAS: female hyenas have penises/large clitorises that are longer than males. They give birth through them but also mount other females, and female-female relationships play an important social role in hyena packs. These hyenas are depicted hanging out with cheeky grins.

SEAHORSES: in many species of seahorse, the male seahorse gestates the fertilized egg and gives birth. FYI "seahorse dads" is a recent term for Trans men who give birth, as in the recent documentary *Seahorse* about the journalist Freddie McConnell and his pregnancy. Depicted is a pregnant male seahorse.

CLOWNFISH: all clownfish are born male. They are sequential hermaphrodites, meaning they produce both sperm and eggs at subsequent phases of their lives. When a female clownfish is removed from a group, then the most dominant male will become gonadally female and take her place in the hierarchy. This clownfish is depicted hanging out in their anemone.

SNAILS: most species of snail and slug are true hermaphrodites; they only have one sex and, when mating, both snails penetrate and potentially fertilize each other. These snails are courting.

PENGUINS: bonded male–male couples are common in many penguin groups. Depicted are Roy and Silo, a male–male couple of chinstrap penguins at Central Park Zoo, New York City, who famously raised a chick together.

WHIPTAIL LIZARDS: many species of whiptail lizard are partly or entirely parthenogenetic, meaning entire communities or even species are all female and reproduce asexually. Female whiptail lizards in these communities are often observed to mount other females, which while it does not inseminate can provide a bonding and social function, and may also stimulate egg production.

LOBSTERS AND BUTTERFLIES: species which display gynandromorphy and particularly bilateral asymmetry undergo a split very early in embryonic development which leads to different halves of the body with different sex-related chromosomes. The left–right split depicted exists in nature, a striking and beautiful variation.

The Maps

We created the city and world maps to suggest the breadth, richness, and variety of queer culture and lives across history and geography. A hundred more cities, a thousand more points on a single city map, could easily be created. LGBTQ+ people have struggled, thrived, loved, created themselves, and made community in every human culture. We hope that marking a very few places of significance on the queer globe will inspire pride, respect, and belonging and, like the rest of this book, spark further curiosity and learning.

LONDON MAP: Summing up two thousand rich years of queer life and love in the city is impossible—this is a tiny sampling of places significant to many over the last three hundred years. The map is annotated and scattered with largely 1980s political badges from the collection of Paul Hegarty, proprietor of Gay's the Word Bookshop, which are reprinted with the kind permission of Gay's the Word. Gay's the Word and the RVT remain lively and essential contributors to LGBTQ+ London today.

THE WORLD IN SEVERAL IDENTITIES: Another impossible summary of hundreds of forms of human love and self-expression over thousands of years. The Femminielli and Takatāpui communities, while both have ancient roots, are active and thriving today. The title crest features in heraldic form some of the creatures celebrated in the endpapers of this book.

NEW YORK AND SAN FRANCISCO MAPS: These annotated tourist maps present a tiny sample of moments, people, and places of pilgrimage. The explosion of Black artistic, intellectual, cultural, and political work that was New York's Harlem Renaissance was home to many queer artists. Black and Latin American ballroom culture has its roots in Harlem. While the Stonewall Inn is marked, I have chosen to highlight the explosion of political work and community building that came in the years afterward. Meanwhile, on the other seaboard, three years before Stonewall, Trans and gay sex workers rioted against cops in a late-night cafeteria. The after-effects and protests sparked a political, legal, and cultural shift that transformed LGBTQ+ life in San Francisco. Armistead Maupin chronicled this era and beyond in his loving, celebratory novel series, Tales of the City.

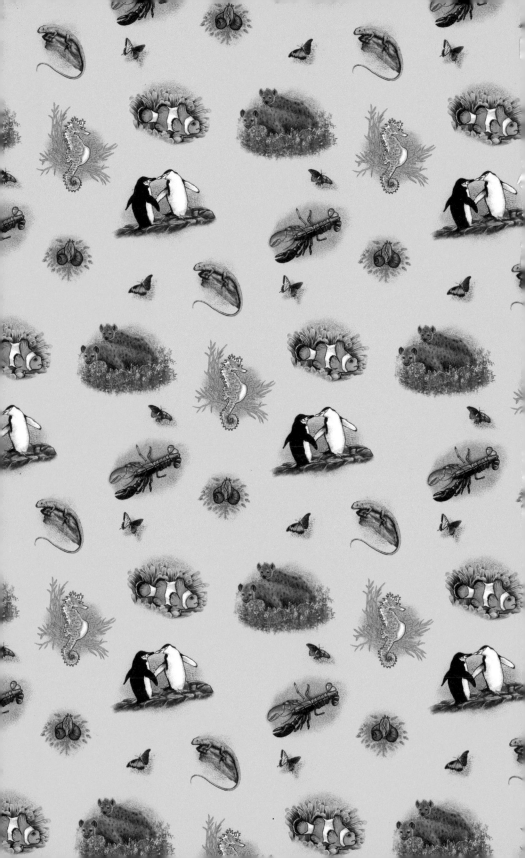